Introduction to World Forestry

Introduction to World Forestry:
People and their Trees

Jack Westoby

Basil Blackwell

First published 1989
Reprinted 1991

Basil Blackwell Ltd
108 Cowley Road, Oxford OX4 1JF, UK

Basil Blackwell, Inc.
3 Cambridge Center
Cambridge, Massachusetts 02142, USA

British Library Cataloguing in Publication Data

A CIP catalogue record for this book is available from the British Library.

Library of Congress Cataloging in Publication Data

Westoby, J. C. (Jack C.)
    Introduction to world forestry / Jack Westoby.
        p. cm.
    Bibliography: p.
    Includes index.
    ISBN 0-631-16133-3
    ISBN 0-631-16134-1 (pbk.)
    1. Forests and forestry. I. Title.
SD373.W48 1989
333.75--dc19

Typeset in 10 on 11½pt Sabon
by Dobbie Typesetting Limited, Plymouth, Devon
Printed in Great Britain by TJ Press (Padstow) Ltd, Cornwall

Contents

Preface

Much is heard today about the shrinking tropical forest. Now there is a new concern about the way in which the forests of the affluent temperate countries are beginning to wither and die. How far can we allow trees to disappear? How important are trees to us? When did the forests start to shrink? If trees are important, what can be done to save the forests?

If it had been possible for us to observe the evolution of the earth's surface over the 4.5 billion years of its existence, we would have seen enormous changes. Once trees had appeared we would have seen the forests ebb and flow, shrink to limited areas, and then spread out again. All these changes in forest cover took place over millions of years, but in the last few centuries we would have witnessed the most rapid shrinkage of forest area in the earth's history. We may also have observed that this reduction coincided with a dramatic increase in the numbers of one particular species – *Homo sapiens*.

Today there are large areas of the earth's surface without either people or trees (the polar regions, the deserts, the high mountain areas). But elsewhere, usually where there are a lot of people, there are few forests; and where there are many forests, there are few people. At first sight there appear to be two possible reasons for this. One is that people settle and multiply only when there are no forests; the other is that when they settle and multiply they clear the forests.

Although the second reason is closer to the truth, the process has not been a straightforward one. There is no simple relationship between the extent of the forests and the size and distribution of the human population. Instances can be found in which large numbers of people live in harmony with their forests, and others where forests are devastated although few people are present. As well as the many examples of human beings destroying forests, there are also many examples of people recognizing their dependence upon forests and preserving or even creating them.

These facts suggest that it is not so much the number of human beings that has the crucial impact as the way in which human society is organized. Different social groups and classes seek to use the forest for different purposes. Sometimes these can coexist; but at other times they conflict. One purpose may require the forests to be conserved, another may entail their destruction.

The fate of the forests during human history, therefore, is not traceable simply to the growth of population, even where that is rapid. It has been very strongly affected by changes in the forms of economic organization and exploitation. And it is some of these changes, more than the growth of population as such, which are today having such destructive impacts on the world's trees and forests.

This book is about forests and people: about the origins of trees; about the development of the human species, its uses of trees and its relations with the forests; about the ways in which human societies have destroyed forests, and also the ways in which they have learned to manage, preserve and create forests; about where the forests used to be and where they are today; about what state they are in, how they came to be that way, what is happening to them now, and why it matters to us.

J.C.W.
July 1988

Acknowledgements

I am grateful to many more people than I can mention. However I should like to record my particular thanks to Dr Jeff Burley and other friends at the Oxford Forestry Institute; to Dennis Cullity, Geoff Elliot, Alf Leslie, Melanie McDermot, Norman Myers, Dennis Richardson, Bob Sutcliffe and Peter Wood for their help and encouragement; to my sons Mark and Adam for helping to construct this book from my sometimes disorganized drafts; and above all to my wife Flo, my sternest critic for half a century and my rebellious typist for the last few years.

To three generations of foresters who taught me
all I know about forestry

Part I   About trees

1   Trees before the coming of humans

To understand how forests have evolved, it is helpful to look at the stages through which life developed on our planet. The earth is reckoned to have been formed about 4.5 billion years ago. By then it had assumed something like its present mass and shape, along with its captured moon. There have been subsequent accretions, as the earth has passed through dead comets, but these have done little to add to the material of which the earth is composed. Billions and millions are not easy to envisage. To make it easier, in figure 1.1 (which obviously is not to scale), these 4.5 billion years have been translated into the familiar six days which the biblical Creation is supposed to have taken.

The six days run from just after midnight on Monday morning to midnight Saturday. Although a great deal happens during Monday to Friday, it happens very slowly. Also, all the important things – from Monday through Friday and well into Saturday – happen in the seas. By late on Monday the first forms of life appear and before the end of the day the trick of photosynthesis, of capturing and converting solar energy, has been learned. By noon on Thursday modern cells, with their DNA organized into chromosomes, have come into existence. Friday morning brings the first true plants, modern cells which have incorporated photosynthetic bacteria. The next step is for more complex structures to be built by groups of cells combining together, and by mid-afternoon on Friday seaweed has appeared. On Saturday morning the first multicelled animals arrive. Changes which would be apparent to us are coming faster now, with the development of vertebrates, then fishes, but all life forms, plant and animal, are still in the water. Life ashore starts at about 10.30 a.m. on Saturday, about 425 million years ago, the first substantial land plants being liverworts and mosses.

By noon on Saturday vertebrate animals have come ashore and horsetails and progymnosperms – the first real trees – have appeared, to be followed within the hour by true gymnosperms (naked-seeded plants), the durable conifers or cone-bearers. About the same time appear the Cordaitales, some of which reached a height of 36 m, but which were to die out 100 million years later. Not long after the Cordaitales there arrive the gingkos and cycads, some of which still survive. We are now in the

1

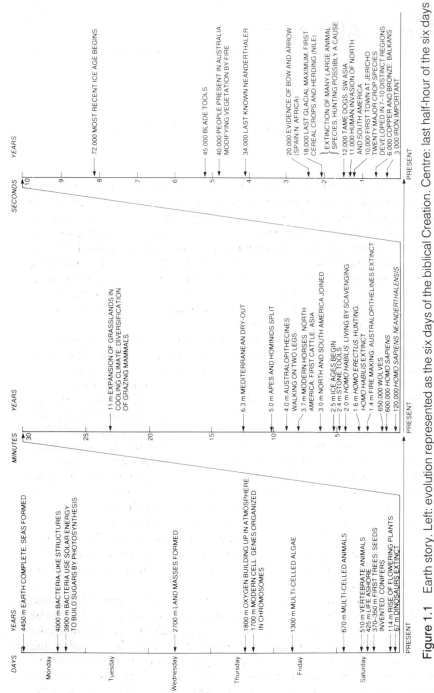

Figure 1.1 Earth story. Left: evolution represented as the six days of the biblical Creation. Centre: last half-hour of the six days expanded. Right: last ten seconds of the last half-hour expanded. (After Nigel Calder, Timescale)

carboniferous age which gave rise to the earliest of the coal seams mined today.

Lunged fishes evolved variants which could exploit the resources on land, leading to early amphibians and eventually to mammal-like reptiles. In the middle of the afternoon some reptiles developed wings and took to the air, the precursors of modern birds. At about the same time there appeared some early flowering plants, the Bennettitales, which, though doomed to extinction later on Saturday evening, made use of insects for pollination. The modern flowering plants, angiosperms, which today dominate the earth's plant life and include all broadleaved trees, made an appearance only four hours before midnight, 123 million years ago, to break out and start their takeover less than half an hour later.

The age of the dinosaurs lasted about 160 million years, from 3 p.m. to 10 p.m. on Saturday. These included a succession of giant herbivores and the well-armed carnivores who preyed upon them. For some reason not yet fully explained, all of these as well as most other reptiles suddenly disappeared about 67 million years ago. Among the few survivors of this catastrophe were the ancestors of today's mammals, placental mammals having evolved from mammal-like reptiles at about 8 p.m., at more or less the same time as modern flowering plants came on the scene. Tree-dwelling primates, the direct ancestors of humans, arrived at about 10 p.m.

Then, 24 million years ago, just under an hour before the week is up, came the grasses. The grasses were able to take advantage of any climatic changes or other disturbances unfavourable to trees, and still do. With the spread of grasses evolved the ancestors of all modern herbivores. On this one-week time scale, the precursors of the human race itself, the hominids *Homo habilis*, *Homo erectus*, and finally *Homo sapiens*, delayed their appearance until the last five minutes before midnight.

The earth's land-masses have been moving, with continents separating and coming in contact, throughout the evolution of modern plant life. For example, early during the evolution of flowering plants, the-land-masses which today form Antarctica, Australia, South Africa, South America and India were joined as a great southern continent of Gondwanaland. These southern continents today have in common certain plant groups which evolved before they separated, such as the southern beeches Nothofagus which occupy cool mountain forests in Australia, New Zealand and Chile. At the time when Gondwanaland was united, there was another great continent of Laurasia, including present-day North America and Eurasia; this has not divided into separate continents to the same extent, and North America has been linked to Asia by a landbridge in recent times. By about an hour before midnight on Saturday the continents had reached roughly their present arrangement.

There is a relationship between the appearance of grasses and the descent of our arboreal ancestors the apes from the trees. With the advent of a fairly prolonged dry period, grasses, less vulnerable to naturally caused fires, gradually spread at the expense of trees. As they spread, a grazing fauna developed, with teeth adapted to crop grass tufts and legs adapted to escape from predators by speed rather than by hiding.

During the last two to three million years the earth's climate has fluctuated considerably, and there has been a succession of ice ages. During each ice age temperate forests shrank back, to spread towards the poles again as the ice receded. And periods of extended ice caps were cooler and drier in the tropics, so tropical forests, too, shrank into smaller areas and expanded again when warmer and wetter conditions returned. The world's forests which existed when people started to make a significant impact upon them consisted of varying mixtures of broadleaved trees and cone-bearing trees, together with a few survivors of earlier evolutionary forms, cycads and tree ferns; some of these forests were interspersed with areas taken over by the grasses. As the ice retreated, conifers came to dominate, so that the broad belt of northern (boreal) forests, across North America, northern Europe, and the USSR consists mainly of conifers. The forests in the moist tropics (and especially the areas to which the forests retreated in drier, cooler times, the forest refugia) are the most heterogeneous. Among the reasons which have been advanced for this are that they are the longest established, so evolution, and speciation, has been at work longer; and that higher temperatures and humidity make for greater biological activity, so that evolution proceeds faster. But of the many alternative explanations that have been offered no single theory has as yet won general acceptance.

Indeed, scientists are far from agreed on what accounts for – even what is meant by – diversity of species. It is possible, for example, to have a wide variety of different species of tree in an area of a few hectares, but with that or a somewhat similar mix extending over hundreds of square kilometres: a homogenized heterogeneity, as it were. On the other hand, there are forests where the composition of the forest itself changes radically over relatively short distances, the composition in any particular location frequently being determined by the nature of the underlying soil. These points are mentioned here since, as we shall see later, they led to great differences in the way in which forests came to be, and presently are, used.

Thus there were very great changes in the earth's forests before ever people came on the scene. But some (though not all) of these changes took place very slowly indeed. And when one of the several lines of hominids which sprang from the great apes finally gave rise to our direct ancestors, they multiplied and spread so slowly that it is difficult to know when their impact on the forest began to outweigh that of climatic change.

There was a time when the principal life form on earth was the tree. Even today trees cover a large area of the earth's surface, and account for most of its biomass. To understand why trees came to dominate, it is necessary at this point to explain what distinguishes trees from other plant species and to say something about how they work.

2 How trees work

One way of looking at a tree is as a particular kind of factory. Its basic production process is like that of most other plants, but it differs from them in factory layout and in the way the product is allocated to different activities.

The raw materials plants use are carbon dioxide; energy, in the form of sunlight; and various other nutrients – nitrogen, phosphorus, potassium, and yet others needed in smaller amounts.

Some of the light energy falling on the plant is captured by pigments in the leaves. The light which is not captured is reflected, and looks green to us. Leaves are sheathed in a thin cuticle which lets light through but is almost impermeable to gases and water. Carbon dioxide nowadays makes up about one third of one per cent of the atmosphere. To get at it, plants have to expose a wet surface so the carbon dioxide can dissolve in the water and be absorbed into the plant's cells. The problem for plants is that water evaporates from the wet surface. They control the process as follows.

The carbon dioxide gas enters through microscopic, adjustable pores in the cuticle. Immediately after entering it is still in gas form in the spaces between the cells that make up the leaf, but then it dissolves in the water on the surface of those cells and the cells absorb it in solution. Meanwhile, water evaporates from the surface of the cells and escapes through the pores. Carbon dioxide is taken in quickly when the pores are open wide and the temperature is high. These same circumstances make the plant lose water fast. By closing the pores plants can greatly slow down water loss, but then they cannot take in carbon dioxide and they stop growing. So the more carbon dioxide plants take in, the more water they must spend. That is why plants grow fastest where there is plenty of water and temperatures are high. As water evaporates from the leaves it needs replacing. Fresh water is drawn up from the soil into the roots and up a ring of 'pipes' to the leaves. This water also brings mineral nutrients up from the soil.

The leaves represent the factory floor (see figure 2.1). Here the energy from sunlight is used to build carbon-based molecules from carbon dioxide. These molecules can be used in the leaf where they are built or they can be transported through another system of pipes to other parts of the plant. They can be consumed as fuel to drive the plant's activities, or combined with each other and with minerals such as nitrates to make the building blocks of the plant's structure. Woody plants differ from others in how they allocate their growth to different activities. The materials for new growth can be spent on the new productive machinery of leaves, and the roots and interconnecting pipes to go with them; on flowering and fruiting to produce offspring; or on building woody stems. Woody plants

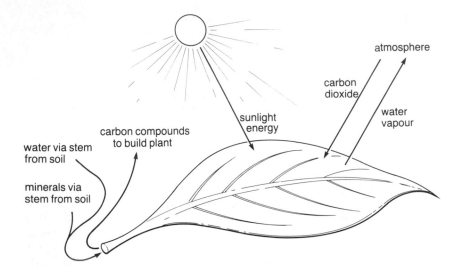

Figure 2.1   It is on the leaf that the production process of the tree takes place; here, solar energy enables atmospheric carbon dioxide to combine with other nutrients to build the carbon compounds that will be distributed throughout the tree

are those that invest a substantial proportion of their growth in a structure which can persist from year to year, and on which leaves can be supported higher in the air so that the plants can outreach their competitors in capturing light descending from above. Trees have a single main stem, the most economical way of achieving height. The new growth is actually laid down by cells multiplying at the tip of the shoot (for lengthwise growth) and in a thin cylinder around the stem. The new cylinder consists of piping to and from the new leaves. Meanwhile, the previous piping in the cylinder inside the new growth turns into wood, so the core of the stem is an ever-expanding tapered rod of wood providing structural support. As piping, the outer cylinder consists of thick-walled tubular cells, a honeycomb structure in cross-section, reinforced with bundles of fibres. This is already a good recipe for structural strength combined with lightness. But all plants have this. Woody plants have gone further. They have increased the thickness of the walls and the number of fibres, and have impregnated with chemicals the older tissue which is being left behind inside the stem. These chemicals – the most important is known as lignin, which comes from the Latin for wood – stain the wood dark and protect it against decomposition, that is against the bacteria and moulds which would otherwise consume it. The protection is not complete, because wood can decay, but it decays very much more slowly than leaves or fruits or softer plant tissue in general. This *lignification* is the key device acquired by plants during evolution that made trees possible. It means that the height gains made in one year's growth can be protected and therefore built upon in future years.

So wood (1) contains energy, (2) is structurally strong, considering how light in weight it is, and (3) resists decay. This is why trees have been successful over the long haul of evolution by natural selection. It is precisely these same properties which make wood useful to people as an energy-containing fuel, and as a light, strong, durable structural material. Nowadays we can mine fossil fuels for energy and metal ores for structure, and make plastics from petrochemicals. But trees have two advantages. Given land and time, wood will grow itself without labour. And some tree or other can be grown, and grown again, in almost any environment. So the potential is there for people almost everywhere to have supplies of energy and structural materials available literally in their backyards.

We have seen that the essential feedstock for the tree-factory consists of carbon dioxide, energy in the form of sunlight, water, and certain mineral nutrients. Shortage of any of these significantly affects the way in which the tree-factory operates; total absence obliges the factory to close down altogether. Thus in areas where there is a marked seasonality, that is where there is an annual shortage of light or water or both, the factory slows down or even closes down. Different kinds of trees bring about this slow-down in different ways. Many broadleaved trees are deciduous, that is they shed their leaves; in so doing they temporarily reduce the area of the factory floor or eliminate it. The litter in the forest is broken down by micro-organisms, restoring nutrients to the forest soil. Once enough warmth, light and water become available again, building activity is resumed, starting with the factory floor – the sprouting of new leaves. Cone-bearing plants, which have leaves shaped like needles, do not lose all their needles at once when water is short, or cannot be pumped (because it is frozen). These needles simply close up their pores so that they do not lose water: this of course also stops work on the factory floor.

These annual shut-downs and slow-downs show up in the cross-section of the tree as annual rings (figure 2.2). By examining carefully these annual rings it is possible not only to estimate how old the tree is, but to gauge changes in the climate, which can be traced back through the tree's life, even for hundreds of years.

This has given rise to the science of dendrochronology, which enables us to probe the past for thousands of years and is a valuable tool for archaeologists and historians. The rings vary in thickness from year to year, with the vagaries of the weather. These tree ring patterns are discernible in old timbers too, for example in oak beams which survive from mediaeval times, and in timbers which have somehow or other been preserved from even earlier times. These 'weather charts' (which is what the tree-ring patterns are, in effect) can be spliced on to each other, giving a

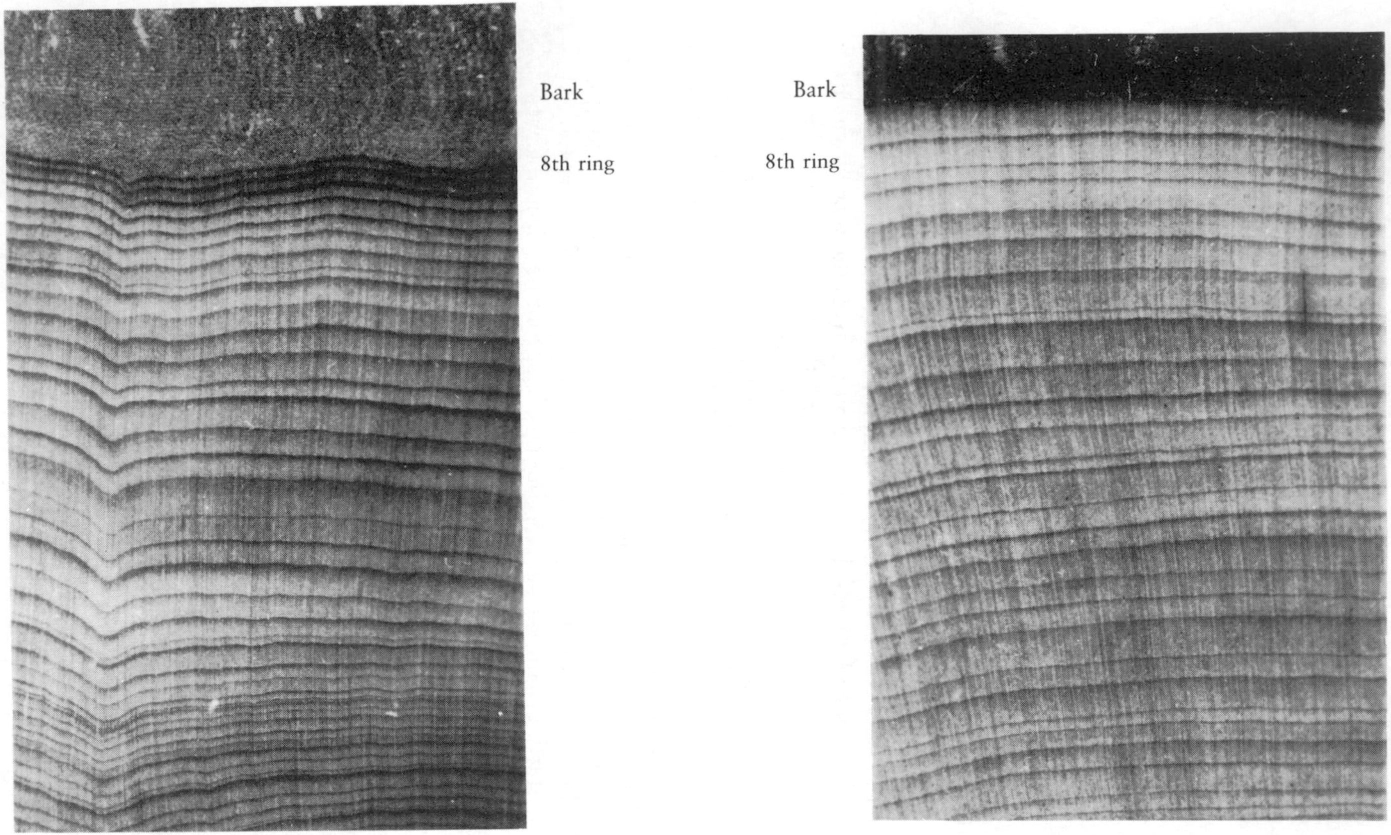

Figure 2.2 These examples of tree rings are from two celery-top pines felled in 1973 near Hobart, Tasmania. The very narrow eighth ring (counting inwards from the bark) corresponds to the drought of 1966 – 7, when fire swept the suburbs of Hobart. Several hundred houses were burnt and more than 50 people died. (photograph courtesy Don Adamson)

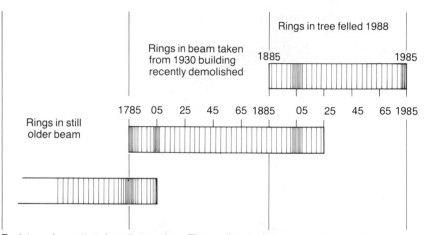

Rings in tree felled 1988

Rings in beam taken
from 1930 building   1885   1985
recently demolished

1785 05   25   45   65 1885   05   25   45   65 1985
Rings in still
older beam

Each tree-ring pattern is a climate chart. These climate charts can be spliced on
to each other as above, reaching back in time.
Not all trees have discernible tree rings. In Arizona, using the bristle-cone pine (very long-
lived, very slow growing), dated climate charts have been constructed up to 9000 years BP

Figure 2.3 Dendrochronological splicing: the linking together of tree-ring evidence from many sources can produce a datable record spanning centuries

continuous, datable record running back several thousand years (see figure 2.3).

Annual rings are the result of seasonal slow-downs or shut-downs. But quite apart from this, in every tree there is a built-in obsolescence in the sense that certain parts lose their effectiveness and are discarded, while new parts take their place. The longevity of leaves varies with latitude, climate and soil conditions; but there are evergreens (that is to say, trees which never lose all their leaves at once) in all latitudes.

Just as the tree can be regarded as a factory, the forest can be looked upon as a complex of factories. Though the basic production process is the same in all of them, the output, and the proportions among different outputs, vary from factory to factory and from complex to complex. A few figures will serve to illustrate the differences.

Three forest types

Let us compare three forests: an oak forest in Belgium, a mixed tropical lowland forest in Thailand, and a spruce-fir forest in Canada (see figure 2.4). Although the trees look very different, there are considerable underlying similarities. In all three cases the canopy is between about 25 and 30 m high, though a few trees are taller in the tropical forest. In each case the greatest weight of biological material is accumulated in the stems

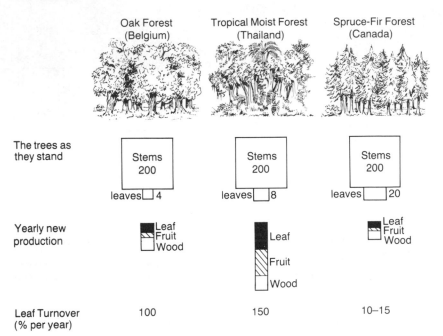

Figure 2.4 Three types of forest compared. Areas of blocks are proportional to quantities in dry tonnes per hectare. Branches typically account for 40 per cent, and roots 20 to 30 per cent, as much weight as main stems. Although the three types of forest produce different quantities of new material each year, they also allocate it differently, with the result that the quantity and annual increment of standing main stems is quite similar in each of the three forests

of the large trees; about 200 tonnes in a hectare (ha), which is the area of a square 100 m by 100 m. There would be about 150 such large stems in a hectare of each forest. Smaller amounts of wood would be present in the form of branches, leaves and roots, and smaller trees: there could be 1000-2000 saplings and understorey trees in each hectare. Branches would account for about 40 per cent as much biomass as the large stems, and roots for 20 to 30 per cent as much.

So the main framework of the biomass of the forests is similar. But the foliage, which captures light energy and synthesizes new growth, does not account for a big proportion of the biomass, and is rather different in the three cases. In the oak forest, at the peak of summer, leaves weigh about 4 tonnes/ha, and have a total area (measured on one side) of about 6 square metres (m^2) for each square metre of ground. In other words light which reaches the ground has been filtered through several 'layers' of leaves, though of course they are not in fact arranged in tidy layers. The leaves are shed each autumn and a new set emerges each spring. The tropical forest carries about 8 tonnes/ha of foliage, twice as much as the oaks, and in terms of area this amounts to about 11 m^2 of leaf per m^2 of ground area. Seedlings starting at ground level in the tropical forest receive substantially less light as a percentage of full daylight, but of course the light impinging on the top of the canopy is stronger in the tropics than in Europe. The spruce-fir forest has about 20 tonnes/ha of needles. This corresponds to about 15 m^2 of needle-coverage. However, this does not mean that shading in the spruce-fir forest is even more intense, because more light gets by a square centimetre of needle than a square centimetre of broad leaf. Light tends to bounce off the needles at an angle, but still travels downward through the canopy and is therefore useful to other needles lower down.

The total amount of new growth created is also different between the three forests. It is about 13 tonnes/ha per year in the oak forest, about 8 tonnes in the spruce-fir, and fully 30 tonnes in the tropical forest. As you can see, the amount of new tissue produced is not greatest where there is more foliage, rather it responds to the warmth and moisture available. But from the point of view of wood production, the three forests are not nearly so different – each lays down about 5-7 tonnes/ha per year of new wood. In the case of the oak forest, only about two tonnes of this is on main stems, and most goes on to branches, because oaks are trees which branch a lot as they grow old. In the tropical forest and in the spruce-fir, most of the new wood, about 4 tonnes/ha per year, goes on to main stems. The differences between the forests in total yearly production of new tissue comes about because different amounts are put into producing foliage, fruits and roots. The spruce-fir only produces 2 to 3 tonnes of new foliage per year, replacing only 10 to 15 per cent of its foliage each year. It maintains a large mass of leaves, but on average they are rather old and not very efficient. The oak forest replaces all 4 tonnes of foliage each spring. The tropical forest produces about 12 tonnes per hectare of new foliage each year, so it is actually replacing its 8 tonnes of leaves in about two-thirds of a year. The extra productivity made possible by these leaves goes heavily into fruit – 12 tonnes/ha per year, compared with 1 tonne or less in the other two forests.

The contrasts among the proportions of different 'outputs' in these examples suggest something else: the great variety of ways in which trees and forests make use of the raw materials or 'inputs' available to them. One of the most essential of these is water. Because this is possibly of greatest importance not only to the tree, but also to us, discussion of this is reserved for a later chapter (chapter 5).

Trees are not immortal. Like people they grow old, sicken and die. In a virgin forest, dying, dead and rotting trees may lie scattered everywhere; new growth each year may well be offset by loss through fire, pests and diseases, so that there is no net growth. If we think of wood as the principal product of the tree factory, then another characteristic of the tree is that the factory and the product are identical. Chop down the tree, to realize the product by releasing it from store, and the factory itself has been chopped down. But simultaneously soil, water, air and light have been freed for new factories to grow.

This is what is happening all the time in a 'natural' forest. Tree falls, whether through simple ageing or because of natural hazards, both create light and space for new growth and return nutrients to the soil. Some trees need light for seeds to germinate and saplings to prosper; others need shade. When hurricanes cause widespread treefall, light-demanding species tend to fill the vacant space. Hence it is not unusual to find in natural forests considerable areas which are even-aged, that is of roughly the same generation. These areas will not be permanently taken over by the species which first occupy them. Such species are typically fast-growing with low-density wood (as a rule, the faster a species of tree grows, the lighter its wood). If more than 200 to 400 years should pass without a disturbance which clears the canopy again, these faster-growing species will tend to die and fall. Meanwhile, other species with denser wood and longer-lived trunks, tolerant of the dense shade, will have been establishing themselves and growing beneath them; these will come to dominate the forest. In wet tropical areas it is mainly hurricanes, earthquakes and landslides which open large gaps and create even-aged stands over wide areas. In temperate zones fires are more important.

Natural catastrophes explain why, within most of the world's mixed forests, there are substantial areas of relatively even-aged forest. It is much more difficult to explain why many different *species* of tree can live in the same or similar locations, with roughly the same availability of the essential feedstocks, and yet grow at different rates and build in to each of their factories different kinds of timber. The fact is that no convincing single explanation for this has yet been forthcoming. Fortunately, the wood of different species does vary greatly in the uses to which it can be put: there are differences in density, in colour, in strength, in chemical composition, in resistance to decay, in odour, in workability, and in numerous other qualities. This range makes wood a most versatile material.

Another advantage shared by almost all trees is that they need not be harvested when they are 'ripe'; they can be left standing until it is convenient or opportune to harvest them. In fact, the pattern of growth of the particular species determines the most sensible time to harvest. Through the life of a tree the rate at which wood is added first accelerates, and then declines. In due course, therefore, less extra wood is gained each year by leaving the tree to grow. On the other hand, the older and bigger a tree becomes (provided it does not become senile or sick), the more valuable is its wood for certain purposes. For example, long beams and wide planks can be cut from it, or long strips of veneer can be peeled from the log. However, size makes little difference for other uses, such as woodchips or paper pulp.

Mention has been made of germination and early growth. But there are many trees which reproduce by sprouting as effectively as from seed. This ability probably evolved through the need to survive frequent natural catastrophes, and is valuable because it means that wood can be harvested without destroying the tree. Some species send up new shoots from the stool: coppicing; others from the crown: pollarding. As every gardener knows, propagation, or vegetative reproduction, provides progeny closer to the parent stock than does sexual reproduction by seed. Some trees lend themselves more than others to vegetative reproduction. But in recent years tremendous advances have been made in extending propagation to a wide variety of tree species hitherto considered only capable of reproduction by seed. It is even possible that tree seed orchards may become a thing of the past; they will certainly decline in importance. This does not, however, mean that the quest for new strains of particular tree seed will become less important; they will still be required for selective breeding, to produce varieties with qualities deemed more desirable or with enhanced resistance to various pests and diseases.

All these very diverse characteristics mean that the options open for manipulating the forest so that it produces the kind of wood (and other things) that people need are many and various. The way in which these options have been exercised in the past, and the bewildering variety of options open today in various parts of the world, will be discussed in later chapters.

3   About wood

Every year about 3000 million m³ of wood are harvested and used. Of this amount, slightly more than half is burned as fuel for heating and cooking, most of it directly but some in the form of charcoal. Over half the world's peoples still depend on wood for cooking and heating (see figure 3.1). In the industrialized countries, very little wood is used as fuel, though with the steady depletion and rising costs of fossil fuels like coal, lignite and petrol there is growing interest in fuelwood plantations as a renewable source of energy.

For those who live in the industrialized countries, wood which is not burned, generally termed industrial wood, reaches the user in numerous different forms, generally after having passed through one or more wood transformation factories. As recently as the nineteenth century most of the wood used in continental Europe was cut and shaped by those who were going to use it: for fencing, for farm tools, for house construction, for household utensils, etc. It is worth reminding ourselves of this fact since this is still the case over large areas of the world today (see figure 3.2).

Figure 3.1 The dependence of over half the world's population on wood for cooking and heating often leads to soil erosion and declining soil fertility. These Ethiopian peasant farmers have no other source of energy (WFP photo by F. Mattioli, 1983/FAO)

In the industrialized countries, there is still some wood which is used without undergoing considerable transformation: as pit props, telegraph poles, fencing and the like. These are still recognizably parts of a tree, although they may have been treated with preservative. But most of the wood used today has been transformed in a wood processing plant. Sometimes it has been so transformed that its wood origin is no longer recognizable. Until recent years, most wood was processed in sawmills (see figure 3.3), and lumber (that is, sawn wood) is still the form of wood most familiar to us. It goes into house and building construction, furniture, packaging, boat building, and so on. But today even more wood is used in a reconstituted form, and the most important of these forms are pulp, paper and paperboard. (Paperboard is thick, strong paper made on papermaking machines. Its thickness and strength may vary from that used for postcards to that used in folding cartons.)

The process of making paper is an essentially simple one. The wood is broken down into its constituent fibres and mixed with water to form a pulp. This breaking down can be done by mechanical means –

Figure 3.2 Traditional timber processing: pit sawing on the eastern slopes of Mt Kenya (photo John E. Hall, Oxford Forestry Institute)

Figure 3.3 A modern sawmill complex on Cowichan Lake, Canada (photo R. A. Plumtre)

grinding the wood – or by chemical means – dissolving away the lignin which holds the fibres together. The pulp so formed can be semi-dried for transporting or it can pass directly on to a papermaking machine. There most of the water is drained off and the remainder squeezed out or dried out as the paper passes through a series of heated rollers. In the course of adding and subtracting water, the individual fibre bundles hook on to and intermesh with each other, thus giving the paper a strength which is related to the inherent strength of the fibres themselves, and the ways they are arranged relative to one another. The process for all types of paper and paperboard is basically the same, though various additives are used to give different qualities to different kinds of paper (such as its writing surface, printability, strength and colour). Wood has long been the most important papermaking material, but it is of interest to note that the Latin word *liber* (book) was originally the word for another forest product, namely bast, the inner fibre of trees, which preceded papyrus as a writing material. Another precedent of papyrus was waxed boards, sections of trunks, caudex; hence the word codex.

Wood pulp, besides being the intermediate stage in papermaking, can also be moulded and used for a variety of purposes, including the familiar trays for storing eggs.

Other products

Of growing importance are the various forms of wood panels. Wood can be sliced very thinly to give thin sheets of veneer. Some woods give highly decorative veneers, by virtue of either their figure or their colour, and the art of fixing beautiful veneers on more common wood is almost as old as the furniture trade itself. Thin veneers can also be produced in a continuous length by rotating a cylindrical log against a knife, that is by peeling. If these thin sheets are glued together, with the grain of the wood running in alternate directions, the result is plywood, producing panels of great strength. There are very many end-uses of wood for which plywood is both more suitable and cheaper than solid lumber. Sometimes the outer layer or ply can be a decorative veneer, making possible the manufacture of handsome furniture much more cheaply than if the more expensive wood were used in solid form.

Another panel product is fibreboard, which can come in different thicknesses. Here the wood is chipped and defibred mechanically, more or less as in the mechanical pulping process. Before the pulp is formed into mats, small quantities of resin are added, then the mats are formed into boards at high temperatures and pressures. Fibreboard is widely used for the backs of carcase furniture (wardrobes and the like), for kitchen furniture, for flooring and partitioning, and for many other similar uses in which they have replaced solid lumber.

A late comer to the range of wood panel products, invented before World War II but expanding very rapidly since then, is particle board, or chipboard as it is known in the UK. In particle board the wood is first converted into shavings, chips, flakes or particles. These are then sprayed with a thermosetting resin, formed into mats and pressed into boards at high temperatures and pressures. Particle board can be given different facings or coatings; it can be of different thicknesses and densities; it can be of different strengths, depending on the shape and distribution of the flakes or particles. It has proved a very versatile material and is widely used for such purposes as construction, furniture and flooring.

Table 3.1 shows how these various uses of wood changed relative to each other in Europe over the seventy years until 1980. The consumption of all these forms of wood in Europe has risen faster than has population, with the sole exception of sawnwood. The slower rise in sawnwood use is attributable to its replacement in very many end uses by wood panels: by plywood and fibreboard up to the mid-century; more rapidly by both these and particle board thereafter. The decades after World War II also saw a very striking rise in the consumption per head of paper and paperboard, though since 1980 the rate of rise has been slowing down.

The foregoing paragraphs do not exhaust the forms in which this incomparable material, 'built by nature for her purpose', can be used. The

Figure 3.4 The rotary peeling of Western Australian Karri (Eucalyptus diversicolor) for the production of structural plywood (photo courtesy D. Cullity)

faster a tree grows, the softer and lighter is its wood as a general rule. Woods from different species differ in colour, odour, the mineral and organic compounds they contain, and in workability by various tools. They differ in pattern and figure according to the way in which they are

Table 3.1   Europe: consumption of forest products, 1913 to 1980 (million m³)

Product type	1913	1950	1980
Sawnwood	55	62	102
Paper and paperboard	5[a]	11[a]	49[a]
Plywood	0.1	1.4	5.4
Fibreboard	–	1.1	4.4
Particle board	–	–	24.1[a]

[a]million tonnes.
Source: Food and Agriculture Organization, Forest and Forest Products Yearbook, various years.

cut, sawn or sliced. This is why wood has proved such a versatile construction material throughout history. There are some woods which are less than one-fifth as heavy as water; others are nearly twice as heavy. Some woods, such as quebracho and chestnut, contain chemicals which, once dissolved out, are suitable for tanning leather. Another wood, sandalwood, has such a pleasant and delicate scent that, in addition to its use for incense, it was for generations highly prized by rich Chinese for coffin making. Today sandalwood has virtually disappeared from the forests of Asia.

Most forms of processed wood make direct or indirect use of the inherent strength of the individual fibre bundles and of the forces binding those bundles together. Special qualities can be given to reconstituted products by orienting the chips, flakes, or other elements in particular directions. Also, with modern glues solid lumber can be assembled into roof members of a size and shape which no individual tree could ever provide: thus very large buildings, without pillars, can be constructed with timber roofs (see figure 3.5).

But this is not all. The wood of many trees can, by chemical treatment, be reduced to pure alpha cellulose. This is the feedstock for a variety of industries: rayon, tyre cord, transparent cellulose wrappings, explosives and so forth.

It will already be apparent that each species of wood has its own characteristics, often discernible from the way in which the species makes use of the inputs which contribute to its structure. When very thin slices of wood are examined under a microscope it is possible to identify the tree species from the cellular structure thus revealed. And surprisingly, charcoal (burnt wood) retains sufficient characteristics of the original tree to allow similar identification. It has thus proved possible to identify, from charcoal remains found in caves in southern Africa, the tree species used as fuel by people, not only hundreds of years ago, but even 20 000 to 30 000 years ago. These findings may prove to have great significance for Africans

Figure 3.5 Timber building technology, old and new: (a) Massive timbers in an historical barn in southern England; (b) A modern glulam structure from the Swan Centre, Dublin (photos copyright Timber Research and Development Association)

of today, many of whom, as will be explained later, face fuel famine which is not being alleviated by solutions presently advocated.

Trade in wood

Although wood is so versatile it is still, in most forms, bulky in relation to its weight. This means that transport costs bear heavily, both on getting wood from the forest to the wood processing factory, and on getting the wood product to the final consumer. It is these costs – the costs of getting wood to where it is wanted – which have always influenced the ways in which wood has been used, how wood has been taken out of the forest, and consequently the impact on the forests themselves.

When the forest was no man's land, or anybody's land, wood was a free good. People went further afield for wood only when woods of the kind they wanted were not available nearby. But wood of special kinds or dimensions has been the subject of long-distance trade from ancient times. The Pharaohs brought cypress, juniper and cedar, by sea, from the forests of what is now Lebanon and Syria, and ebony up from the south. The wooden pillars of the Summer Palace in Peking came from far away Szechuan. Successive maritime powers have sought ship timber far afield once local supplies became exhausted. Thus Venice, in her prime, depended on the forests of Dalmatia, and issued regulations to control exploitation in those forests. Similarly Britain was importing ship masts from the Baltic, delivered by the Hanseatic League, as early as the end of the fifteenth century. With the expansion of the fleet and the advent of multi-masted ships this trade steadily grew. In the mid-seventeenth century Samuel Pepys, as secretary to the English king's navy, was arranging the import of masts from Norway, and in the second half of the century Norwegian timber, mainly for shipbuilding, made up more than half the total tonnage of British imports; the trade shifted to North America towards the end of the century only because of the exhaustion of suitable stems near the western Scandinavian ports. Later on, it was British Admiralty needs that led to major incursions in the forests of India and Burma.

Some highly prized luxury woods occur only sparsely in heterogeneous tropical forests. The rich merchants and the nobility in England valued mahogany so greatly that it was worthwhile employing mahogany hunters in the forests of Central America to locate these rare and valuable trees. The country of Brazil owes its name (originally *terra de brasil*) to a prized species of wood which was discovered there and which became its first major export of wood. Similarly, though much later, in the moist temperate forests of Australia, cedar-getters searched out specimens of the valued red cedar *Toona australis* (not to be confused with the Western red cedar *Thuja plicata* from North America).

Historically the price of wood has generally been determined by the cost of getting it to where it was wanted, not by the cost of growing it, renewing it, or replacing it. This was true of the northern temperate forests until quite recent times, and it is *still* true of the tropical forests. However, as the temperate forests began to come under strict management, with greater heed to ensuring that they renewed themselves, the price of wood relative to that of other materials rose. A consequence of this has been that wood has been used more thriftily. Thus various forms of reconstituted wood have replaced solid lumber in a wide variety of uses. As we saw from table 3.1 the rapid expansion in the use of wood panel products this century has taken place largely at the expense of solid lumber. Thus 1 m^3 of particle board can replace 2.5 m^3 of sawn wood, which in turn requires close on 4 m^3 of roundwood to produce. Since the particle board itself can be manufactured largely from wood residues – formerly regarded as wood waste – this represents a considerable saving in wood. As recently as the 1940s the wood waste accumulating at saw mills and plywood factories was simply a nuisance, a fire hazard to be eliminated periodically unless it could be used as fuel to power the factory. Today no-one speaks of wood waste, only of wood residues: technologies are being developed to make use of the last fraction of sawdust.

The same considerations have prompted the drive for more complete utilization of the forest, that is of the various species which compose it, and of the tree itself, including the tops, branches, twigs, bark, stumps and roots. It used to be said, of the meat processing factories in Chicago, that nothing of the pig was wasted except the squeal. Something analogous to this occurs in many of the forests and wood industry complexes of North America and Europe. Small trees, tops and branches that were formerly not worth bothering to cart out of the forest are converted into wood chips on the spot by portable chipping machines, and are transported to the pulp or particle board factory to be used in the same way as wood residues arising in saw mills and plywood plants. Sawdust and wood chips mixed with green material are often compressed into briquettes for fuel; such briquettes are superior to fuel firewood, as they have a lower ash content, are easily transportable, and do not require special furnaces. Bark can be processed for use as a compost or mulch, and is thus widely used in forest nurseries, in hothouses, and in gardens. It can also be used as fuel. Because up to 12 per cent of the wood biomass of a tree is to be found in the stump and roots, it has become worthwhile, in some circumstances, to devise machinery for grubbing out stumps with their roots, to be washed and chipped for further processing.

This by no means completes the catalogue of wood uses. Though mention has been made of certain chemical extractives obtainable from special woods, nothing has been said about wood chemistry and the many products that can be derived from wood distillation. Trucks and automobiles converted to run on wood gas may seem museum pieces, but this practice was general in Scandinavia during World War II when petroleum supplies were cut off.

In the 1940s, before the petrochemical industries had taken off, many scientists argued that we could not afford to burn coal; its potential future use as a feedstock for a wide range of chemical industries far outweighed its value as a fuel. Today an analogous argument is being put forward by some scientists on behalf of wood: its potential for giving rise to a vast new range of materials is such that it may be wasteful to sit upon it, read it, or burn it. It may be doubted whether advances in wood chemistry have enhanced the value of wood to this point, but in the long term the fact that wood is renewable offers great advantages.

However, the old adage that the least valuable use to which wood could be put was to burn it was never valid for most of the Third World. While the vagaries of oil prices and supply will mean that some industrialized countries may have to reappraise their plans for growing wood for energy, over much of the Third World there is no alternative fuel to wood yet in sight. For many decades yet, more than half the wood harvested in the world is destined to be burned.

4 Other forest products

Most of us think of wood as the most important product of the forest. But there are many other products and services which come from the forest, and sometimes these are more important, and of greater value, than wood. There are a number of trees which yield valuable saps, resins, gums and the like, and which can be managed to yield these on a continuing basis.

The most important of these commercially is the rubber tree, whose milky sap is induced to run by cutting V-shaped notches in the bark (see figure 4.1). Originally the rubber tree occurred sporadically in the forests of the Upper Amazon. It was the discovery of rubber's properties and the collection of rubber from those forest trees which gave rise to the rubber boom which at the close of the nineteenth century turned Manaos into one of the world's richest 'boom' towns. However, after rubber seeds were smuggled out of Brazil, disguised as orchid seeds, by the English botanist Henry Wickham, and developed at Kew Gardens, near London, plantations of rubber trees were established in Malaya and other parts of Asia. The plantation rubber proved much cheaper than that collected from the natural forest, and Manaos rapidly fell into decay.

Several pine trees yield resin, on which whole 'naval stores' industries were built up in past times. The sugar maple yields maple syrup, while one of the acacias, growing in Sudan and Ethiopia, yields gum arabic, a constituent of jellied confectionery. The wild bees of Tanzania, which make their nests in rudely constructed cylindrical hives made of bark, hung in the trees, provide honey for export in enormous quantities, representing a value many times that of the wood produced in Tanzanian forests. Nuts, berries, and a wide variety of edible fungi (as well as truffles) are to be found in or associated with forests and woodlands. Some of these are largely consumed locally; others have given rise to important export industries.

The Mediterranean cork industry, based on the bark of the cork oak, has declined in importance with the advent of synthetics, but still survives in Portugal and North Africa (see figure 4.2). It has been estimated that in India the ubiquitous *bidi*, local cigarettes, rolled in leaves of a particular native tree, *Diospyros melanoxylon*, contributes over £200 million sterling to the national economy, in income tax, costs of leaves and tobacco, excise duty, freight, and wages to 3 million part-time workers.

The tropical forests provide a whole variety of leaves, bark, roots, nuts, berries and the like, which form one of the mainstays of the modern pharmaceutical industry. By 1974 the United States was importing pharmaceutical materials from the tropics to a value of US$24 million, and this raw material entered into a drug output with an estimated retail market value of US$8 *billion*.

In many forests, from the warm temperate to the tropical, an important component is bamboo, which is not a tree at all but a special kind of grass. In some countries vast areas are covered by bamboo. There are many species of bamboo but broadly speaking they fall into two classes: those which throw up stem after stem from the same stool; and those which spread underground by rhizomes, throwing up single stems at intervals. Some of these hollow stems reach such a length and have such strength that they are widely used as scaffolding poles and for constructional purposes. The forests of Asia also shelter many species of climbing plants known as rattans, which can attain lengths of up to 100 m or more and range in diameter up to 10 cm. Bamboos and rattans are put to a great variety of uses by people living in and near these forests. Exports of furniture and woven goods made from bamboo and rattans have multiplied enormously, and by the 1980s certain species of useful rattans in southeast Asia were becoming very rare.

All types of forest shelter a wide variety of fauna. To the people who live in the forest, many of these are of more than scientific interest: they represent a principal source of animal protein. In some west African areas today the local people still depend on forest game for up to three quarters of their animal protein. On the other side of the globe, a recent study showed that the Dyaks and other tribes of the Sarawak rainforest consumed or sold the meat of over 700 000 wild pigs and about 75 000 deer each year. A parallel study showed a very sharp drop in the average

Figure 4.1 (opposite) Rubber being tapped for latex, Kedak, 1986 (photo I. M. Turner)

Figure 4.2 Plastics have replaced cork in most of its traditional end uses. These cork oaks in Morocco's Mamora forest have now been replaced by pines and eucalypts for the development of timber and paper industries (photo R. Rouget/FAO)

consumption per person of wild meat after areas had been logged. Indeed, throughout history people have depended on forest fauna for all or much of their protein intake. Apart from meat, forest-dwelling animals have always provided furs and skins. There were vast areas of forest on the European continent and in North America which were penetrated by hunters and trappers to feed an important international trade in furs and skins long before significant areas of them were cleared for settlement. Where settlements spread, those wild animals inimical to farming were, of course, hunted, often to the point of extermination.

Furs and skins were among the important items traded internationally in medieval times, royalty, the nobility and the high clergy being the final consumers. Thus the Skinners' Company, founded in the fourteenth century, is one of the oldest of England's livery companies; centuries later it was to invest in the East India Company. In Russia, the town of Nijni-Novgorod owed its importance to the fur trade of which it was the most important centre.

Hunting and trapping for furs and skins still survives in the wilder areas of the cool temperate and boreal forests. And it continues in the shrinking tropical forest, in spite of attempts to outlaw it. Furs and skins continue to be traded internationally. But in recent decades another significant product of, and export from, the tropical forests has been live monkeys for medical and other research (including research into cosmetics and space flight). The value of this trade to research may be debatable; the manner in which the bulk of it is presently conducted is wholly to be condemned. The proportion of deaths in transit rivals that among slaves when slaves were a principal item of international commerce.

Yet there is one 'product' of the forest which in many countries, both tropical and temperate, outranks all these, and even wood itself, as the most important: clean water. Since water can be regarded either as a product of the forest or as a service which the forest can provide, we take it as the starting point for our next chapter.

5   Further benefits from trees

Ever since classical times writers have observed that whenever there has been a loss of forest cover, perennial streams have given way to oscillations between drought and dry river beds on the one hand, and disastrous floods carrying away topsoil on the other. It is easy to see why this happens. The leaves of a tree intercept a proportion of falling rain; that which penetrates to the ground does so at reduced speed when it reaches ground level, so that soil disturbance is minimized. The interstices within the soil created by tree roots offer ample room for water absorption and storage. Thus the tree, while consuming some of the water through its roots, allows the rest to penetrate slowly towards the water table, reducing surface run-off to quantities and speeds which do not spell soil erosion. Of course, trees are not the only form of land cover which can help to regulate and provide clean water supplies. Today hydrologists know enough about the water-regulating abilities of different kinds of forest in the temperate zone, and other forms of green cover, to ensure that watersheds are planted with the combinations of cover most apt for providing community needs.

However, the relationships between water and forests are more complex, and are as yet far from being well understood. Some notion of these complexities can be gathered by reverting for a moment to the tree–factory analogy. To carry out photosynthesis leaves need to transpire water, water which is pumped up from the ground via the tree's plumbing system. The availability of water for pumping is one of the main factors which controls the rate of production. The leaf, the tree, the forest as a whole, thus transpires water in the form of vapour.

When rain falls, some rain is intercepted on the leaves, evaporates, and never reaches the soil. Thus the total amount of moisture going back into the atmosphere is the sum of evaporation and transpiration. What proportion of rain is intercepted depends on the frequency and intensity of storms, less being intercepted where storms are very intense. Generally speaking, three-fifths to four-fifths of the rain that falls reaches the soil. Some of this drains off into aquifers or runs off into streams; the rest, which may be as little as a fifth or as much as three-fifths of the total rainfall, remains in the surface soil and is available to the tree (see figure 5.1).

In the three kinds of forest mentioned in chapter 2 – tropical rainforest, spruce-fir and oaks – evapotranspiration per ha per year might amount to about 14 000, 5000 and 4000 tonnes respectively. This is more than a hundred times as much water as is actually tied up in the trees' bodies at any one time. Thus, though trees do use water as a resource for constructing their bodies, this is quite insignificant when compared with the amount they need to spend exposing wet surfaces in order to absorb carbon dioxide from the atmosphere. Put another way, the water used for processing on the factory floor is more than a hundred times as much as that which goes into the product.

Many experts believe that widespread deforestation can seriously affect climate – the macroclimate, not simply the microclimate (about which there is little argument). Such records as are available suggest, for example, that rain in Brazil's northeast is rarer and sparser today than before that area was deforested and converted to sugar plantations centuries ago. The argument is lent force by the fact that the amount of water entering the atmosphere from the forest is immense as compared with the amount incorporated in the forest structure. Controversy goes on and much still has to be learned about the complex interactions, but whether or not forests decisively influence climate, near or far, there is no doubt that they do determine what happens to the rain which falls upon them. That is the key to the most important influence of forests.

In the tropical forest, rainfall is often extremely heavy, while the soils are thin and lacking in nutrients because of the rapid recycling. Thus when these soils are bared, especially on slopes, they are easily carried away and the process of degradation begins. There is plenty of evidence that deforestation reduces infiltration and increases run-off, especially if the soil is compacted. For example, it was discovered that the run-off from cultivated bare soil in West Africa (as a percentage of the total annual rainfall) was more than twenty times that from forest land. There are sizeable areas in the Brazilian Amazon which have been converted to pasture and subsequently overgrazed, leading to soil compaction; this has brought about such severe erosion that it has been described as a 'ghost

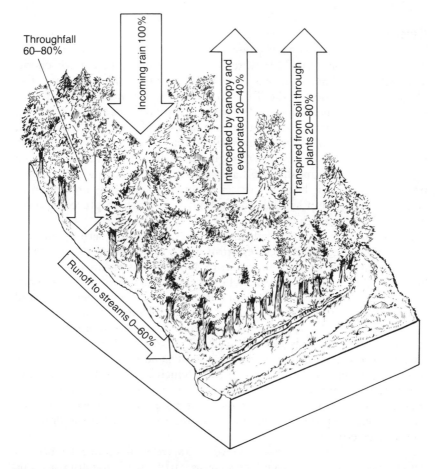

Throughfall
60–80%

Incoming rain 100%

Intercepted by canopy and
evaporated 20–40%

Transpired from soil through
plants 20–80%

Runoff to streams 0–60%

Figure 5.1 The water transactions of a forested watershed

landscape'. One of the lessons to be learned from this is that any conversion or exploitation of tropical forest should be carried out so as to leave as complete a vegetation cover as possible. The unfortunate thing is that, for reasons discussed in later chapters, very little is known about most tropical forest ecosystems, and in particular about forest-water-soil relationships. What is known is that most of them are much more vulnerable when interfered with than are temperate forests. There are some forest types, and there are forests in particular locations (by no means all in the tropics), where the water-regulating and soil-holding functions of the forest are so important that any intervention may be dangerous and substantial clearance can be – and in some cases has been – catastrophic.

Other benefits

Trees are not only vital for watersheds. They can prevent, or check, avalanches and landslips; they can curb snowdrift and sand drift. The ubiquity of television in the Western world, which makes news global, instant, but ephemeral, has made it seem that mud slides and landslips are occurring more often, and with more serious effects: in Peru, Brazil, Ecuador, Colombia; in Switzerland, Italy, Austria, France. The phenomenon is not simply the consequence of more efficient media. It is a very real one, and landslides in Latin America are reaching catastrophic proportions. This is because greater numbers of peasants are driven to cultivate steeper slopes, while the upland forests which protected them and their land are being cut down.

In the European Alps the effects have so far been less serious. But the underlying cause, upland deforestation, is the same, and without prompt action even greater tragedies are in store. Not all disasters are preventable. Small scale mud slides and avalanches occur frequently in the Alps. They can gather force and become serious if and when there is persistent and exceptionally heavy rain or snow. But the Alpine scenery and the possibility of skiing virtually all year round attracts more and more tourists, and forest has been cleared to make way for roads, hotels, chalets, shops, cable cars and ski pistes. Austria now has a greater mileage of ski slopes than of railways. The trees which damped the water flow, which checked avalanches in their early stages, which cushioned falling rocks, have gone. Studies have shown that pistes even above the tree line can so affect the ground vegetation as to interfere with natural drainage and lead to erosion.

In the form of shelterbelts and windbreaks, trees can reduce the speed of desiccating winds that would otherwise carry away thin topsoil. The profile and pattern of windbreaks can be so constructed as to counter the effects of winds that vary in strength and direction through the seasons. These are some of the reasons why trees play an enormously important role in rehabilitating marginal land, in halting and reversing encroachment by the desert. Trees alone will not accomplish these things, but combined with other measures, they can and do.

Moreover, there are trees suited to a bewildering variety of hostile environments (see figure 5.2): trees that will grow under near desert conditions, providing browse for animals, either *in situ*, or in the form of leafy boughs cut for penned or tethered animals; trees that will grow in saline conditions where misapplied irrigation has ruined the possibility of other forms of vegetation; trees that fix nitrogen and that can serve as 'green manure'. There are trees capable of providing wood for fuel within two to three years, and of supplying biomass energy that can be adapted to industrial scale needs as well as for household purposes.

Figure 5.2 Corsican pine being used to revegetate spoil from an open-cast coal mine in south Wales (photo P. S. Savill)

There are large areas of the world, especially in the tropics, where sustainable agriculture is only possible with the aid of trees, whether as part of the crop rotation, as shade trees, or as fodder. Only since the 1970s has there been a determined effort to learn from and extend the traditional methods arrived at by trial and error in the course of centuries, and to scientifically devise new systems capable of being applied to lands presently considered marginal. Trees have an important part to play in land reclamation. The 'great green wall' being erected in northern China is no figment of the imagination. It exists, and it exists where before there was nothing but sand. For many hundreds of miles there is now a belt of forest shelter, and within the forest, natural regeneration is sufficiently advanced to ensure the forest's survival.

In all continents, but particularly in Asia, Africa and Latin America, there are today vast areas of land which have been so badly misused in the past that they are no longer capable of growing food and fuel for the people who live there. In all these critical situations, trees have a significant contribution to make to land rehabilitation; in many cases their contribution will be decisive. This is about the most important job that trees have to do in the world today.

Another function of certain types of forest, and especially of the tropical moist forests, is as a reservoir of genetic material. Because many of our staple foods and important drugs originated in these forests, this function is vital. Its significance will be discussed in the chapter on tropical forests.

Before leaving, for the time being, the services which trees render, just a word about what trees can do to improve the quality of urban life. In every continent, there are some cities which, through the accident of history, or as a result of wise planning by the original city-builders, have made sensible use of trees. Yet the majority of the world's cities are concrete jungles or featureless shanty towns. Only recently has it been recognized how careful use of trees can reduce levels of dust, chemical and noise pollution, heating and maintenance costs, and road accidents; and can provide play space and shade and other amenities. At the time of writing urban forestry is still taught at only a handful of forestry schools, but already it is beginning to make life healthier and more pleasant for millions of urban dwellers.

6   The scope for management

Given the thousands of different ways in which trees can serve people, and understanding something of the way a tree grows, it should be clear that there is an almost infinite number of ways of manipulating the forest, the woodland, or the individual tree so that the trees serve the particular needs required, and serve them better. In fact, forests have been 'managed' (perhaps it would be better to say purposefully manipulated) in certain simple ways ever since prehistoric times. Often this was done simply by encouraging the growth nearby of those kinds of trees which serve particular food, fuel, or shelter needs. The pollen record has demonstrated that many of the lake dwellers of Western Europe deliberately encouraged, and perhaps even planted, hazel and other preferred species near their homes.

Primitive peoples not only felled some species and planted others, they developed coppicing and pollarding – arts which are still extensively practised today. Instead of raising a new tree from a seed or sapling, or by planting a slip, coppicing involves the encouragement of new shoots from the stool at ground level. The wood is harvested periodically, but the root is not destroyed and several shoots are always maintained in production. Pollarded trees are those in which new shoots are fostered, not from the stool, but from a point on the main stem 2 or 3 m from the ground (see figure 6.1). Pollarding has the advantage that the new shoots are less susceptible to the depredations of livestock, but of course harvesting the wood is slightly more difficult. Wood from coppice and wood from tall individual trees (standards) served different purposes. Until quite recent times many European forest inventories distinguished between coppice, coppice with standards (figure 6.3), and high forest.

So forests can be moulded to human needs in many different ways.

Species that are not wanted can be eliminated. This can be done by felling, poisoning, or ring-barking. (Because the tree gets its water feedstock from the roots via a ring of pipes just under the bark, a cut through the bark and just below it encircling the trunk necessarily kills the tree.) Preferred species can be encouraged by various means. The spacing between trees can be altered, directly affecting the quality of wood (if little light gets to the lower branches they wither and die off: this is self-pruning). The age at which the tree is harvested can be varied, thus changing the characteristics and dimensions of timber which can be obtained from it. The production of wood can be combined with grazing or browse for domestic or wild animals; in the Domesday Book, many forests were measured by the number of pigs that could be fed from the acorns or beechmast in them.

Scientific management

Even the most primitive peoples built up empirically some rudimentary knowledge of how to manipulate forests, woodlands and trees to meet their needs. But the codification of this knowledge, a true understanding of the dynamics of the forest and the biology of the individual trees which compose it, had to wait until modern times. Forestry science is still relatively young. Forest management requires not only a detailed knowledge of how trees behave, individually and collectively, when subject to various kinds of intervention; it also requires a clear understanding of the functions which the forest is to serve, and the priorities accorded to those several functions.

Wood is not only versatile; it is also a renewable resource. It is something which we can have, if we go about it the right way, as far in the future as we wish. Many European and North American forests are primarily managed for wood production, and the key principle is that yield should be at least maintained. This principle of 'sustainable yield' was only established after a hard battle at the end of the last century. In establishing it, foresters won the first battle in the twentieth-century conservation movement. Because the factory and the product are identical, care must be taken that trees are not felled at a time and in a way which lowers the capacity of the forest to go on producing wood (and providing its other services). Forestry science has now advanced to the point where it is known how to do this for nearly all kinds of temperate zone forests. This does not mean that all such forests *are* properly managed. But mismanagement arises more often from confused ideas about the purposes for which the forests should be managed than from ignorance about how to manage.

The different functions which trees serve call for different forms of management. Since many forests have to serve more than one purpose,

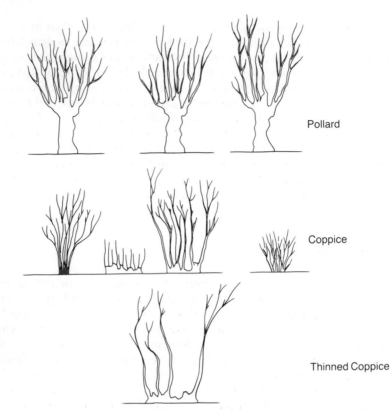

Figure 6.1 Coppicing is one of the earliest forms of tree management. Many trees will coppice, i.e. throw up new shoots from the stool (figure 6.2); stumps are cut off near the base to provide small-diameter wood for domestic purposes. During the growth of each cycle, some shoots can be cut small while others are left to grow larger. Pollarding was a later development; new shoots are kept out of the reach of browsing domestic animals

compromises have to be reached. Multi-purpose management is possible, but not all the functions of the forest can be realized in full simultaneously. A forest can provide recreation and amenity services, regulate stream flow, protect farm land and shelter wild life, while still producing timber. But the optimum for each service requires single-purpose management: to manage for some or all these services necessarily requires trade-offs. Most disputes between foresters and environmentalists have arisen because of the difference in importance each side assigns to the various functions of the forest.

One of the complicating factors is that what happens to a forest depends

Figure 6.2 Mallee is a growth form of Australian eucalypts in which several stems coppice naturally after the fires to which the vegetation is prone. The species shown is *Eucalyptus salubris* in south-western Australia (photo courtesy D. Cullity)

Figure 6.3 Modern coppice with standards at Iphofen in West Germany. The coppice has recently been cut, and the resulting smallwood is in stacks; the standards are still in place (photo P. S. Savill)

not only on what is taken out but on how it is taken out. The technology of harvesting timber – logging and transport – progresses and becomes more complex year by year as new machines are invented to reduce the very high labour cost of getting wood from where it grows to where it is to be processed. A modern forestry operation will involve felling by chain saw, trimming off the branches, dragging or 'skidding' the stem by tractor to a suitable landing or clearing in the forest, and sawing it into suitable lengths, to be finally loaded on to trucks and taken to the wood processing factory along roads which have been specially built into the forest. The operation is somewhat simpler if the forest is even-aged and of a single species, so that the area can be clear-felled. Where the topography is difficult, other means are available for getting the timber out. Skyline logging enables bundles of logs to be lifted and winched by cable to a landing point. Even logging by balloon has proved economic in some exceptional situations. Water transport, historically, was always easier and cheaper than transport by land, so wherever suitable waterways were available, these were employed to float the logs down to where they were to be used or exported. Sometimes streams were redirected into artificial wooden waterways, called flumes, down which logs could be speeded.

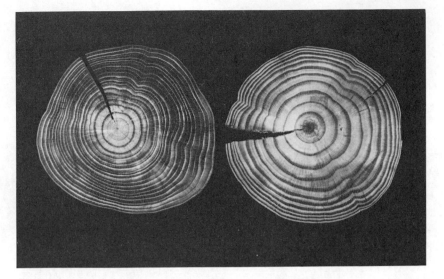

Figure 6.4 Cross-sections of *Pinus caribaea* grown under natural conditions (left) and plantation conditions (right). The wider growth rings of the latter show the faster growth achieved under plantation conditions

When trees are removed from a forest, scope for new growth is created. There is more light near the ground, more water in the soil where roots are no longer pumping, and more mineral nutrients as the cut-off roots, leaf litter and slash from the logging decompose. Harvesting methods affect not only what remains, but also what is likely to develop in the space created. Highly selective logging creates gaps the same size as individual tree falls, while clear-felling creates gaps from a few hectares upwards. Depending on the forest type in question, either of these gap-sizes may mimic gaps created by natural events and so provide suitable opportunities for regeneration of tree species which grow there. Sylvicultural systems which aim for natural regeneration seek to create gaps which are similar to those naturally exploited by the tree species in question. For example, eucalypt forests which naturally regenerate after crown fires are logged to create fairly large gaps, and the slash is burned to make an ash bed suitable for seedling establishment. There are other forest types where regeneration is favoured by leaving the slash to decompose. But the slash can constitute a fire hazard which must be guarded against.

Though forests have been manipulated from time immemorial, there are still relatively few forests in the world which are managed in the modern sense. When forestry science did develop, its application extended but slowly, and only to those countries or parts of countries where problems of timber supply became acute. Planted forests are, of course, much easier to manage than natural forests. Selected seed can be used;

growth is uniform; the spacing is regular; the wood material for industry is homogeneous. There are even circumstances where it is as profitable to fertilize forests as to fertilize farm or garden crops. Though the practice is not, as yet, widespread, it could extend were the relative price of wood *vis-à-vis* artificial fertilizers to change in favour of the latter. There are still some people to whom planted forests are anathema. But a forest plantation is no more unnatural than a field of wheat or a herd of Black Angus cattle; all three are similar manifestations of humans moulding nature to their purpose. Moreover, there is no doubt whatever that the world is going to depend – indeed will have to depend – more and more heavily on plantation forests in the future: not only for its wood supplies, but for fuel and for the management of its water needs.

The domestication of trees, like the domestication of food plants and animals, brings, along with manifold advantages, new problems: constant controls and preventive measures against pests and diseases, and the need for periodic selection and breeding to maintain vitality and resistance to disease. Some of the most important recent advances in forestry science echo the forward strides of agricultural science generations ago. It is now possible to 'farm' trees in 'artificial' plantations so as to produce up to ten times the volume of wood or fibre as would be produced in a 'natural' forest on the same area. But this procedure, whether applied in the temperate zone or in the tropics, has costs which must be taken into account and risks which must be guarded against, for example in the progressive exhaustion of important nutrients, or in reduced water regulating capacity.

The problems of managing the tropical forests are particularly complex. In general they are much more heterogeneous than are temperate and boreal forests (though not invariably so). They comprise many different and complex ecosystems. So far there has been but little systematic effort to understand the dynamics of these forests, and practically no attempt to manage them. It took many centuries before, in the temperate zones, it came to be accepted that the cost of wood should bear some relation to the cost of replacing it. That notion has scarcely begun to penetrate the minds of those who exploit the tropical forests.

Figure 6.5   (opposite) Managed beech forest about 140 years after planting, near Nancy, France (photo R. A. Plumtre)

Part II People and trees

7 The origins and spread of humans

Chapter 1 described how, before the continents assumed their present shape and location, the original land mass (Pangaea) wandered over the face of the earth as it gradually broke up. Over vast periods, slow changes in the pattern of land and sea were accompanied by long term changes in climate, to which both flora and fauna adjusted through evolutionary change.

It is generally thought that the emergence of the hominid line was linked from the outset to the availability of open grassed country. Unforested country began to spread starting about 25 million years ago. The dryopithecine lineage, from which apes and humans are thought to have derived, divided from the lineage leading to other monkeys by about 20 million years ago. Species in the ape/human lineage were tailless and spent increasing amounts of time on the ground. Eventually this lineage split in Africa into three branches, leading to gorillas, to chimpanzees, and to Australopithecines and thence to humans. These three branches used different parts of the landscape, with gorillas in dense forest, chimpanzees in open forest, and Australopithecines in sparse forest or grassland.

Nowadays in the tropics and subtropics, the boundary between forest and wooded grasslands is set by fires, in conjunction with climate. The main elements of the situation are these. Tall forest is not fire-resistant, nor is it particularly flammable. Outside tall forest, vegetation is fire-prone and carries a variable mix of woody plants with grasses. Generally, woody plants are favoured where there are intervals of ten to a hundred years between fires. Grasses can tolerate fires as often as yearly but are suppressed by high densities of woody plants, therefore they are indirectly favoured by intervals between fires of less than ten years. Dry grass makes good fuel, so country with a continuous grass cover carries fires easily. This relationship of mutual support between fires and grasses can produce sharp boundaries between fire-prone (grassy woodland) and fire-sensitive (forest) vegetation. Within grassy woodland vegetation can vary from nearly pure grass to nearly pure woody plant dominance, depending on the fire history over the previous ten to a hundred years.

All this is true even in response to lightning-strike fires. However, in the presence of hunter–gatherers or pastoralists, a large proportion of fires are set by people. After fires, new green grass shoots ('green-pick') attract game for hunting, or favour livestock. Fires are also set to drive game, or to make country easier to travel through. Therefore the boundary between forest and grassy woodland, and the mix of woody plants with grasses within grassy woodland, has been strongly shaped by people in recent history. The influence of hunter–gatherers on vegetation via fire is so strong and so deliberate that it has been called 'firestick farming'.

It seems certain that this shaping of the forest–shrub–grass mixture goes far back in human emergence, but there is no direct evidence on this point because fossil materials do not allow lightning-strike fires to be distinguished from firestick fires. In Australia about 40 000 years ago, shortly after modern *Homo sapiens* evolved, pollen evidence shows there was a shift to more fire-prone vegetation, and increased charcoal shows that there were more frequent fires. Archaeological evidence of human occupation has been found from dates not long after that, and the period was one when sea-level was low, so it would have been relatively easy for humans to reach Australia from south-east Asia. These items of evidence all seem to hang together well, and it is thought that the shift in Australian vegetation around that time was due to the arrival of humans and their use of fire.

In Africa, where humans are thought to have evolved, it is not possible to attribute changes in vegetation or fire frequency firmly to firesetting by humans rather than to changing climate. However, humans are known to have had the use of fire for a very long time. Burnt clay has been found in association with bones from animals butchered by stone tools, implying a campfire, at a date of 1.4 million years ago, well before *Homo sapiens* replaced *Homo erectus*. It is hard to believe humans could control fire for cooking without having some idea how to use it to manipulate the landscape or to drive game. Most likely the distribution of vegetation in landscapes has been affected by human use of fire for a long time.

Much more recent has been the human impact on forests through the physical felling of trees and the clearing of land. It was thought at one time that the clearance of forests for agriculture had to await the invention of iron. This is not true. There is ample archeological evidence for both stone axes and stone saws, while there are contemporary surviving palaeolithic tribes which can fell trees and scoop dugout canoes with stone. It does seem certain that primitive agriculture, wherever it did invade the forest, was swidden agriculture, or slash and burn. The reason for slash and burn, however, was not (as in most shifting cultivation in the tropical forests today) that the fertility imparted by the wood ashes was quickly exhausted; it was that the battle to keep weeds at bay soon became more onerous than clearing a fresh piece of forest. So slash and burn was as typical of early forest clearance in Europe as it is characteristic of much tropical forest clearance today.

But settled agriculture and the domestication of plants and animals did not start in the forest, but in fertile river valleys. The architects of the neolithic revolution were those who observed that collected seed, when scattered on the fertile silt, flourished, thus saving endless hours of gathering. The significant aspect of the transition from gathering to gardening was that surpluses could arise and be saved, giving the family or clan a measure of security. It was precisely the possibility of creating food surpluses, the surpassing of the hand-to-mouth mode of existence, that rendered specialization within early human societies possible. Individuals or families could develop and transmit particular skills, knowing that their pottery, textiles, tools, and so on were always exchangeable for food. Settled agriculture thus fostered technological progress in many directions. This was important for the forest because it gave rise eventually to new tools which would facilitate forest clearance.

But permanent agriculture had another aspect. With the growing power to accumulate surpluses came the possibility for particular individuals, families or castes to appropriate those surpluses for their own ends; hence the evolution of hierarchical societies. The ends to which the ruling castes in hierarchical societies chose to devote the surpluses varied. But they eventually came to include, as civilizations developed, specialized fighting groups to maintain the rulers in power, priesthoods to promote ideologies which would justify the rulers' right to rule, durable monuments, sometimes on a gigantic scale, as well as all forms of what today would be called conspicuous consumption. But whatever the ends, all hierarchical societies, from the most primitive clans or tribes to mighty and complex civilizations, required growing numbers of non-food-producers to be fed out of the surplus extracted from those who did produce food; in other words, there was a continuing drive to expand the surplus. It was this drive which was to have the greatest impact on the forest, in the earlier phases of human history as today. It applied to those civilizations which originated on alluvial plains or fertile river valleys and which had to reach out into neighbouring forests; that same drive is destroying vast tracts of tropical forest today. Because of that reaching out, some early civilizations fell into decline and all but disappeared; the fertility which had given them birth was undermined by deforestation. That is one reason why much of the area known as the Fertile Crescent is today infertile. Once the land was green, with early agriculture stretching from the Egyptian border and Syria, through Mesopotamia to the Persian Gulf. Today the course of irrigation canals which helped to feed the ancient cities can be faintly traced under the windblown sand. The famed cedars of Lebanon, once used to build Solomon's temple in Jerusalem, are now restricted to a few tiny scattered groves.

Gardening instead of gathering started at roughly the same time in several different parts of the world. As gardeners spread along the river valleys, population grew and technology spread out: rice in Indochina, millet in Africa and China, beans and maize in the Americas, wheat and barley in the Middle East. The domestication of animals may have started by herding for meat, but it progressed to dairy farming and the harnessing of animal power. When the two joined together, so that the ox-drawn plough supplanted the hoe, the stage was set for further substantial inroads into the forest.

Hierarchical societies

The shift to settled agriculture, bringing about permanent forest clearance, was facilitated by iron, animal power, and rudimentary crop rotation. Even so, for many centuries after the neolithic revolution, much of the land surface of the main continents was covered by forest, and a good deal of this was dense, closed forest. Although the clearing of forests for agriculture took place very slowly at first, it accelerated in places where, and at times when, expanded societies with a hierarchical structure developed.

How many people a given area of land will support depends not only on the land's innate capacity; it depends also on the technology employed and on the socio-economic structure of the society using that land. This is why the expression 'land capability' is so unsatisfactory. When so-called 'land capability' surveys are carried out, the classifications they adopt invariably assume current technology. Sometimes they even fail to raise the question whether the technology assumed ensures sustainable use of that land.

Some have argued that it is only when population increases to the point where the land available will no longer support it with existing technology that technology takes a forward leap. In other words, technical revolutions in agriculture spring from population pressure. The principal weakness in this argument is the same as that which lies at the heart of the Malthusian thesis. Neither thesis gives sufficient weight to the influence of social relations. While the relation between the size of population and the availability of resources is important, whether and how problems arise from rising population depends very much on how social and economic life is organized.

While it may be true that a natural increase in population obliges a clan or tribe to clear a corresponding area of new ground for agriculture, what happens more frequently in history is that societies become reorganized in ways that require a very much higher proportion of non-food-producers (ruling groups, the priestly class, armies, household servants and slaves, craftsmen and tradesmen) as compared with the numbers actually producing food. If dominant groups are to strengthen and maintain their power and wealth, they must organize a food surplus. This can be done by more intensive exploitation of the rural producer, whether slave, serf or tenant; by putting more land and people into food production (which may mean clearing forest); or by importing additional food supplies (which may also prompt further forest clearance in the region the food is imported from).

The 'population pressure brings agricultural innovation' thesis fails to explain why, in many parts of the Third World today, completely different technologies are being applied on lands which are similar and adjacent. Those technologies are being applied by different people, for different purposes, within different systems of social relations. Thus on one stretch of land, small independent peasant producers may be employing a traditional and primitive technology to feed themselves and their families on a sustainable basis. On an adjacent stretch of land, modern, more sophisticated, technology is producing cash-crops for people in distant lands, and is also often steadily reducing the soil's inherent fertility.

Human progress, whether defined in material or cultural terms or as a mixture of both, stems from the ability of food-producers to feed not only themselves but a host of others who either create material goods or provide services which spell rising welfare. This is true, of course, of all forms of society. But historically the drive to increase the food surplus has accelerated when dominant and dynamic strata of hierarchical societies have striven to expand their wealth and power. This is why the periods of most rapid deforestation in the past have not necessarily been at the times when population was most rapidly expanding. They have occurred when the exploitation of subordinate groups (as well as of resources) has intensified. It is an oversimplification to regard deforestation as the consequence of population growth. It is nearer the truth, as the following chapters will show through a number of historical examples, to regard deforestation and population growth as joint manifestations of exploitative social relations.

That is why the World Bank (1977) was wide of the mark when it stated:

Growing population pressure has always been a major cause of forest depletion. Such adverse effects are now most pronounced in developing countries, a reflection of their typically greater population densities, more rapid population growth, their rural based economies, with large numbers of relatively low income people, and lack of conservation measures.

As we shall see, there is much evidence indicating that this view is erroneous. Deforestation, both historical and contemporary, is a more complicated matter than the World Bank at that time assumed. This is not to deny that in many parts of the world there exists a very real population problem, one which cannot be sidestepped or ignored, and which demands action if millions are not to suffer. But forests are disappearing today not simply because human numbers are growing. Their disappearance can spell catastrophe for people now living and for future generations. If we want to avoid that catastrophe, we must understand why the forests are disappearing. Only in the light of that understanding can measures be devised and action taken to avert disaster.

8   Britain up to Roman times

Roughly 10 000 years ago trees came back to Britain. With the ending of the last ice age, as the ice cap receded northwards for the last time, Britain was recolonized by trees from the European continent, to which it was then still joined. Ireland was also connected to England so some of the recolonizing trees from the continent got as far as Ireland. First came birch, to be followed after a dozen centuries or so by pines. After the conifers came alders, hazel and then the other broadleaves, oak and elm. Trees with needles transpire less than trees with broad leaves: they retain their moisture better. That is how they survive long, cold dry winters, and why the boreal forest – right across Canada, Europe, the USSR, and northern China – is mostly conifers. In the warmer parts of the world, we find the conifers up in the mountains, where they chased the receding ice.

How is it known what kind of trees were around so many thousand years ago? By means of pollen analysis. Tree pollen is practically indestructible. There are well-preserved specimens of pollen from peat and the mud of lake beds, through well-dated geological sequences. Looking through a microscope it is easy to tell the pollen of one species from another (unless the species are closely related, when the picture can get a bit confusing).

The various species spread north and west. Alder, for example, reached Ireland just before the sea cut it off. Last to come was lime: it spread only through the lowlands of south-eastern England. There followed a few thousand years (this was the warm Atlantic period) during which the several species battled it out among themselves. By 3000 BC Britain was covered with virgin forest. What did this look like? Possibly something like the Bialowezie forest on the Russo-Polish border, the central part of which has for many years been protected to remain in its natural state. If so, it must have been a tangled mess of both broadleaved and coniferous species, with trees of all types and all ages, healthy, sick, dying and dead. At any given time some giant trees have already crashed, and are rotting and clearing space; others still standing are rotting on their feet and nearing collapse.

Between the forests of three thousand years ago (what Oliver Rackham (1986) has called the wildwood) and the woodlands that survive today – a miserable few per cent of the forests that once covered Britain – there is a

Figure 8.1   Europe, Asia Minor and North Africa, showing places mentioned in chapters 8 – 11

direct line of descent. Mesolithic people followed from the continent soon after the trees came back, but they made little impact on the forest. The neolithic peoples, however, with their stone axes, made substantial clearings of wildwood for agriculture. There is evidence of the appearance of farmyard weeds from about 3000 BC. It is interesting that about that time elm went into a temporary decline for several centuries; this decline probably stemmed from the use of elm as browse rather than from a predecessor of the Dutch elm disease which has devastated Britain's elms in recent decades.

There was an acceleration in clearance of the wildwood during the Bronze Age, about 1700–500 BC, and again with the arrival of the Celts around 400 BC. Thus, particularly in southern England, quite significant inroads had been made in the wildwood for agriculture before the Romans came. And, indeed, a number of elementary forms of woodland management were already being practised: coppicing, for example, especially for poles for corduroy roads (constructed from logs laid transversely), and for forest grazing. This pre-Roman investment in forest clearance took a great deal of effort. Of England's trees, only pine could be destroyed by fire; other species had to be grubbed out, with rudimentary tools and a large expenditure of labour.

The Roman occupation

Yet four centuries of Roman occupation had a greater impact on England's forests than all that had gone before. Under the occupation the population is estimated to have doubled; it also turned England and Wales into a major grain exporter to the Roman Empire. The rivers, which served as effective waterways, greatly reduced the cost of transportation, thus facilitating trade. Southern England was much more closely studded with Roman villas than was once thought. Most of them were, in effect, export farms. They were established not only on the light soils that had previously been worked, but also on new lands of heavy clay, rendered workable by improved iron ploughs. In addition, a good deal of dense forest was cleared.

Apart from clearing forest land for agriculture, the Romans needed wood for a wide variety of purposes: civil and military building and construction, and fuel for salt, mining and metallurgy, bricks and so on. The extent of iron working by the Romans in England and Wales suggests that much of the woodland was already managed on a coppicing system. Had 'cut and burn' been the rule, many of the forges would have run out of wood supplies much earlier than they did. As far as we know, the Romans introduced no great technical innovations in agriculture, though some modifications to the iron plough were made to enable it to cope with the heavier soils of the northern Roman provinces. But the colonizers' ability to produce an export surplus seems to have rested mainly on organization and administration. The importance of these factors in major economic changes has been evidenced by later historical examples. When plantation slavery expanded from the fifteenth century on, it depended on organization rather than on technical innovation or mechanization. Indeed, even the first phases of the industrial revolution depended not so much on power or mechanization as on the more effective organization and supervision of the workforce.

Though Roman rule extended far beyond Wales and the southern half of England, it is not clear how far northern England and southern Scotland were incorporated into the imperial wealth-extraction machine. The Romans were obliged to push further and further north to protect themselves from persistent border raiders. The remains of corduroy roads show they reached as far north as Fife and Perthshire. Much of the lowland forest was cleared for areas of tillage and pasture; some of these may have been 'buffer' settlements of subjugated tribes whose tribute helped to offset the costs of occupation.

The forests of England and Wales thus suffered their sharpest reduction in serving Roman imperialism, as did much of the accessible Mediterranean forest. Though there have been slight fluctuations in the amount of forest cover in Britain since the Romans left, Britain has remained one of the least forested countries in Europe. As a Roman colony, Britain typified the processes at work elsewhere in the Roman empire; but it was not altogether typical in the consequences of these processes. If deforestation in England and Wales did less permanent damage to the land than in the Mediterranean, this is because Britain enjoyed a more equable climate. With a mild climate, adequate rainfall, and reasonably fertile soils, deforestation had much less disastrous consequences in Britain than in some other parts of the Roman empire. Where – as in Spain, for example, another major Roman colony – temperature contrasts are greater and rain less well distributed during the year, bared soils were subject to greater erosion, to the extent that considerable areas became infertile and remain so to this day.

9   Mediterranean forests in classical times

In the Mediterranean area the kind of pressures which accelerated forest clearance in Britain have had a longer history. They have occurred over three millennia, and there is a continuing thread which links classical times, through the Middle Ages, to modern colonialism.

Russell Meiggs, one of the few classical scholars to have closely studied forests in ancient times, observed: 'The conversion of forest to agriculture is a natural response to an increase in population, and it continued throughout our whole period [i.e. from the Bronze Age to the fall of the Roman Empire]' (Meiggs, 1982). Yet, as he goes on to show, this is far from being the whole of the story. In his account of deforestation in the ancient Mediterranean world he makes it clear that the stripping of forests for building fleets, for erecting imposing public buildings, and for growing export crops, was at least as important as the need to feed more people.

The neolithic peoples, when they spread through the Mediterranean, occupied the narrow coastal plains. Their influence on the tree cover did not extend far up the mountain slopes. There was sufficient timber on or close to the Mediterranean littoral to generate long-distance trade in it, by rafting and floating. In Egypt, timber was sledded by large gangs of slaves. Timber rollers made possible the movement of the blocks which were used to build the great pyramid of Cheops, which weighed about 500 tonnes each, over a distance of 100 km. Sometimes timber was towed behind ships, and rafts of dense timber were supported by inflated sacks.

When the Greeks came to dominate the Eastern Mediterranean, their influence extended in all directions then accessible by sea, and their direct and indirect influence on the forests was much greater. It is common knowledge that the Greek world, to which we owe not only the idea of democracy but the very word for it, was in fact a slave society. Even if free and independent farmers and craftsmen accounted for most production, the essential surplus, as De Ste Croix (1981) has pointed out, was squeezed out of slave labour. As the Greek city states expanded, the forests on the plains and low hills were cleared for agriculture. Not all this agriculture was devoted to raising grain to feed the cities. Some large landowners found it more profitable to grow olives for export than to grow grain. This is an additional reason why the expanded production had to be increasingly supplemented by agricultural imports from other parts of the Mediterranean.

The growth of a small city-state into the Athenian empire would not have been possible without maritime supremacy. The naval fleet which defeated the Persians, and the trading ships which carried merchandise to and from all parts of the Mediterranean, were built of wood. This too had a considerable impact on the forests.

A number of writers of classical times, both Greek and Roman, registered an awareness of forest–soil–water relationships. The father of botany, Aristotle's student Theophrastus, who wrote *Enquiry into Plants*, can also be regarded as the father of dendrology. Alexander the Great, also a student of Aristotle, took scholars with him on his expeditions, from whom Theophrastus collected botanical information on their return.

As Rome grew in power, steadily asserting its domination over the Italian mainland, its army and corps of administrators swelled. More food was needed to feed more non-food-producers. Greater incentives were offered to those willing to clear forests for agriculture. During the struggle with Carthage, full legal right to ownership was offered to anyone who would clear the equivalent of about 50 ha of forest. In the middle of the second century BC, Rome finally conquered Carthage, more or less at the same time as it brought Greece firmly under its control. Neither would have been possible had not Italy been sufficiently well forested to build a fleet capable of dislodging the Carthaginians from Sicily and commanding the Mediterranean. A couple of centuries later the African provinces were shipping enough grain to Rome to feed a million people for two-thirds of the year. The long arm of Roman imperialism reached out in all directions for grain, with consequent forest clearance. As we have seen, Britain was not immune. The deforestation of the Iberian peninsula also accelerated under Roman rule, though its present deforested state owes most to the inroads of the Middle Ages and the later period of the Iberian domination of the seas. Iberia was a centre of ship-building and metallurgy in Roman times, exporting gold, silver, copper, zinc and iron. Other exports to Rome included cork, wool, wine and ceramics.

Feeding Rome's populace was a recurring political problem for its rulers. It might have been less of a problem if more of Roman agriculture had been directed to that end. But, just as in Greece, there were periods when farms were left untended, returning soldiers flocked to the cities, land fell into the hands of the rich and much of that land was converted to pasture. Grain was imported from Sicily and Africa to feed the urban population, but large Italian landowners found it more profitable to produce other crops and luxury items, employing slave labour to raise cattle and to cultivate vines and olives. Warming the populace of Rome in winter, and fuelling some of its industries, also took toll of the forests. Fuelwood was carried to Rome, by mule or donkey, from hills over 100 km away. In addition, some of Rome's timber supplies came by sea to the port of Ostia Antica, where surviving mosaics indicate the traders' posts.

Homer, and such Roman writers as Virgil, Lucan, Horace and Ovid, were well aware that deforestation of watersheds could lead to devastating floods and siltation below. Upland areas, inaccessible to transport, retained their tree cover, but elsewhere conversion to agriculture, supplemented by metallurgy and natural fires, progessively diminished the forest area. Strabo tells how ore from Elba had to be transported to the mainland for processing because the forests of Elba had been exhausted.

It was transport difficulties which limited the extent to which wood (for construction or for fuel) could be moved, and these shaped much forest clearance. Nevertheless, wherever Imperial Rome established permanent colonies, whether in the Mediterranean or in Europe, the original forest was heavily cut, for example in the Rhone valley, in Spain, in southern England and Wales. Beyond the Alps, a vast expanse of forest spread north to the Baltic and west to the Atlantic, to survive until the growth of towns in the Middle Ages.

Throughout the classical period, where coastal plains were limited in extent it was natural for agriculture to move up into the hills. When times were difficult, farms would be abandoned, and some kind of forest would creep back. This process continued throughout succeeding centuries, the forest border ebbing and flowing. Even today, in many Mediterranean countries, terraces painstakingly built centuries ago to sustain hill farming are collapsing and giving way to mixed hardwood forest of little value. After the fall of Rome the Roman population fell, there were no great building programmes, and there was opportunity for some of the mountain forests to recover. Thus there was no great difficulty in obtaining large timbers for the basilicas of the tenth to the fourteenth centuries. But this was not the case everywhere. In some parts erosion had already gone too far.

Not all the loss of tree cover and forest degradation in the Mediterranean is attributable to the ancients, but they started the process. In the following centuries clearance for agriculture, overgrazing, fire and the goat have in many areas degraded the forest into *maquis*, or have destroyed the thin soil cover and pushed the land to the point of no return: to bare karst rock, or to arid desert.

10   Britain after the Romans

When King John signed the Magna Carta at Runnymede in 1215, he undertook to discontinue certain traditional practices. These affected the material interests, and had increasingly aroused the hostility, of the barons, who were for the most part landed nobility. Some of the principal clauses of that charter had to do with the forests. Quarrels between the king and the barons about the forests were nothing new. However, hardly was the ink dry at Runnymede than John had second thoughts, tried to wriggle out of his commitments, and sent off a messenger to seek the Pope's permission to release him from the oath he had just taken. Permission was granted, but it arrived too late. Early in 1216 John died, to be succeeded by the nine-year-old Henry III. The barons lost no time in getting the boy-king to bind himself to Magna Carta, and a year later spelled out their most important demands in the Forest Charter, which the boy king also signed.

Why had the forests become so important? The Romans had turned southern England and Wales into a very productive colony, a valuable piece of real estate – one, moreover, where most of the heavy work of clearing forest to grow food crops had already been done. Though the land was still well wooded, forest cover was down to around 15 per cent; very different from continental western Europe, still 90 per cent forested. This is one reason why, with the departure of the Romans in the fifth century AD, the Britons were not left in peace. Jutes, Saxons, Danes and Vikings invaded various parts of England, and many settled. Though contact with the Roman Empire ceased, and tribute was no longer paid, there was still an agricultural system from which a surplus could be squeezed and which petty kings fought over for centuries. The Anglo-Saxon takeover was gradual and not always violent. The invaders often settled on land which, with the collapse of the Roman Empire, was no longer needed for growing export crops. Most of this land was already farmland, and though the wooded areas may have been denser, they were little more extensive than they were centuries later. The Romans had gone, but there was still good land and labour to be exploited, and this led to rivalries, alliances, wars.

In fact, the Norman Conquest of 1066 was not the watershed in English history that some history books have led us to believe. William did not bring with him a feudal hierarchical system and impose this pyramid on a land of small, free, independent farmers. Well before 1066 the various

Anglo-Saxon kings had a firm, exploitative system in force. Indeed, at court level, interchanges, including intermarriage, with the Normans had been going on for half a century before William the Conqueror took the throne. For the average Briton working the land, serf or free, the Norman Conquest probably meant little change at first. William rewarded his followers, organized an effective administration, and, in what came to be known as the Domesday Book, began the first detailed survey of national wealth, aimed at finding out the extent of his possessions and how far the nobility could be expected to contribute to the king's expenses. The Domesday Book was, in effect, an agricultural census, a forest inventory, and an income tax assessment. It is from the Domesday Book, which listed arable land, woods, pastures, commons and waste, spelled out title, and often therefore recounted much of the previous history of the land, that it is possible today to make reasonable guesses about the extent of the forest in the eleventh century and earlier. Woods, for example, were often recorded not by area but by the number of swine they would maintain on acorns and beech mast. But there are many difficulties in interpretation; for example, sometimes the number cited was not the number of swine which the forest would support, but the annual fee payable in number of swine for the right to run swine in the forest.

The Norman kings have become famous for their afforestation. Today the word 'afforestation' means the creation of new forest on bare land by tree planting. But when land was afforested in Norman times, this simply meant that the king decreed that a certain area of land (whether that land belonged to him or not, and whether it carried trees or not) was henceforth Royal Forest, reserved for 'vert and venison' at the king's pleasure. Thereupon it became subject to separate Forest Laws, administered by separate Forest Courts. It was once thought that this Norman afforestation, like the Norman exploitation of peasant cultivators, had its precedent under the Anglo-Saxon kings. This view, it now transpires, was mistaken, being based on documents forged in the Middle Ages (Rackham, 1986, p.130). Before William of Normandy's time a wild animal was not owned: it became the property of whoever subdued it, and Customary law settled any disputes over wildlife. William changed all that. The forgery just mentioned, alleging 'afforestation' precedents by King Canute, was intended to lend greater antiquity and legitimacy to the Forest Laws.

The 'king's pleasure', to which end land was designated Royal Forest, was not for the Norman kings simply a matter of hunting for fun. The forest was an important source of food. Venison was preserved by salting and sent to the court. Poachers were punished severely not because they were spoil-sports, but because they were stealing from the king's pantry. It is possible, too, that certain blocks of territory were afforested – brought directly under the jurisdiction of the Forest Laws – for defence purposes.

The Forest Charter which followed close on Magna Carta not only took all the lands which Richard and John had afforested out of the jurisdiction of the Forest Law; it also reduced the maximum penalty for trespass against the kings' venison to imprisonment for a year and a day. Much emphasis has been placed by some writers on the reduced penalties embodied in the Forest Charter. But Rackham (1986) maintains that maximum penalties were seldom applied, and that for most offences rigorous penalties could be commuted into fines. The purpose of Forest Courts was thus not so much to punish as to raise revenue.

What upset the barons about royal afforestation was that it hit them where they least liked it: in their pockets. They resented the limitations to what they could do with their own property. Afforestation restricted access to their own game; it could involve destruction of their crops; it could limit their right to license the taking of timber and the conversion to arable land. At the same time the barons remained responsible for the upkeep of the land and in many cases were obliged to lodge and feed the king, together with his whole entourage, when the court made its peregrinations through the land, administering the law and deciding cases.

What was even worse for them, the king would appropriate the nobles' privilege of exacting fines and fees. Indeed, as time went on, many of the fines inflicted on commoners for various practices became more in the nature of fees paid for the licence to pursue those practices. Thus the royal forest became increasingly a prime source of the monarch's revenues, rather than an area reserved for the court's recreation and food. Fees and fines covered such things as the right to take dead wood, small wood and timber, the right to cut turves, the right to pasture livestock, assarting (permission to grub up trees and cultivate the land), licences to quarry, to make charcoal, to establish wood burning industries, and so on. Assarting was of particular importance, because it gave rise to money rents. Thus in essence, when the barons forced the Magna Carta and then the Forest Charter on John and Henry II, they were asserting their right to do what they liked with their own land. In addition it rid them of the burden of periodically lodging and feeding the court, and returned to them the right to be as severe as they liked with peasants who presumed on their privileges.

Peasant resistance

The twelfth and thirteenth centuries, in England as in Europe, were a period of fairly steady growth in population and wealth. Crafts multiplied, trade, both local and distant, grew, and small towns, fairs and markets prospered. This required a greater surplus from agriculture, with greater exploitation of peasant labour, an extension of land under the plough, or both. In England this did not involve further forest reduction on any great scale, the forest having been largely cleared in earlier times. But it was a period of rapid forest clearance in France and Germany: the process was led by the Cistercians and imitated by the temporal powers in France, and promoted by deliberate colonization eastwards and southwards by the German nobility. Thus by the middle of the fourteenth century much of Germany had been cleared and serious inroads had been made into the frontier forests of Poland, Bohemia and Hungary.

In the fourteenth century, successsive waves of bubonic plague swept across Europe. One of its effects was to seriously deplete the work force, rendering it easier for peasants to escape from the land and find work in the nascent towns. But another consequence, all over Europe, was that the lords and landowners attempted to tighten their hold over their peasants and to increase the extent to which they exploited them.

The Peasants' Revolt in England, in 1381, was in many ways typical, and foreshadowed the kind of struggles which were to take place in Europe for centuries to come. The deeds of Wat Tyler and Jack Straw, the charters and promises they extracted from the boy-king Richard, and their subsequent betrayal and atrocious deaths, are well-known parts of English history. Less familiar is the story of William Gryndecobbe, who rallied the common people of his area against the rapacious Abbot of St Albans. This time the peasants were not merely angered about what had always been one of the most burdensome requirements in feudal society: this was labour rent or labour service, the duty to provide so many days' labour on the fields of the overlord at haymaking and harvest, precisely the times when peasant families most needed to be busy on their own plots. They were also opposed to the Abbot's ban on them grinding their own corn, which he enforced by confiscating their millstones. They were obliged to carry their corn to the Abbot's mill and pay the necessary fee in kind. Similarly, the Abbot insisted on the peasants taking their home-woven cloth to the abbey for fulling – again, at a price. Marshalled by Gryndecobbe, the peasants tore up the abbey floor, which had been paved with their millstones, and demanded the original charter (which they assumed to exist, and in which they presumed their customary rights were enshrined) from the terror-stricken Abbot.

But it is clear from some of their actions that they were also resisting the Abbot's attempts to curb their customary rights in such woodlands as remained in the area. When the procession of townsmen and some 2000 peasants from the Abbey's lands swore an oath to be faithful to each other, they also broke down fences, burned down a forester's house, handed round branches of trees, and fixed a live rabbit on a pole on a pillory in the town: actions symbolizing the reassertion of ancient rights which had been taken from them. Throughout the counties where the peasants and some townsmen took up arms, they exacted vengeance only on those who were deemed to have cruelly exceeded their powers. The toll they took was negligible when compared with the exemplary punishment meted out to all the revolt's leaders and many of the participants once the established power succeeded in reasserting its authority.

Customary rights in the forest, in England as in Europe, were always a matter of high importance to the peasant. Throughout history they have figured in, and sometimes triggered, peasant resistance and struggle. The English experience in these years is one example among many of how the forests are affected by human social relations, with different classes and interest groups struggling with each other over how they are to be used.

11 The poor man's overcoat

The rural populations of these areas are imbued with the idea that they have been unjustly despoiled of property rights they have held from time immemorial.

These are the words of the chief government prosecutor in Toulouse in 1848, reporting on the forest fires which were being set, and the mutilation of trees, within the area of his jurisdiction. Similar words have applied, however, throughout Europe at various periods, though perhaps earlier in England than elsewhere, and apply even today in much of the rest of the world.

Peasants have seldom revolted simply because they were being exploited. Almost invariably they have regarded exploitation as their natural lot. Only when it has become too harsh have they been moved to collective anger and action. That is why their demands have always been limited, relatively modest, and backward-looking: the restoration of rights they have enjoyed from time out of memory; the removal of some particularly cruel or unjust administrator. In so far as their demands have been political, have looked for a re-shaping of society, they have frequently looked backwards to some mythical 'golden age' rather than forwards to a new Jerusalem. But almost always, among the measures which pushed them to desperate action, have been restrictions of what they conceived as their rights in the forest.

When, in 1381, the Kentish peasants revolted against the nobles and the landowning clergy, they were seeking the restoration of rights to which they considered themselves entitled by custom and by charter. They profoundly believed that King Richard, when he heard their complaints, would ensure that justice was done and rights were restored. Even though power was within their grasp, they were not asking for a new society; simply for a return to a past that had seemed supportable. Their faith was misplaced, as it has been countless times in the centuries which have followed. When peasants have succeeded in overthrowing the established power, it has usually been when they have allied themselves to other elements in society intent on changing power relationships: the fact that their strength and resolve has been decisive has not necessarily meant that they have reaped the reward. The peasant revolt in England in 1381 was in many ways typical of what was to come in later centuries.

Folk-tale and ballad, too, frequently express the resentment of the common people at the landowning classes' attempts to monopolize the forest. The targets of Robin Hood's exploits were the forest laws, the royal foresters, and the royal game. But also dating from the thirteenth century is the Norman-French poem *Roman d'Eustache li Moine*. Eustace, like Robin, was an outlaw who took refuge in the forest. His adventures almost exactly parallel those which go to make up the legend of Robin Hood.

It is impossible to be definite about the real-life originals of such legends. In all probability both Robin and Eustace, 'noble robbers', sprang from the lesser nobility and became outlaws because they had offended against the forest laws. Though not peasants themselves, they were joined by peasants on the run for analogous offences. Their daring deeds, always concerned with the righting of wrongs and with robbing the rich to give to the poor, were made possible by their ability to melt into the forest, and the refusal of common people to betray them made them popular heroes. Robin and Eustace, under other names, have reappeared time and again in many different countries, often in the flesh, but sometimes conjured in the popular imagination.

Just because the forest has afforded shelter to those at odds with the established power that power has, on many occasions through history, deliberately destroyed the forest, or tried to. In 1399, McMorough, king of Ireland, hid with 3000 of his men in the woods west of Kilkenny. Richard II proposed burning them out; he was dissuaded only because it was pointed out to him that the woods, mainly deciduous and in leaf, were not sufficiently flammable. In modern times, the US armed forces succeeded in inflicting considerable forest damage using napalm and Agent Orange in Vietnam, but that forest destruction did not save them from defeat.

Forested land does not generally become property until such time as those holding power decide that the forest, or the land on which it stands, or what lies in or under that land, has a material value for them. It is not until then that land titles are established, and that land markets arise. It is then too that the process begins of exterminating, expelling, or simply dispossessing those whose present occupation of the land stands in their way. But title apart, in many parts of the world, and in particular in feudal Europe, dwellers in and near the forest held certain customary rights in the forest, even when possessing no title to the land. These have included, at different times, the right to graze animals in the forest or in forest clearings, the right to cut turf and peat, the right to fuelwood (sometimes only dead wood or snapwood), to a certain amount of wood for farm and home use (to build and repair, to make tools and instruments), and the right to wood, osiers and bark for various crafts; the right to take game; the right to gather fruits, berries, nuts and fungi; and so on. These rights were always important; in years when harvests were poor or when winters were particularly rigorous they could make the difference between survival and death. This is why the forest became known as 'the poor man's overcoat'.

It was not only the farmer who depended on the forest. Rural craftsmen and artisans also depended upon the commons, woodlands and waste to provide secondary means of support. This recourse became critical for them in bad times when trade was slack and demand for their goods and services low. Thus deforestation, and the curtailment of rights in the forest, was a matter of life and death for them too. This is why artisans were usually heavily involved in peasant uprisings.

Although England and Wales lost most of its tree cover much earlier than did continental Europe, the English peasant, free or unfree, and later the small tenant farmer depended heavily on the common or waste, whether treed or not. Through medieval times there were wood motes, courts concerned with the forest and with the determination of contested rights in the forest. But it became difficult to maintain these rights once the large landowners discovered the profits to be made out of wool and started to enclose the commons. This process continued through the fifteenth and sixteenth centuries, so that by the time of the Civil Wars in the 1640s the wood motes had lapsed. By then, however, the rural social structure in England had become very different from that on the continent. Not only had the landowning class asserted political power; the peasantry had been replaced by tenant farmers and landless agricultural labourers, while those expelled from the land sought work in the towns or became itinerant beggars.

Henry VIII's dissolution of the monasteries in the 1530s had accelerated enclosures. When the Reformation spread to England it had little to do with theology, and much to do with the wealth accumulated by the monasteries, and the flow of money, through the church, to Rome. The rich pickings from dismantling the monasteries in England were redistributed among the landed aristocracy, who found the wool trade more profitable than traditional agriculture, and proved strong enough to frustrate the efforts of the monarchy to keep people on the land and prevent the threat of a growing class of landless and restless labourers.

While commons and waste were being enclosed in England, the poor man's overcoat in Ireland was also being sharply cut back. The English colonized Ireland in Tudor times and strengthened their hold in the succeeding century. Ireland was never as heavily wooded as Britain. Much of the land area was too high, too rocky or too boggy to be tilled or even to support tree cover. As English colonists took over the land from Irish subsistence farmers they met with resistance, and an Act of 1612 obliged owners to clear all trees and bushes growing on highways and passes (tracks) through their land. Many of the displaced Irish took refuge in the woods, became outlaws or woodkernes. Some years before the Act a settler had written 'the woods and bogs are a great hindrance to us and help to the rebels' (McCracken, 1971). Wolves and woodkernes were regarded as the most serious danger to the colonists, and manhunts were recommended to track the human wolves to their lair. The rewards for the destruction of wolves and woodkernes were much the same. The woodkernes came later to be known as tories, from the Irish *toir* (to search), and tory hunting continued to the end of the century. The shelter which the forests afforded the outlaws was one more reason for destroying the forests. These are the reasons why Ireland's forest cover, 12 per cent in 1600, had fallen to 2 per cent by 1800.

Much has been written about the seizure of common lands by the landowning classes in England; less has been written about the extinction of common rights. But the forests of England, like those of the continent, continued to be the scenes of bitter struggle until those common rights were effectively suppressed. Resistance took the form of poaching, wood stealing and tree destruction. This was usually done by night, and the lawbreakers blacked their faces to reduce the chances of their being recognized – at times they even wore gowns. In 1723 the British Parliament under Walpole rushed through, in the record time of four weeks, and without debate or discussion, the Black Act. This created fifty new capital offences, including hunting, wounding, or stealing deer in the royal forests, or anywhere else if the offenders were armed or disguised; cutting trees 'planted in any avenues, growing in any orchard or plantation'; and a variety of similar offences. As if this were not enough, within a year court judgements had widened the scope of this Act to make disguise – the blacking of the face – a capital offence in itself.

In Britain the economy had developed very differently from that on the continent. Consequently the rural social structure was very different, and the offenders were not peasants (as on the continent) but small tenant farmers, agricultural labourers, rural unemployed and the like. It is hard for us now to imagine the savagery with which property was protected in England but a few generations ago. In 1748 two young men were caught raiding deer in the park of Viscount Cobham. Their wives begged the nobleman to spare their husbands' lives. He promised to return their husbands to them the following day. So he did, sending home their corpses on doors. Yet the Black Act did not succeed in safeguarding the forests, the timber they contained, or the deer. Gamekeepers led schizophrenic lives: sometimes they struck terror into the hearts of poachers and marauders; sometimes they were terrorized in their turn by the victims of the laws they sought to administer.

Forest struggles in Europe

The forests of much of continental Europe survived longer than did those of England and Wales. The major part of the forests bordering or close to the Mediterranean had substantially disappeared in classical times. In other parts of Europe where Rome established permanent colonies, the original forest was also heavily cut: for ship-building, for the treatment of ores, and for the establishment of export farms. This happened in the Rhône valley, Spain, southern England, and Wales. However, that still left a vast expanse of forest spreading from the Alps north to the Baltic, and west to the Atlantic. These forests remained intact until the spread of towns in the Middle Ages, and those in northern and eastern Europe remained a bar to overland transport until the German nobility started to colonize Prussia and Eastern Europe.

During the Middle Ages the Church was one of the largest owners of property throughout Europe. It extended its wealth and power by clearing forested land for conversion to agriculture, usually with scant regard for peasant needs in the forest. The Cistercians were exceptional in that they recognized the interdependence of forestry and agriculture and normally ensured adequate woodland areas around their clearings.

Besides being the largest landowner, the Church was often savagely punitive when it considered its rights trespassed. The significance of landed property to the church is exemplified by Archbishop Michael of Salzburg, who in 1538 sentenced a man to death simply for eating a stag that was shot by someone else, but found dead in his field. The actual poacher was publicly executed by being sewn into deer skins and thrown to hungry blood hounds.

In Europe, the mainstream Reformation changed the beneficiaries, but little of the harshness, of rural exploitation. When, in 1517, Martin Luther nailed his Theses to the church door at Wittenberg he was railing against the vices and commercialism of a corrupt Roman church; he was not calling into question the established social order. Nevertheless his Theses did imply that even the poor were God's children. In the towns the ideas of the Reformation fed anti-clericalism and resentment against the social and economic privileges of the clergy. In the countryside notions of equality spread like wildfire, and set alight the smouldering social discontent which led to the Peasant War of 1524–6.

The 'charter' around which the peasant movements of southern Germany coalesced, the 'Twelve Articles' adopted at Memmingen in 1525, was a fusion of religious and social demands, partly inspired by Luther's former follower and radical critic, the anabaptist preacher Thomas Munzer. It sought freedom from serfdom and feudal burdens, and the right to elect clergy. In addition, a number of the demands aimed to restore commoners' customary rights, eroded by landlords' use of

Roman law: rights to cut wood and take game in the forest, and to fish in streams.

The peasant movement was suppressed by the union of Protestant princes, the Swabian League, with appalling brutality, perhaps as many as 100 000 (including Munzer) being killed. Luther, however, was enraged to see his doctrines being put at the service of the rural poor, and swiftly took the side of landed property. His abusive pamphlet of 1525, 'Against the murdering, thieving hordes of the peasants', drove home his conviction that salvation was to be had only in the next world, and gave theological justifications for the extermination of peasants that the German princes' armies were engaged upon.

Germany was not the only European country where landlords and forest owners sought to spread their title to the land and what stood on it and lay under it. France, too, experienced peasant risings which continued into the nineteenth century, and in which peasants' claims to uses of the forest were almost invariably an issue. Few roads crossed the forests, and brigands and outlaws found safe haven there. Rural crime was widespread, much of it the consequence of conflicts between poachers and gamekeepers, smugglers and customs men, peasants and forest guards. Country people strove hard to retain their traditional practices. In the Pyrenees friction over forest rights, with attempts to arrest locals, led to what were described as 'insurrections'.

Nor was it always simply a question of defence of traditional rights. When, in the French Revolution, much of the monarchy's forest land was confiscated for 'the Nation', villagers were prone to interpret this in an all-too-immediate sense, drawing the conclusion that the woodlands had become common property. In 1793 it was reported to the *Convention* from the area of Corbeil that whole villages, led by their mayors, were stripping the forest for timber and fuelwood, and chasing away the gendarmerie. In other rural areas in the Paris region the Revolutionary Army spent much of its time searching houses for pilfered wood.

The harsh winters of 1795 and 1796 much aggravated the problem. Public prosecutors expressed their despair at the scale of theft from the forest and local justices' connivance at forest crime. The people of Morville and neigbouring communes, wrote the *commissaire* of Hazebrouck court to the Minister of Justice, 'consider the forest [of Nieppe], because it is national, as their own, and, holding this view, daily commit devastations and degradations that it is impossible to describe to you . . . this court . . . is presently faced with at least 200 indictments for forest crimes.' His colleague from Marchiennes declared bluntly that the countryside was reduced to misery, and that the inroads into the forest could not be halted without a considerable armed force.

With such tensions, the profession of forest guard could be a perilous one if pursued with too much zeal. One guard was stabbed to death in broad daylight in the main square of a village in the Mons area in the spring of 1796 and, added the report to the Minister of Justice, 'the assassin is known, but it is impossible to arrest or try him because in this area no-one dare testify or tell the truth.' The forest guards were themselves extremely savage, empowered to carry weapons and displaying an alarming readiness to kill. In certain areas they succeeded in establishing little local despotisms, reserving to themselves traditional monopolies over hunting rights. (These incidents from the years of the French Revolution are described by Cobb (1975, chapter 2).)

Well into the Empire it was the most heavily forested areas of France which continued to present the authorities with the greatest problems of public order. And the late years of the Restoration saw the conflicts rekindled by the Forest Code of 1827, which sought further to limit access to the forest, and threatened to deprive many poorer peasants of rights indispensable to life. The foresters, rangers and guards recruited under the Forest Code came mostly from the unemployed. The aim of the code was to preserve existing stands and create new forests to build ships for the navy (however, the advent of iron hulls around the middle of the nineteenth century meant that ships were not, in fact, built of wood by the time the new plantings matured). For peasants, the Forest Code meant that their rights to graze their animals and to gather firewood were further curtailed. All over France, rural crime soared once more: and again, not merely trespass and theft, but also acts of vengeance against the guards and against the forests themselves. Army and national guard had to be called in to quell riots (as in Gens in 1828 and Cantal in 1839) in which the poor cut down thousands of trees. Crimes connected with forestry ran high for years and began to fall only after the 1850s, when offences began to be treated with greater leniency. But this period left its mark in popular tradition and the rural poor continued to view the forest guard as an enemy.

Perhaps one of the most spectacular episodes occurred at Ariège in the Pyrenees in 1829. Here a new iron smelting operation caused all the local forest owners to insist on saving, for sale to the smelters, every stick of available firewood in the forest. Forest policing was stepped up, and punishments likewise. Violence erupted, and the Demoiselles – bands of men disguised in long shirts and bonnets, often with blackened faces to avoid recognition – ranged the countryside at night to strike against gendarmes, forest guards, jails and harsh landowners. Thus the Demoiselles echoed the offenders against the Black Act in Britain a century earlier. Moreover, they had a somewhat savage way of exacting revenge on foresters. They would cleave a log, force the forester's hand into the cleft, and hold the hand there until they had withdrawn the axe. Often the forester was left with a permanently maimed hand to remind him of the dangers of enforcing unpopular laws. In 1848 the General Council of Ariège explained that the peasants had grown to hate the forests themselves, and now thought that the more they ravaged them the sooner they would get rid of their oppressors.

However, towards the end of the century forest crimes in France had fallen to near zero. The yearly average in the 1830s was 135 000, in 1910 only 1798. The draining of population from the countryside, the fact that new sources of revenue became available, and the course of time itself, had finally 'turned past injustice into present usage'.

Uprisings or resistance against local princes and church dignitaries occurred repeatedly in the centuries following the late Middle Ages throughout most of continental Europe north of the Alps. And almost invariably, among the peasants' demands were, besides the right not to be called away from working their own lands to working the lord's lands at critical seasons in the farming calendar, demands directly related to restoring rights they had formerly held in the forest.

Such struggles had one very significant and little-realized consequence for the history of political thought. It was thefts of wood in Germany which led Karl Marx to study more deeply the socio-economic basis of political action. The rising value of wood, and the consequent clampdown of large land and forest owners, meant that five-sixths of all prosecutions in Prussia concerned wood thefts, while the proportion in the Rhineland was even higher. Marx in an article for the *Rheinische Zeitung* in 1843 attacked the proposal that keepers should have sole right to decide when an offence was committed and to assess the damages. He argued that the state should defend customary law against the rapacity of the rich. The *Prussische Staats-Zeitung* had advised law givers 'that, when making a law about wood and timber, they are to think only of wood and timber, and are not to try to solve each material problem in a political way.' It was this issue that brought a turning point in Marx's thinking, leading him to concentrate on socio-economic realities rather than on strictly legal issues. Later on Engels confirmed that he had 'always heard from Marx that it was precisely through concentrating on the law of thefts of wood and the situation of the Mosel wine growers, that he was led from pure politics to economic relationships and so to socialism.'

As we shall see in later chapters, the process of suppressing common rights in the forest is confined neither to the historic past nor to Europe. When the forest is seen as having commercial value, realizing that value frequently involves extinguishing pre-existing rights. This was true of the colonizing powers throughout the colonial period, and it is equally true of the regimes which have succeeded them.

'The poor man's overcoat' is a European expression, and reflects the age-old dependence of the rural population and of some artisans and craftsmen on the forest to supplement their living and at times ensure their survival. That dependence has, in the direct sense, almost vanished today. There are still, in some European countries, pockets of rural poor who would be hard put to it to get by without access to the forest for supplemental income, but these are getting fewer each year.

Over much of the Third World, however, the expression still has a very real significance for rural people, including forest dwellers, and efforts to strip the poor of their rights in the forest continue to evoke resistance and sometimes armed uprising.

There is a certain irony in the fact that European peasant risings (in which rights to the forest were almost invariably involved) found their ideological justification in that most subversive of books, the Bible; while today, as peasants are being thrown off their land in Brazil and other Latin American countries, in the Philippines, Indonesia and elsewhere in Asia, they find their strongest allies in the lower ranks of the priesthood.

12   The European assault on the tropical forests

We have seen that when the Mediterranean civilizations blossomed, they could no longer feed themselves. That meant they had to colonize other areas: either by the direct settling of labour to produce food in foreign lands; or by the moulding of markets in the colonies to generate the surplus required. Grain imports by the Greek city-states presaged the much greater impact of the food requirements of Imperial Rome. In Rome as in Greece, when cheap grain imports became available, large landowners turned to more profitable crops: olives, vines, pasture for cattle.

In the centuries that followed the conquest of Rome by the Huns, some of the Mediterranean forests had time to recover. Over the last two millennia, tree cover in the Mediterranean has fluctuated against a steadily downward trend. During periods of depression, the natural forest crept back, except in areas which had become too eroded or arid. When more prosperous times returned, land was reclaimed from the forest once again.

The Mediterranean continued as the centre of 'western' civilization for many centuries, though the locus of power continuously shifted. The eastern Mediterranean came into prominence following the fall of Rome, but by 1200 the Italian trading cities had won back much of the Eastern trade, and successively dominated the Mediterranean. With this upsurge of trade and population, foreshadowing the fourteenth-century Renaissance, deforestation accelerated. The expanding maritime republics – Pisa, Venice, Genoa – took over much of the eastern trade from Jews, Syrians, Greeks and Arabs. Their fleets, naval and merchant, required ample supplies of ship timber; Venice, for example, drew timber supplies from northern Italy, from what is now Slovenia, and from the Dalmatian coast. Their growing populations made it necessary to step up food imports as well as to convert suitable nearby forest land to agriculture. These city-states also represented growing internal markets for luxury imports such as spices, silks, indigo and sugar, and for slaves.

Moreover they had ample funds to invest. The Italian colonies in the Levant and the Black Sea became, in Verlinden's phrase, virtual laboratories for the testing of commercial companies, colonial administration and finance, for long-distance trade and plantation agriculture (quoted in Davis, 1984, p. 54).

In particular, the commodity which centuries later was to become the main factor in tropical deforestation – sugar – came to play an important role in the deforestation of the Mediterranean. It was the Crusaders who met with sugar in Palestine and carried back the taste for it to Europe. It was the Muslims who had brought back sugar from India via Persia, making the Middle East a sugar growing and refining centre by the thirteenth century. Sugar was still a luxury good: it is reported that under the Mameluke Sultans, the Cairo court consumed 300 tonnes monthly. When the Crusaders were finally dislodged from the Holy Land in 1291, many of the princes and nobles settled in Cyprus. They proceeded to turn Cyprus into a sugar island. Soils and climate were right for growing cane, water was available for power and processing, the forests supplied fuelwood for energy, and the peasant population was harnessed to the task.

Two centuries later, as Venice steadily gained ascendancy in the eastern Mediterranean, the Venetians joined in the Cyprus sugar trade, first as shippers and agents, subsequently obtaining concessions for the creation of plantations and the erection of refineries. Finally, in 1491, the Venetians took possession of the island, turning it in effect into a huge Venetian sugar plantation-cum-refinery.

The Black Death had sent up the demand for slaves in Europe, but these slaves were still predominantly white, drawn from the Balkan and Black Sea areas, as in classical times. Only when the fall of Constantinople in 1454 cut off that supply did the Mediterranean switch to black slaves from Africa. By the late fifteenth century the plantation areas, mainly sugar and vines, in Sicily, Majorca and elsewhere were predominantly worked by blacks. In other words, the American form of slavery was invented shortly before America was discovered.

Thus, Mediterranean deforestation was not, as some have supposed, a simple affair of ship timber, the goat, and the progressive clearance by ever-increasing local populations of their nearby forests to make more farm land. Certainly hillsides were stripped to build ships. Certainly from time to time the spread of goats ensured that the forest could no longer regenerate. But equally certainly the periods of most rapid deforestation coincided with the pressing new need to feed growing empires and support the consequent build-up in the categories of non-food-producers.

In the second half of the fifteenth century the development of a sea-route round Africa by Portuguese navigators and merchants enabled this small country to displace Venice as the major power in trade with Asia. In the 80 years following Diniz Diaz's discovery of Cape Verde in 1445, Portuguese traders penetrated round Africa, along the coasts of India (which Vasco da Gama reached in 1498) and, by 1516, to China. Equally momentous was the development of Portuguese colonialism in the Atlantic islands and the Americas. At the centre of this lay the massive expansion of sugar cultivation. Hitherto, sugar in Europe had been a luxury commodity rather than a foodstuff, sold in small quantities by apothecaries, and included, on occasion, in royal dowries. The warm and humid climates of the Atlantic islands, in combination with African slave labour, made it possible to grow sugar cheaply enough for it to enter widely into western European town-dwellers' diets. Sugar-cane growing, and with it deforestation, spread from such centres as Cyprus, Crete, Malta and Sicily to the Atlantic islands, and it was there that the early stages of European imperialism were built. By 1490 the output of Madeira, the first sugar monoculture based on black slaves, exceeded that of the whole Mediterranean. In due course the change involved massive forest destruction in Madeira, San Tome, the Canary Islands, and the Azores. Following Columbus's transatlantic navigations of the 1490s, it was these islands which provided the pattern for New World plantation slavery.

The drive to the west

Europe's first economic interest in the Americas was in looting precious metals. This objective, genocidally pursued by a series of Spanish freebooters, powered the European banking system and economy and furnished, as a spin-off, fortunes and nobility to a number of British pirates. But commercial production soon became comparably important. Of the many colonial crops from which European fortunes were made in the sixteenth to eighteenth centuries it was sugar – 'white gold' – that proved the most important. It was also the most destructive of forest, for not only did it require the clearance of land to grow the cane on, but converting the cane to sugar devoured vast quantities of fuelwood.

One of Columbus's landfalls on his second voyage was the island which he christened Hispaniola (today Haiti and the Dominican Republic). He was delighted to find that the sugar cane roots which he had brought from the Canaries rapidly took hold when he planted them. However, it was again Portugal, in conjunction with Dutch capital, which took the lead in planting sugar. The Portuguese developed plantations for the European market in the highly fertile coastal area of high rainfall in north-east Brazil (claimed for Portugal by Pedro Cabal in 1500) in the early sixteenth century. At first, the planters experimented with indigenous slaves, but the South American Indians proved uncooperative labourers, and soon Portugal was exploiting its west African possessions to ship negro slaves across the Atlantic.

Eventually Portugal declined and was incorporated into the Spanish

Figure 12.1 The European assault to the west

monarchy in 1580, to be displaced by Spain's economic and religious
enemies – first the rebel Dutch, and then the English. In the early
seventeenth century many of the sugar lands of Brazil passed by concession
to the Netherlands, and thus to the Dutch merchants who had been
involved in the trade from much earlier. Later, Holland was supplanted by
Britain, establishing her dominance over Portugal; at the same time the
Dutch, the British and later the French were establishing large numbers of
sugar plantations in the West Indies. The Caribbean was closer to the
European market, but another important reason for the shift was the
denudation of forests and the exhaustion of soils in the Brazilian
plantations. Monoculture dominated to the extent that, even in the late
sixteenth century, food was being imported from Europe to this
immensely fertile region to feed the plantation owners and their staffs.
Coastal Pernambuco continues to this day, due to the destruction begun in
the sixteenth century, to be one of the world's most impoverished sugar-
producing areas, still known as the 'forest zone', despite the fact that its
original rich forests survive only as pitiful traces.

A similar pattern was repeated across the Caribbean from the middle of the seventeenth century onwards, the plantation economy destroying the ecology of island after island, then moving on. Deforestation took place everywhere, and was in some of the islands devastatingly rapid. The extensive forest cover in Barbados, for example, had gone within four decades of the start of English colonization in 1627. The first settlers, helped by Arawak Indians brought from Guiana, cleared coastal areas for food and small scale commercial crops. Two decades later the island's agriculture was revolutionized: small-scale cotton and tobacco estates gave way to large sugar cane plantations, requiring much more capital and large numbers of negro slaves. By 1666 the island had 800 plantations and over 80 000 slaves. The greater profits yielded by the new plantations, together with the increased population required to operate them, inaugurated the final intensive phase of forest destruction. A 1671 report observed that 'at the Barbadoes all the trees are destroyed, so that wanting wood to boyle their sugar, they are forced to send for coales from England.' That did not prove economic; instead they imported wood for fuel, first from New England (which by the end of the seventeenth century was becoming a substantial exporter of both timber and fuelwood), and later from adjacent islands.

The cost of such imports, however, together with the fact that soil fertility was declining, pushed the price of Barbadian sugar to uncompetitive levels. After Barbados it was the turn of other islands: the Leewards, Trinidad and Tobago, Jamaica, the Guianas on the South American coast. In the second half of the eighteenth century Saint Dominique became the focus of the shifting boom in importing slaves and exporting sugar: in the year 1787 alone 40 000 slaves were brought into the French colony. The scale of brutality, together with the opportunities presented by political turmoil in France, engendered the Caribbean's first successful slave rebellion, led by Toussaint L'Ouverture, and graphically described in C. L. R. James's (1980) *The Black Jacobins*; later, in 1825, the territory, crushed under a huge French indemnity, was to be given independence as Haiti.

The wars of rebellion, and subsequent blockades of Saint Dominique, however, drove up the price of sugar in Europe, and brought about the conversion of Cuba to its almost total dependence on sugar. The price of lands for plantations in the Oriente region increased more than twentyfold in the late eighteenth century. The island which the first European explorers described as so richly forested – its fine hardwoods were cut for the window frames of the Escorial and the doors of the royal palace in Madrid – had its forests ruthlessly cut down or burned. Well into the twentieth century *palanqueros* made a living on the Rio Sagua, searching with iron-tipped poles for hardwood logs in the river bed, and disinterring the remains of trees that the rush for sugar land had felled and discarded.

The fortunes made by despoiling the West Indies and South America were usually enjoyed abroad; some of England's finest landscaped parks, as well as the magnificent Codrington Library at Oxford, arose from despoiling the forests of the Caribbean. But it was not only the 'renewability' of the forest that was ignored: the whole plantation economy rested, until the early nineteenth century, upon the massive and barbaric transport of slaves from West Africa. Even with the horrific death rates on the slave ships it often remained, as a Jamaican planter remarked, 'Cheaper to buy a nigger than to breed one.' The fate of the indigenous peoples at the hands of plantation colonialism was even worse. The *entire* aboriginal population of the Caribbean was exterminated by the early European settlers. Conquering *bandierantes* in colonial Brazil hunted Indians like animals; genocide was given a gruesome further twist by the rubber collectors in the Amazon basin in the early twentieth century, who, like some colonists in North America over a century earlier, distributed smallpox-infected blankets to the Indians. As so often subsequently, it was the same forces that devoured people and forests.

Sometimes – and this was particularly the case for Central America and Mexico – the initial impact of the European assault was much more disastrous for the people than it was for the forests. The volcanic soils of the hills and alluvial soils of the upland valleys sustained a fairly dense population before the Spaniards arrived; the moist evergreen forest of the Caribbean and Pacific coasts sheltered scattered shifting cultivators. With the Spaniards came the implantation of export-oriented agriculture and a variety of diseases which ravaged the indigenous population. Of the cash crops for the European market, only sugar was new. This had but little impact since, more distant from Europe, it was insufficiently competitive to spread widely. The other products, indigo and cochineal, did not involve forest destruction. The decline of Spain entailed a decline in Central American exports, and for two centuries the region remained a backwoods. Its revival came in the nineteenth century as first the hill forests were cleared for coffee for the English market, then next, the lowland forests were cleared for bananas for the US market.

Even so, in 1950 the region still retained 40 billion ha of forest. The next four decades saw this figure halved. The reason for this accelerated clearance has been the growing concentration of land holding in the hands of a limited number of rich landowners. To earlier export crops have been added cotton and beef. Peasants have acted as land-clearers for the local beef barons, only to be subsequently dispossessed and pushed into the hills. There they have no alternative but to hack away at the remaining forest, bringing about widespread erosion. Though the 'hamburger connection' (beef exports to the USA) peaked in 1980, the highly skewed land distribution, coupled with rapid population growth, means continuing pressure on the remaining forests. Even in Nicaragua, the only country in the region to have carried out land reform, land hunger has not been assuaged. Further forest clearance for agriculture seems inevitable.

Sugar planting was only one of the most spectacular, and earliest, components of the European assault on the tropical forests, which began in the sixteenth century, and became widespread in the seventeenth. Coffee, cacao, tea, abaca, indigo, palm oil, fruit, rubber – all engendered both direct and indirect destruction of forests not only in South and Central America, but also throughout Asia and in Africa. The assault has concentrated on different areas at different times. Sometimes the impact on the forests has been immediate; sometimes it has been long delayed.

Reaching out to the east

The account of the European assault given so far may have created the impression that the Europeans were the first to clear tropical forest, that the forests they cleared were empty of people, or nearly so, and that the objective of forest clearance was always to establish plantations. But this is not so. Over much of Asia, and to a certain extent in West Africa and in parts of Central America, there had already been substantial clearance of tropical and subtropical forest before Europeans came on the scene. The country profiles set out in the chapters of Part III provide glimpses of the manner and extent of pre-European deforestation. But the impact of Europeans on Asian forests, directly and indirectly, was both more far-reaching and more shattering.

It was the immense profits to be made from luxury products of the east when brought to Europe that motivated the early explorers. Even the westward drive described above was sparked off by the search for a new way to the east; hence the general description, 'West Indies'. For centuries, luxury goods had found their way to the Mediterranean and to Europe. The journey was long, partly overland, and perilous. But demand was rising and profit prospects were unlimited.

These commodities were not, of course, the products of barbarians. Long before Europeans came on the scene, there had already been built up over much of Asia many petty kingdoms and several important civilizations. Firmly exploitative systems were already in place, with the efforts of local rulers to expand the agrarian surplus entailing continuous forest clearance by slaves or petty cultivators. These systems were mainly based on wet rice cultivation using irrigation which provided a large rice surplus. In Central Java, for example, kingdoms had risen and fallen for centuries before the Dutch arrived in 1641. Some of these societies had left remarkable monuments: Borobudur on Java (dating from the ninth century) was paralleled by Angkor Wat (Kampuchea), Haripunjaya (Thailand) and others. Thus, when the Europeans arrived, Asia was no empty jungle waiting to be discovered. There were developed societies, and a considerable volume of inter-Asian trade. The luxury goods which had been finding their way to Europe were of no great importance in the total Asian context. But with the arrival of the Europeans, local rulers

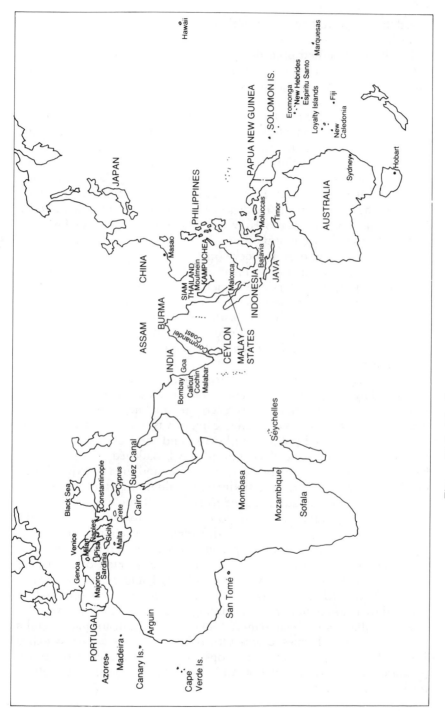

Figure 12.2 The European assault to the east

seized their opportunities and negotiated with the merchant venturers and other intermediaries.

The Portuguese had been the first to establish trading posts on the African coast and at many points in Asia: Cape Verde, Arguin, Sofala, Mozambique, Mombasa among many in Africa; Goa, Calicut, Cochin, Malacca, the Moluccas, Timor, Macao and elsewhere in Asia. When all Iberia was consolidated under the Spanish Hapsburgs late in the sixteenth century, Spain dominated all Latin and Central America, Milan and Naples, Sardinia and Sicily, and the Philippines. With the Spanish decline, coinciding with the diminished flow of wealth from the Americas, the Dutch began to take over. They had already reached Japan in 1600 and China in 1601. The Dutch East India Company, established in 1602, excluded the English, the Portuguese and the French from India. Batavia (now Jakarta) was settled in 1619 and Dutch domination of Java was assured by the massacre of the English at Amboyne in 1627.

The key to taking over and developing trade and to establishing the kind of colonial domination which would build up the wealth of the mother country, its traders and settlers, was mastery of the seas. The empire on which the sun never set was not acquired in a fit of absence of mind; it was built up gradually, with a number of setbacks, as British naval power steadily grew and coped successfully with its rivals: Spain in the sixteenth century, the Dutch in the seventeenth, and the French in the eighteenth.

In the early stages of the eastward drive, merchant enterprise was sponsored by the metropolitan nation states (as in the drive to the west); subsequently private capital was accorded any necessary military or naval support by the state; finally, capital was amalgamated with the state, which assumed political authority, and took over possession of the conquered lands. The objectives steadily broadened. At first the aim had been to take over existing lucrative trade, and then to expand it by developing trade in other commodities. In addition to the profits from trade, the European traders sought to siphon off some of the agrarian surplus normally taken by local potentates, all too evident from the conspicuous consumption which characterized their courts. Then, over and above any profit accruing to private individuals and companies, the metropolitan state itself needed to exact tribute, in kind or in cash. It had to finance its machinery of control, civil and military; and, of course, it wanted a share of any available profits. To this end, it resorted to a variety of devices, including land taxes and poll taxes. But to exact tribute in this way required an economic transformation and a money economy. Domestic agriculture had therefore to be switched from subsistence crops to cash crops. The consequence was greater pressure on the rural population and on the land, leading inevitably to further forest clearance.

The quest for wood

The experiences of Indonesia, India and the Philippines (see Part III) reveal that on the whole it was the indirect impact of the Europeans on the forests which was most severe. But the direct impact, from quite early days, included not only clearance for export crops and clearance to expand the area of land under agriculture (and hence land revenue), but also the felling of valuable forests for timber. In this, it was the British who had the greatest overseas impact: her 'wooden walls' required immense amounts of first class timber, and wooden ships had no great longevity. Besides, Britain was the least forested of all the metropolitan powers.

Timber had been of some importance in the westward drive. For example, long before Cuba became a sugar island it was a major shipbuilding centre for the Spanish navy. The long period of Iberian domination of the seas had severely hit the more accessible forests of both Spain and Portugal, causing faster deforestation than at any time since the peninsula had formed part of the Roman Empire. Much later, the North American colonies were a principal supplier, both before and after independence, of ship timber to Britain. But, apart from the Caribbean and North America, there were, in Central and South America, few forests of the quality encountered in South and South-east Asia. Thus, during the westward expansion logging was not a significant cause of deforestation. There were, of course, valuable species, but these were nowhere found in concentration: that is why mahogany was 'hunted'.

In the east, even before India had become 'the jewel in the crown', a dispatch in 1805 from the Court of Directors of the East India Company enquired how far the British Navy could depend on a permanent supply of teak timber from Malabar. Soon afterwards the Company succeeded in having transferred to it all the royalty rights in teak trees claimed by former governments. Unauthorized fellings were prohibited, and a Captain of the Police was appointed the first ever Conservator of Forests on the subcontinent, with the task of extinguishing all private rights in the forest. Later on, British wood needs, both for the home market and the expansion of the infrastructure in the subcontinent, made giant inroads first into the teak and sal forests of Northern India and finally into the Himalayas.

In Burma the main attraction for the British was the magnificent teak forests, which had long supplied timber in inter-Asian trade. In 1847 staff from the Pembroke dockyard arrived to buy Admiralty teak. Moulmein became both a shipyard and a timber export centre. Ships built there included a 1000 ton frigate for the Royal Navy, and exports of teak rose to 12 000 tons annually. Pleas for conservation were ignored; there was tremendous waste in the forests (rarely visited by representatives of the Company) and no efforts to replant.

Forest clearance for timber occurred only where the forests were rich in desired species and reasonably accessible, as in Burma, parts of India, and later Siam and the Malay States. But forests were penetrated, though not necessarily cleared, for particular species which were highly prized. One such wood, formerly found in many parts of tropical Asia, has now almost completely disappeared. Sandalwood has a strange history, worth recounting because of its surprising consequences.

Sandalwood

Sandalwood is highly valued for many secular purposes, but above all as an incense wood. The Buddhists of India had their own sources of sandalwood: Malabar, Coromandel. But ever since Buddhism flourished in China, that country has constituted the greatest market for sandalwood. From the sixth century onwards traders – Arab, Persian, Chinese – carried sandalwood from India and the East Indies to China, exchanging it for silk. From the fifteenth century first Portuguese, then Dutch and English, carried on the same trade.

As supplies dried up, European explorers, traders and whalers discovered sandalwood scattered through the Pacific Islands. Though less valuable than Indian supplies, the new finds were cheaper to acquire. When the demand for tea in Britain rocketed towards the end of the eighteenth century, China was the only source (it was another century before tea plantations in Assam and Ceylon provided an alternative). China spurned all Britain could offer, even Lancashire cottons, and to fill Britain's tea cups traders raided sandalwood throughout the Pacific.

This story had a surprising postscript. British settlers in Australia became even more addicted to tea drinking than Britons in the homeland. But this one-way trade with China became an extravagant drain on currency. As soon as the East India Company's monopoly on the China trade was broken in 1834 the merchants and mariners of Sydney and Hobart seized their opportunity, and scoured the Pacific for this saleable commodity. First, Fiji's sandalwood was cleared. Then the Marquesas (discovered in 1814) were stripped within three years. Next came Hawaii, to be followed by the clearance of supplies in the then virtually unknown islands of southwest Melanesia: Eromonga and other southern New Hebrides, the Isle of Pines, Loyalty Islands, New Caledonia, and Espiritu Santo.

All these were areas carefully avoided by Europeans since Cook's voyages because of the ferocity of the inhabitants and the fear of cannibalism. Only the prospect of quick riches from sandalwood broke down the barrier of fear. Thus it was sandalwood that brought many Pacific islanders their first sight of Europeans, and introduced to these stone-age cultures the iron objects which they most prized: fish hooks, nails, axes.

The ravages of the sandalwood traders brought this tree close to extinction, and efforts to save the species by establishing sandalwood plantations have not yet succeeded.

The assault continues

Colonial exploitation has taken many forms. The surplus has been extracted differently at different times. Tribute has been exacted in cash or in kind. Poll and other taxes have been levied in order to compel peasants to undertake export commodity production. The pattern, however, has generally had recognizably similar components. Wherever land was found capable of growing the crops increasingly in demand in the expanding European economy, the forests were cleared to establish those crops. If the land was already being tilled, some or all of it was converted to growing the new crops, obliging further forest clearance to satisfy indigenous food needs. The pattern varied from country to country and with the colonial power. To the British administrator, any inferior forest with no obvious commercial value, any jungle, waste or commons, was repellent. It represented idle land which if put under the plough could yield revenue in the form of export crops and land taxes.

Though it was the teak forests which had first attracted them to Burma, once the Suez Canal opened in 1869, the British promoted by all possible means the clearance of the botanically rich but commercially uninteresting evergreen and mangrove forests of the Irrawaddy delta in order to grow rice for export. The incentives offered to peasants from Upper Burma and to immigrants from India differed little from those offered by the Roman rulers in classical times to those who would clear forest and plant.

The methods used by the Dutch to extract an exportable surplus included forced labour, restrictions on crop cultivation, and the collection of coffee 'tribute' through local rulers (the Dutch introduced coffee in 1699). When the Dutch East India Company went bankrupt in 1799, the Dutch government took the company over and took political control of Java in 1830. Control was subsequently extended to the other islands. With growing political control, Indonesian goods came to be collected by forced deliveries, with the local rulers becoming, in effect, Dutch civil servants.

Of course, neither the forest nor the jungle, neither the commons nor the waste, was empty land. All were the habitat of tribal peoples; and everywhere on the fringes were small cultivators who depended heavily on what the forest could yield, in the way of food or fodder, tools, building materials and fuel. Not all administrators, and certainly not all foresters, were oblivious to this. But that did not prevent them from continuing to encroach on traditional uses of the forest.

Local manufactures had to give way to provide markets for the manufactured goods of the metropolitan power, as manufacturing developed in Europe. This could be accomplished in various ways. Often European manufactures were sufficiently cheap to displace hand-crafted goods in the local market places. But sometimes it was necessary to devise other means of handicapping indigenous products in order to give free range to European manufactures. When the British accelerated the clearance of the Deccan, the hinterland of Bombay, to encourage cotton growing, most of that cotton went for export, not to expand the native textile industry. The British were trail-blazers of the Industrial Revolution, and British classical economists carried the flag of free trade, enunciating the doctrine of comparative advantage. But when Ricardo cited the example of British textiles exchanged for Portuguese wine, he was providing plausible justification for a state of affairs which the British rulers had imposed. The Treaty of Methuen, which nailed down Portugal in 1703, was a treaty between the lion and the lamb. It opened the doors of Brazil to Britain and it effectively stifled Portugal's own textile industry. Though Portugal hung on to remnants of its empire until after World War II, this was mainly because none of the other maritime powers felt sufficiently strongly about them to dispossess the Portuguese.

The European assault had a continuing thread. Whenever indigenous handicrafts were displaced by imported manufactures, there was invariably a knock-on effect on the forests. Native craftsmen deprived of their livelihood had to seek a living elsewhere. If there were no employment opportunities, urban or rural, they were obliged to break fresh ground; more often than not this was in the forest. The penetration and destruction of tropical forest for export crops spread as Europe grew in power, population and affluence. Where indigenous peoples were few, or resisted enslavement, slaves were imported, and the indigenes either exterminated or pushed deep into the forest. With the ending of slavery, nominally or otherwise, came the turn of indentured labour. A large and docile labour force was sought: in slave-based planting, when slaves became too expensive, then the breeding of slaves was encouraged. When technology changed, when the land deteriorated, when even the climate was affected (as in Brazil's north-east), then production would shift to new areas. Each shift left behind peasants with no, or inadequate, land from which to wrest a living. Often, settlement on forested land was encouraged, only for the land titles later to be torn up and the peasants driven off once they had cleared sufficient land to make way for plantation agriculture or giant ranching interests.

World War II and its aftermath brought about a series of struggles for national independence, and within a couple of decades scores of tropical forested countries achieved or were granted new flags, new stamps, votes at the United Nations, and sometimes also new borders and new names. Independence did not, however, either halt or slow down the European assault. The Europeans were joined by the Americans, the Japanese, Australians and others, and found accomplices within the newly independent countries. The period since World War II has seen the greatest devastation of tropical forests of all time. The reasons for, and the manner and the consequences of this renewed assault are described in Parts III and IV.

The European assault on the tropical forests, which started in the sixteenth century, continues today, in changed forms but only partly so. In particular the process of evicting the rural population continues: in the Philippines, for example, multinational corporations, aided by the Marcos regime, dispossessed small farmers and drove them deeper into the Philippines' surviving forests. In Brazil, powerful landlords, waving land titles, use their own private armies to expel peasants from forest land they have laboriously cleared, obliging them to move on.

13   The development of forest science

From very early in their history men and women have learned means of manipulating the forest in order to satisfy their needs. Ordinances concerning the forest have a very ancient history. Nearly every civilization which has left a written record has left evidence of decrees or regulations designed to protect the forest. Many paragraphs in Roman law, for example, were concerned with the forest, and these had to do not only with the religious aspects of the forest but also with forest property.

Yet forestry as a science – as a separate science, encompassing an understanding of the biology of the tree and the dynamics of the forest, with the consequent application of scientific principles to managing forests – is relatively young. In fact, the science of forestry, and with it, forestry as a profession, has its roots in Germany in the second half of the eighteenth century. It was there that theoretical work in a number of relevant disciplines led to an understanding of practical forestry, an understanding which was broadened by systematic research and disseminated through a body of students who felt that they belonged to a learned trade.

The first professional foresters were concerned with growing trees, or protecting trees, to the best of their ability, for those purposes deemed important by those who employed them: usually large landowners, a public authority, or the state itself. As time went on, foresters often succeeded in influencing their employers, convincing them, for example, that the function of trees to protect watersheds, to regulate water supply, to reduce the threat of floods and avalanches, was as important as the growing of timber for strategic or commercial purposes. In this they were not always successful; indeed, there are still many parts of the world today where their voices go unheard. Foresters can justly claim credit for being among the first 'conservationists'. Yet their influence has generally been limited to land which had once been, was already, or was intended to be, dominated by tree cover.

We have already seen how forest laws multiplied throughout Europe in the Middle Ages; though these were at first concerned with conserving the forests for hunting, later they became more concerned with the forest as property and with timber. In fourteenth century France, Charles V introduced the first Forest Code, designed to bring about some form of management of the forests in the interests of timber for the navy. As yet, however, understanding of the biology of the tree and the dynamics of the forest was developing very slowly. For some time to come, 'foresters' were to be more concerned with protecting state or private property and with suppressing common rights in the forest than with managing the forest in accordance with any well-understood forestry science.

Perhaps one of the most important steps was the publication in France of Colbert's *Ordinance* in 1669. Colbert had observed that '*faute de bois la France perira*' (for lack of wood France will perish). His *Ordinance* set out general aims (which covered navigable waters, hunting and fishing, as well as timber production) and prescribed management methods which were designed to maintain the forest capital but also to produce clean, straight oak stems for ship-building. There had, in fact, been similar preoccupations in England since early Tudor times, but the desultory measures taken by successive English monarchs, often in imitation of the French kings, failed to stop forest depletion. Even the publication of John Evelyn's *Sylva* in 1664 had little immediate impact.

Evelyn was not the first to publish a major work in Britain on forestry. His work was preceded, among others, by Standish in 1613, and by Hartlib's *Compleat Husband-man* in 1659. But it is *Sylva* which has rightly won lasting fame. Evelyn, for a time secretary of the Royal Society, was one of the band of prosperous, influential and intelligent men of insatiable curiosity, who sought out and endeavoured to apply, in the words of Sir William Petty, 'such knowledge as hath a tendency to use'. The publication of *Sylva* in 1664 was the outcome of intensive discussions in the Royal Society in 1662 on the serious problem embodied in Evelyn's subtitle, *Discourse of Forest Trees and the Propagation of Timber in His Majestie's Dominions*.

If *Sylva* had little impact, this was not because Evelyn lacked influence. In 1661 he had addressed himself to the problem of atmospheric pollution in London, and had put forward a programme for making London's air fit to breathe, in his 'Fumifugium or the inconveniencie of the aer and smoak of London dissipated together with some remedies humbly proposed by J. E. Esq., to his Sacred Majestie and the Parliament now assembled'. Cleaner air was to be accomplished by 'improving Plantations' and by banishing lime burners, brewers, dyers and similar factories from the city. He had the ear of the monarch, and an Act was prepared on Charles II's instructions in 1662 requiring that certain factories should be relocated beyond the city limits – an Act which vested interests succeeded in frustrating.

Sylva still makes fascinating reading, mainly because in his quest for encyclopaedic forestry knowledge Evelyn was at once a beaver, a ferret and a magpie, and included folklore and fable about trees which give the book a flavour all its own. One can only speculate why Evelyn's book and the post-Restoration Parliament had so little impact on England's forests, while in France Colbert's measures did much to halt deforestation and encourage reafforestation. The reason is probably that England with its growing naval power had access to cheap timber, brought by sea from the Baltic and the multiplying colonies. France, lacking naval dominance, was dependent on domestic supplies.

But, though there was considerable concern in other countries about forestry matters and especially timber shortages, it is in Germany that we find the true beginnings of forestry as a significant branch of learning, with a continuous thread of development of forestry science, and the spread of forestry teaching, leading to the development of forestry as a profession. There the first significant technical publication was by Noel Meurer, adviser to the Palatine Elector, in 1561. Towards the end of the century, two more important works were published by Johannes Koelerus, of Brandenburg. But already forest services were building up in several of the German principalities, in accordance with the exigencies of the local wood supply. Thus as early as the fifteenth century, Tyrol had an *Oberforstmeister*, or Forestry Inspector General.

Forestry science really began to blossom in Germany after the Thirty Years War, so that the practical knowledge which had been accumulated over past centuries began to be interpreted scientifically and applied systematically. In 1713 Carlowitz published his *Economic Silviculture*. Later on, Urtelt applied mathematical calculus to the determination and control of forest production. It was the work of such as these which gave rise to the foundation of the early forest schools, the first being established in Ilsneburg by Zanthier in 1768. The most successful and famous of the forestry schools, however, was that established by Kotte in Zillbach in 1795, to be later transferred to Tharandt in Saxony in 1827. This school flourished, and its students later founded forestry schools in France (1825) and Spain (1848). This recital of names and dates serves to emphasize how much modern forestry science owes to its German origins.

Forestry schools were also established early in the nineteenth century in Austria and Russia, both of which countries had closely followed progress in Germany. It was a German, Hartig, who published a famous work on how to obtain a predetermined, sustained yield and how to treat the forest so that it could attain this ideal status. It was a German, Dietrich Brandeis, who, in 1865, first headed the Indian forest service, after a decade in Burma advising the British colonial administration. British professional foresters received a three-year training in England, and from 1878 their Indian subordinates were trained at the Imperial Forestry School at Dehra Dun. In Japan, the first modern forestry administration was headed by a former student of the Eberswalde school. A Prussian immigrant, Bernard Fernow, was appointed as Chief of the Division of Forestry in the US Department of Agriculture and may be considered as having introduced scientific forestry to North America. Formal forestry education began in North America in 1898 with Cornell University's four-year degree programme, and in 1900 the first forestry chair was established at Yale.

There are still many professional foresters today who are reluctant to believe that, down the ages, the forester has usually been looked upon as the gendarme of landed property and rich forest owners. But this is perfectly true, and some of the traditions survive in surprising places. There has always been an association between landed property, forest estates, foresters and hunting, for example. At one time many young men chose the forestry profession precisely for this reason. A few decades ago it was impossible to walk into the house of an old-time forester in many parts of Europe without becoming entangled with antlered trophies on the walls. Even parts of the public forest estate were reserved as hunting grounds for eminent persons. Around this pursuit, a traditional ceremonial developed. City-bred people may find these rituals quaint. But ponder the following quotation, and try to guess where it is from.

A number of usages are observed which impart to the hunt a dignified aspect and influence its course. During the hunt, hunting signals and fanfares are employed and are sounded with bugles. Before the sounding, during and after it, the bugler or buglers take a correct posture so that the hunting signals and fanfares are dignified. Before starting the hunt the hunt-master has all the participants of the hunt line up at a suitable place so that the hunters stand, when he faces them, on his right side in double, or four-fold ranks; opposite them on the right hand side are the buglers, the home sportsmen or employees, and next to them dog-handlers. Behind them stand the beaters. The buglers sound 'Attention' and 'Welcome'. All participants take off their hats, the uniformed ones, wearing a cap, salute and the hunt-master reports to the game manager the number of shooters, beaters and dogs. The game manager thanks him and orders 'Attention' sounded. Then he tells the participants what can be shot, what is the procedure and way of hunting, draws their attention to the hunting signals, reminds them of the correct use of arms, the hunting regulations etc. The bugles sound 'Good hunting' and 'Start hunting' and in this way the hunt is begun. Before each drive 'Begin the drive' is sounded and the 'Finish the drive' when it is ended. To conclude the last drive the bugles sound

'Drive finished' and finally 'The hunt is ended'. All bagged game must be arrayed for the last salute to the game, arranged according to species, rarity and size (first the furred, and then the feathered species.) The game is placed on its right flank and each tenth animal is pulled out a little to make the display easier to view. The participants arrange themselves in the same way as at the beginning of the hunt, the bugles sound 'Attention' and the hunt-master reports to the game-master the results of the hunt. Then the buglers sound again, saluting, thus formally concluding the hunt.

The country is the Czechoslovak Socialist Republic and the quotation comes from *Czechoslovak Forestry*, published by the State Agricultural Publishing House in Prague in 1966. Traditions die hard, and even in the countries of 'actually existing socialism' (for similar traditions survive elsewhere in eastern Europe) top people and eminent visitors can still enjoy noble pursuits! Yet even if contemporary forest science exhibits its medieval and propertied origins more visibly than some other sciences, its achievements are considerable. The directions which research has taken at different periods have been determined by the principal concerns of those who have financed it. Research institutes have been set up by public authorities, but have often become heavily dependent on private funding especially from major forest industries. Similarly, research at universities has come to depend increasingly on industry funding. This is why research into sylviculture and forest management has tended to concentrate on producing the kind of wood needed by industry.

Some of the most significant recent advances have to do with the creation of artificial forests for industrial purposes. Artificial forests are nothing new. The main impulses for the creation of artificial forests in Europe came from the need for ship timber and later, with accelerating industrialization, for fuel for smelting. Elsewhere, as in the USA and Brazil, it was the need for railroad ties (sleepers) and engine fuel. Debates about the quality of plantation-grown wood as compared with that from the natural forest, and about the economics of growing wood in plantations, are nothing new either. They have filled the columns of forest science journals in recent decades, but the terms of the recent debates correspond exactly to the letters appearing from the pseudonymous 'Agricola' in the *Edinburgh Weekly Amusement* in 1791 (personal communication from Dennis Richardson).

Some have compared the progress made since World War II in tree selection, tree breeding and propagation with the neolithic revolution in agriculture, the transition from food gathering to crop farming. This is an exaggeration, but there is a certain analogy; the full impact of recent progress has yet to be felt. Modern forest industries operate most efficiently with uniform raw material, and this can be grown more effectively, more quickly, and harvested more easily, than timber from natural forests. Many countries already depend heavily on 'farmed' trees;

more will come to do so. New Zealand and Chile have important export industries based entirely on plantations; the overwhelming majority of Brazil's industrial timber comes not from the Amazon but from its artificial forests. The new factor which is going to radically transform the role of artificial forests is the application of genetic engineering to tree breeding. The process of creating exactly the kind of new forest which will match particular needs has been speeded up by the creation of new methods of vegetative reproduction, now applied to many species for which previously one had to wait for seeding, with its inevitable attendant variation.

Computers have made it possible to automate commercial forest management, particularly in relation to artificial forests and even-aged natural stands; mixed forests are more difficult to model. With biological data and direct and indirect costs adequately programmed it is possible to feed in market information so as to enable the forest manager to decide what to fell and when, and for which processing outlet or market. A variety of sophisticated programmes are already available, but their practical application is extending only slowly.

Forest industries

Automation has extended its sway much more rapidly to the giant forest industry complexes, so that even sawmilling and timber fabrication, formerly highly labour intensive, have become processes conducted in factories almost empty of people. In some modern complexes, all incoming logs are automatically appraised for size, shape and quality, then directed without human intervention to the processing plant which ensures optimum yield in financial terms. Pulp and paper plants have long been so highly automated that it is possible to tour the entire factory meeting practically no-one between the woodyard and the dispatch department save an occasional maintenance engineer or instrument checker. Other wood processing plants are now moving rapidly in the same direction.

The rising emphasis on artificial forests does not mean that natural forests have been entirely neglected. But here too most research has gone into how best to manage them to meet industrial requirements. Society's ideas about what it needs from the forest are today changing rapidly, especially in the more affluent industrialized countries. Until quite recently, research into how some of these new needs can best be satisfied has lagged. This has led to needless conflicts between foresters and others concerned with natural resource conservation and use.

Labour has always loomed large in the cost of the final wood product. This is why most of the research into forest working techniques (or logging) has concentrated on getting wood out of the forest and to the factory gate as cheaply as possible. Mechanization has gone furthest where labour costs are high, and the drive for economy has, in industrialized countries, been reinforced by labour pressure for safer working methods. Logging has traditionally been a heavy and dangerous pursuit. Today it is much safer than it used to be for the workers engaged, but this progress is less evident in underdeveloped countries where labour is still cheap.

Perhaps the most striking advances have been in wood technology, in all those aspects of processing and using wood already mentioned in chapter 3. Wood has steadily become more valuable in real terms as the more accessible reserves have been used, as labour costs have risen, and as demand has grown. This has meant that research has been devoted to making more economic use of it: use of more species, use of all parts of the tree, use of wood once regarded as waste. It has led to the widespread substitution of solid lumber – first by plywood and fibreboard, subsequently by particle board. The wide variety of characteristics and finishes which can now be imparted to the several types of wood-based panels has done much to multiply the ways in which wood can be used.

At the beginning of the twentieth century, wood had already become the most important raw material for paper making, but relatively few species were deemed suitable for this purpose. Pulp and paper technology has steadily evolved so as immensely to broaden the kind of wood raw material which can be successfully converted to paper. Thus the slabs and edgings from saw milling and the cores from plywood manufacture can all be converted to wood chips and pulped. Indeed, the price obtainable for these wood residues has reacted beneficially on the economics of sawmilling and plywood manufacture. Similarly, technology has made possible the collection and recycling of waste paper and board on an increasing scale.

The advances in pulp and paper chemistry which have broadened industry's raw material base have required very high capital investments to achieve the considerable economies of scale. This has meant that the average size of new pulp and paper plants has sharply risen, particularly since World War II. But it also means that, whereas the price of wood (relative to prices generally) has steadily risen, that of pulp and paper products has remained steady or even fallen. The relative cheapness of paper and paperboard has brought about a revolution in packaging and distribution in the industrialized countries.

Economies of size, the need to make the best use of all parts of a variable raw material, together with the need to produce a wider range of marketable wood products, have all contributed to the evolution of giant forest industry complexes. Higher capital investments, with longer amortization times, have led major forest industries into more vertical integration: backwards into forest ownership, forwards into many kinds of fabricated wood and paper products. There has been horizontal integration too, with mergers and rationalization as in other industrial sectors. Similarly, transnationals and conglomerates have come to play an increasing role in forest products. Of late there seems to be a new trend, as in other industries, for the giant concerns to acquire smaller firms which have already successfully developed new technology based on research findings, instead of conducting their own research and funding university and institutional research. This has a double advantage for them: it shifts some of the burden of research costs on to others; it also enables the buyer either to utilize or to suppress the new technology.

Although forestry and forest products research has been heavily influenced by the interests of its principal paymasters, forestry science has made many other important advances. Much more is now known, for example, about the influence of different kinds of forests on water quantity and quality; about the role of trees in checking soil erosion by wind and water. This does not mean that all the knowledge which has been acquired is actually applied. Afforestation to achieve these ends involves costs which many governments are either unwilling or unable to bear. Thanks to television, everyone is becoming more familiar with the natural catastrophes consequent upon deforestation in all parts of the world. If catastrophes continue, it is not because knowledge of how to prevent them is lacking.

Forestry teaching, as well as forest research, has also been largely market-oriented: devoted to the production of professionals capable of managing forest lands in accordance with the objectives of their prospective employers, for the most part national and regional authorities, large forest owners, and forest industry complexes. The demand has thus been for professionals who could create forests, manage forests, or exploit forests with those objectives in view. Those objectives have not always coincided with, and indeed have sometimes been in direct conflict with, either the long-term public interest or changing social values. Nevertheless, the universities have never been completely suborned. They have sought to keep alive a sense of responsibility about the forest resource heritage. This has meant endeavouring to uphold the long-term public interest where this conflicts with private interests or short-term political expediency. The younger generations of foresters are at least as sensitive to these issues as were their predecessors.

Forestry's uneven development

Generally speaking, forest science in its application to the underdeveloped world remains itself underdeveloped, when compared with the knowledge acquired about temperate and boreal forests in the developed world. In so far as the European powers established colonial forest services, the primary concern of those services was the same as that of the colonial

Figure 13.1 Imperial architecture: the Imperial Forestry School, now the Forest Research Institute, at Dehra Dun in India (photo J. Burley)

administrators who had summoned them, and alongside whom they worked: to identify and organize timber supplies, either to be sent to the metropolis, or to be used for extending the infrastructure of the territory being administered, or for export; to raise revenues; and, where needed and feasible, to create new timber supplies for these purposes. These were the tasks assigned to the colonial forestry services. Inevitably, a good deal of information was collected about some of the tropical forests in the course of carrying out these tasks, but only rarely were resources devoted specifically to research: to learning, for example, how various types of tropical forest ecosystems might be managed on a sustainable basis. Still less was there any systematic attempt to understand the significance of the forests, of woodlands and of trees for the native peoples.

In those tropical countries where the policy pursued by the colonial powers entailed widespread deforestation, rapid population growth and an extension of agriculture to marginal land, it was inevitable that the forests would come under increasing pressure. Thus it was that, under the British Raj, the columns of the *Indian Forester* (probably the oldest surviving forestry journal with a continuous history) were largely filled with statistics of petty crimes against the forest: straying cattle, wood thefts and the like, with figures of transgressors apprehended and penalties exacted. In the interests of the 'reserved' forests traditional rights in the forest had to suffer. Many foresters, British and Indian, were aware of the misery they were inflicting. They were also aware of the dire consequences for agriculture which would attend the stripping of the Himalayan forests. But their warnings were ignored.

With independence, Indian foresters struggled to maintain the tradition and keep their forests intact. It was a vain struggle, since with the delegation of forestry and agriculture from the central government to state governments, electoral pressures persuaded state ministers that the conversion of more forest to agriculture was the easiest way to win votes and hold on to political power. As Indian foresters glumly observed, trees have no votes. Several decades passed before the significance of continuing deforestation to the people of India received full political recognition (see chapter 17) – although India has now become the focal point for what is nowadays called 'social forestry', which will be discussed in Part V.

The decades following World War II saw an unprecedented acceleration of economic development and material standards in what has now come to be known as the First World. Along with this went a very rapid expansion in the demand for timber, and heightened interest in opening up the world's remaining tropical forests for exportable timber. Many newly independent governments in tropical forested countries raced to climb on the export bandwagon. If there are still many glaring gaps in our knowledge of these forests, it is because those who have profited from them, both in the First World and the Third World, have not considered it worthwhile ploughing back any significant fraction of their profits into acquiring the needed knowledge.

Though billions of dollars were earned in export revenues, little was spent either on managing those forests or on finding out how to do so; on controlling the exploitation that was going on in them; or on replacing them. And though forest services were built up, their principal task was to facilitate the operations of the loggers, native or foreign. It was no fault of young foresters that many of them became unwilling accessories to the reckless depletion of their national resource heritage. Young foresters who were overly inquisitive might well find themselves transferred to remote stations; there were even cases of devoted and unbribable foresters being murdered.

World War II brought in its train demands for political independence throughout the colonial possessions. In most of the newly independent countries, new forestry schools were established. These were staffed by expatriates, or by citizens of the newly independent countries who had received their basic forestry training in metropolitan forestry schools overseas. The kinds of forestry the latter learned, and the notions they carried back to their students at home, often had little to do with the real forestry problems confronting their own people. Perhaps the most damaging of these notions was the idea that forestry was concerned with but one particular form of land management: the management of land that was already under, or intended to be put under, forest cover. Only recently have some Third World forestry schools started to consider the significance of shade and fodder trees for pastoralists, the many types of agroforestry adaptable to successful peasant farming on different types of soil, the accelerating fuelwood crisis in the towns, the role of forestry in rehabilitating marginal lands, and so on. In short, only now are they beginning to understand that forestry is as much about people as it is about trees.

Although, historically, the function of the forester has changed in Europe, his allegiance has always been to his employer. Today, worldwide, most foresters are employed by the state or by large forest owners. The latter are now usually forest industry complexes, often huge and transnational, or conglomerates which have taken those complexes over. Their principal concern is the continuing supply of cheap wood for industry. Even where the forests are publicly owned, the public authority or the state still often places its main emphasis on the raising of revenue or on producing wood for industry.

These facts have determined both the directions in which research has been concentrated, and the main content of forestry teaching. They have connoted a definition of forestry which is far too narrow to cope with the many new problems arising today, both in the industrialized countries and in the Third World. Awareness is growing, especially among the new generation of foresters. But as yet neither forest research nor forestry teaching have truly come to grips with these problems. To solve them, notions of what forestry is about have to change more quickly than they have done so far.

Part III The state of the world's forests

Introduction

No attempt has yet been made to set out the dimensions of forest cover in the different parts of the world today. In chapter 14, where basic statistics on the world's forests are presented, one of the significant facts which emerges is that over most of the Third World forest cover is today shrinking, while in nearly all the rich countries the area of land under forest is steadily expanding. This must seem at first sight surprising, since in those areas of the world which are today affluent, forest clearance was closely associated with economic development, sometimes being a prerequisite for it, at other times a consequence of it.

Yet, as we have seen, economic development has for many centuries had a global reach. In this part of the book, after chapter 14, the effects of that global reach upon the forests are traced in several selected country 'profiles'. While the countries chosen do not provide a comprehensive picture of what is happening in the world's forests today, the accounts given are typical, and the processes at work today are often analogous to those operating centuries ago. Only by looking back can the present be understood. And only if the present is understood will it be possible to influence the future effectively.

Though the processes at work are analogous to those operating in former times, the context in which they operate is very different. The first important difference is that the numbers concerned in and affected by the processes are very much greater: the world's population is ten times what it was in 1650, and is being added to at the rate of 87 millions a year. The second is that technology has advanced by leaps and bounds, so that the impact of those processes on the resources on which people depend is very much greater. Finally, among those enjoying more privileged access to the world's material resources, the numbers who feel some kind of responsibility to those less privileged is growing. That sense of responsibility may ebb and flow, but the impact of modern media and instant communications, however those media may be slanted, acts to enhance it.

This has had several consequences. One is a growing and widespread desire to halt the destruction of natural resources deemed irreplaceable, and to manage in a renewable way those which can be managed. Another is a wider understanding of the fact that some limit must eventually be set to the numbers of humans the earth's resources can be expected to support. And yet another is a growing disposition to transfer resources, within countries and between countries, in ways which will help the more disadvantaged members of society to achieve a decent level of life in a sustainable way.

All these consequences carry important implications for forestry and for foresters: for what they do and how they do it. That is why some of the country profile chapters in this part relate not only what has happened to forests in the past, but what kind of forestry problems are arising today and how those new challenges are being met. And in Part IV the various common problems which arise in the case studies will be pulled together and discussed in more general terms.

14   The world's forest cover

It is important to recognize that many of the forest statistics presently available are no more than informed guesses. It may seem strange that, with the technologies currently available, there is still uncertainty about the extent of forest and the rate at which the forest area is changing. But measuring forests is a complex matter.

The first forest inventories in the underdeveloped world were nothing more than what old-time loggers would call timber cruises: that is to say, they were concerned only to find out how much timber there was in the forest of a kind and a size that could be marketed, together with some general information which would help to estimate how much it would cost to get it out. Thus, often only a few species were counted, and then only trees above a certain diameter; all else was ignored.

With the advent of aerial photography, the work of forest inventory could be speeded and cheapened. The photographs taken by successive flights across the forest could be put together to form an aerial map; this map could be interpreted with the help of 'ground truth', physical data collected systematically from sample plots within the forest. Even so, the ground truth established by field teams working in the forest was still far from comprehensive, though more details were added about the composition of the forest as marketing prospects developed for so-called secondary species. Some information about topography, soil conditions, availability of road-making materials, and the like might also be collected, to estimate extraction costs. But still, of course, forest inventory

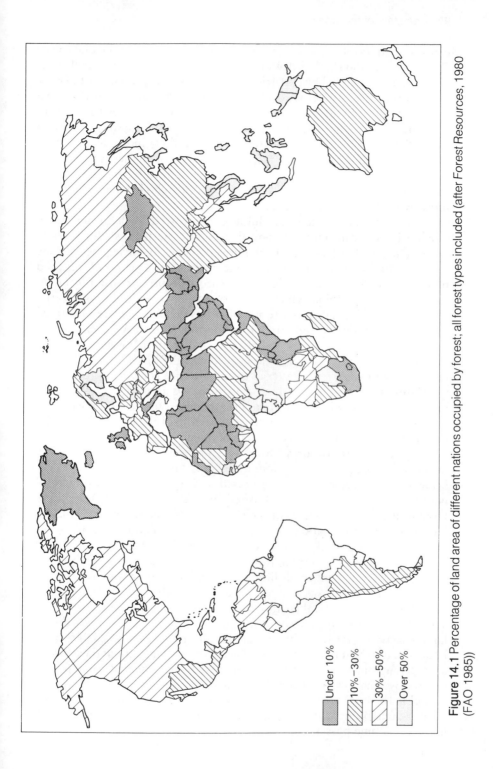

Figure 14.1 Percentage of land area of different nations occupied by forest; all forest types included (after Forest Resources, 1980 (FAO 1985))

Under 10%
10%–30%
30%–50%
Over 50%

concentrated on those forests deemed to have potential commercial value. This meant that in the Third World inventory data were often collected, compiled and analysed by expatriate companies, under contract to either the government, an international development agency or a prospective foreign investor. In the last of these cases, the data might even be withheld from the government – in spite of a long-standing UN resolution entitling Third World countries to all data concerning their indigenous natural resources collected by external agents. In the case of all these inventories, the concern was with how much forest could be converted into cash in the shape of export revenues. The role of the people who lived in or near the forest was of small consequence.

Today, with earth satellites, technology has moved much further. Earth satellite images can tell us a good deal about the forests. But satellite imagery has its limitations, and requires considerable investment in the 'ground truth' necessary to facilitate interpretation. The use of infra-red photography also makes possible the inventory of forests constantly under cloud cover, something which was not formerly possible with aerial photography. How advanced technology has become may be illustrated by the fact that, during high fire-hazard periods, North American forests at risk are systematically overflown by planes taking infra-red photography (thus registering heat as well as light waves); these data are radio-transmitted to a computer at the central fire control; the computer translates the data on to a map which shows immediately the exact location of any sudden rise in temperature. Fire suppression means can then be directed to the exact spot in order to control and extinguish the fire before it spreads and serious damage is done.

For real measures of forest shrinkage, we need comparable inventory data over an adequate time period: a decade or more. These data are now being steadily accumulated, interpreted and analysed. The estimate of world forest cover in 1980 published by FAO (Food and Agriculture Organization, 1985) consists of such national data as are so far available, interpreted by international experts in close collaboration with the national authorities responsible for collecting the data.

The difficulties of interpretation and estimation are considerable. But whatever the arguments and difficulties, understanding the problems of the *world*'s forests makes it necessary to refer to the best estimates so far available of their scale, their distribution and composition, of the ways and rates at which they are changing, of how far these changes are due to human action, and how they might be altered or restrained. Precisely because national authorities have collected information about their forests at different times, for different purposes, have classified their forests differently, and have changed those classifications over time, the figures assembled by FAO are necessarily something of a hotchpotch. But they are the most reliable data presently available: it can be expected that they will improve as time passes.

Table 14.1   Distribution and composition of the world's forest in 1980 (million ha)

Region	Total forest	Coniferous	Non-coniferous	Forest as % of land area	Forest fallows and shrubs
Africa	744	14	730	25	608
N. & C. America	807	533	274	37	94
S. America	915	20	895	51	220
Asia	468	102	366	19	62
Europe	159	98	61	31	0
Oceania	299	16	283	28	46
USSR	929	680	249	42	0
World	4321	1464	2857	32	1030

Oceania encompasses not only Australia and New Zealand but also Indonesia, the Philippines, Fiji, Papua New Guinea etc.: in short, insular south-east Asia. North and Central America includes the isthmus down to Panama, and the Caribbean.
Source: Food and Agriculture Organization (1985)

The least reliable aspect of the figures presented in this chapter relates to changes in forest area, since statistical improvements and changes in definition tend to blur the extent of real changes. Even so, the figures show the direction of change and point to its magnitude. As we saw in Parts I and II, the large-scale human destruction of forest cover did not begin yesterday, but was well under way in Europe, North Africa and the Near East in classical times and it has been spreading on a global scale from the sixteenth century.

It is now time to take fuller stock of these processes; to spell out a simple aggregated picture of the world's forest cover, noting some crucial aspects and pointing to current changes. Table 14.1 shows the general distribution of forest cover in the principal regions of the world. From it we see that South America has about the same area of forest as has the USSR, but is the only region with more than half of its land area under forest cover. Forest cover in Africa (as a percentage of the land area) is below the world average, but forest fallow and shrubland in that continent account for more than half the world total. Forest fallow is forest land which has been cultivated and then left for the forest to re-grow, thus restoring some fertility to the soil; shrub land is land dominated by woody vegetation too low and scrubby to warrant the description of forest. The high figure for forest fallow and shrubland in Africa is an indication of the extent to which Africa's original forests have disappeared and become degraded.

The distinction drawn in table 14.1 between coniferous and non-coniferous does not imply that all forests are of distinct species; mixed forests are classified according to the species which are predominant.

Table 14.2   Type of cover (closed forest, other wooded land, fallow and shrub) as percentage of total land area in 1980

Region	Closed forest	Other wooded land	Fallows and shrubs
Africa	7.8	16.7	20.0
N. & C. America	24.1	12.5	4.3
S. America	37.5	13.9	12.4
Asia	14.3	4.2	2.5
Europe	26.3	4.2	0
Oceania	20.8	7.1	4.3
USSR	35.4	6.1	0
World	22.0	10.3	7.7

Source: Food and Agricultural Organization (1985)

Notice that in the forests of the north temperate zone – Europe, USSR, and North and Central America – coniferous species predominate; in all other regions, non-coniferous (broad-leaved) species predominate.

What has to be remembered is that the figures in table 14.1 cover a multitude of different kinds of forests: so much so that any 'world' table necessarily conceals as much as it discloses. For example, in the FAO statistics a distinction is drawn between closed forest and other wooded land; both are included as forest.

Table 14.2 summarizes the different types of land cover by region. However in order to interpret it it is necessary to remember that its statistical definitions reflect forestry's traditional concerns. Thus from table 14.1 Africa would appear to fare worst in terms of the quality of its wooded land, with under a third of its total forest area being 'closed forest', while in Europe 86 per cent of the forest area is closed forest.

In fact, however, closed forest is not (as the description might lead one to suppose) forest where the canopy is complete; it is defined by the forest statisticians as land with trees whose crowns cover more than about 20 per cent of the area, and which is primarily used for forestry. Other wooded land includes open woodland, areas occupied by windbreaks, shelterbelts and isolated groups of trees, together with scrub and brush not mainly used for agricultural purposes. The regional figures are not broken down by country since it would take too much space. But a few comments will highlight some of the salient features in each region.

Forest cover in Africa varies from zero, or near zero, in Egypt, Libya, the Western Sahara, San Tome, Cape Verde and Lesotho, to over 50 per cent in Botswana, Cameroon, the Central African Republic, Congo, Gabon, Guinea Bissau, Senegal, the Seychelles and Zaire. The last-named has the greatest area of forest: 178 million ha; Gabon has the highest percentage of forest cover: 78 per cent. The high figure for Botswana is misleading: most of this forest is little more than arid scrub land, but since the land is neither tilled nor used for grazing, and has a certain woody cover, it is classified as forest. Similarly, Tanzania has a 46 per cent forest cover, though most of this is treed savannah – open, scattered, myombo woodland.

The regional figures for North and Central America are dominated by Canada, the USA and Mexico, with 436, 298 and 48 million ha of forest respectively. In Haiti (2 per cent forest cover) and El Salvador (7 per cent) the forests have already practically disappeared. Belize has the highest proportion of forest cover (60 per cent) followed by Panama with 55 per cent. In South America forest cover ranges from 3 per cent in Uruguay and 11 per cent in Chile to over 90 per cent in Guyana, French Guiana and Surinam. The South American figures are dominated by Brazil, which, in addition to its 65 per cent forest cover of 553 million hectares, has 163 million hectares of forest fallow and shrub.

Only four countries in the Asian region have over two-thirds of their land area forested: Kampuchea, the two Koreas, and Japan. The last named, the country of the 'wood culture' par excellence, and also the world's greatest importer of tropical woods, has no less than 68 per cent of its land area forested; the highest of any industrialized country. China claimed that by 1980 it had raised its forest cover to close on 18 per cent, well on the way to its 20 per cent target, compared with the estimated 5 per cent cover at the time of Liberation in 1949: this claim will be discussed in chapter 18. The former principal exporters of prime quality logs – Burma, Malaysia and Thailand – now have forest cover of 47, 65, and 33 per cent respectively, that is 32, 21 and 17 million ha of forest. But these figures understate forest depletion in these countries; much of the remaining forest cover is already sadly degraded. Thailand, whose teak graces millions of homes in the industrialized countries, will soon need to import wood to meet its own needs.

In Oceania the figures for total forest cover are dominated by Indonesia (121 million ha of forest), Australia (107 million ha), Papua New Guinea (38 million ha), and the Philippines (13 million ha). But again the common statistical category conceals great differences. Only about 40 per cent of Australia's forests are classified as closed forests, and the vast majority of these are thin and lightly stocked. The Solomons, with 86 per cent, and Papua New Guinea, with 83 per cent, have the highest forest cover.

In Europe, leaving aside Greenland and Iceland, with no or negligible forests, the countries with least forest cover are Ireland with 5 per cent, and the UK with 9 per cent. Finland has the largest percentage of land under forest: 69 per cent. More will be said about European forests in the discussion on forests in the rich countries in chapter 25.

Table 14.3 Annual forest loss and renewal around 1980, by region and for selected countries (1000 ha per year)

	Forest renewal	Forest loss
Part A (by region)		
Africa	108	1,333
Asia	5,545	1,037
N. & C. America	2,528	930
S. America	470	3,191
Europe	978	—
Oceania	342	679
USSR	4,540	—
World	14,511	(7,266)
Part B (countries with forest renewal or loss of over 200 000 ha per year)		
China	4,670	
USSR	4,540	
USA	1,775	
Canada	720	
Brazil	346	
Japan	240	
Sweden	207	
Brazil		1,480
Columbia		800
Indonesia		550
Mexico		530
Thailand		333
Ivory Coast		310
Ecuador		300
Nigeria		285
Peru		253
Malaysia		230

Source: Food and Agriculture Organization (1985)

The discussion so far has alerted us to some of the weaknesses in the data about forest areas. Information about *changes* in forest area is, for reasons which have already been mentioned, even more tenuous, but it may be expected to improve as time passes. Table 14.3 gives estimates of the annual loss and renewal of forests, by region and for some principal countries, around the year 1980. A first glance at part A of the table would seem to suggest that forest cover is spreading in Asia, North and

Central America and Europe, but is shrinking elsewhere. This impression is only partly correct. Thus, for example, the Asian figures are dominated by China's afforestation programme. Moreover, the two columns of figures are not of equal validity. FAO has used the expression 'forest renewal' because it is often not clear whether official national figures refer to new afforestation, or to the reafforestation of formerly forested land. There is a further problem. Forest authorities tend to report area afforested in terms of the work accomplished each year. But it by no means follows that the work is successful. Thus, had China's reafforestation really proceeded at the rate claimed in the early years, then the original aim on Liberation – of raising China's forest cover from 5 per cent to 20 per cent of the land area –would have been achieved some years ago. But in fact, many millions of trees planted never survived, for reasons explained in chapter 18.

It is not only Chinese figures which may be suspect. Some afforestation carried out in the USSR and in North America is done by aerial seeding – easily the cheapest way of creating new forests. Depending on soil conditions and vagaries of climate, this may be wholly successful, partially successful, or an abysmal failure. Or to give another example, in some parts of the world such as eastern and southern Africa, the success of planting will depend heavily on the amount and timing of rainfall, once the seedlings have been planted. In short, though at first sight it might seem that it is a fairly simple matter for countries to state exactly what new area of forest has been created, as yet there is no means of determining whether the reported figures represent effective afforestation, still less whether they represent net additions to forest cover.

If the forest renewal figures are sometimes open to doubt, the figures of forest loss are little more than informed guesstimates. This does not mean that they are simply wild guesses, though it should be borne in mind that they refer only to diminution in forested area: they do not reflect forest degradation, arising from such processes as uncontrolled logging. All these figures should steadily improve as monitoring extends and the importance of having more accurate resource data becomes more widely recognized.

Even so, the FAO figures do point to certain ineluctable facts. Almost everywhere in the Third World the forests are shrinking. The only significant exceptions are China and the two Koreas. However, over most of the First World (though not in every individual country) the progressive reduction in forest area up to the early part of this century has been halted and in many cases reversed.

15 Australia

Australia's most famous tree – some have called it the Wizard of Oz – is the eucalyptus or eucalypt, a genus of hardwoods which comprises about six hundred species. The eucalypt has travelled far and wide. It has formed the basis of important forest industries in both the First World and the Third World. It has been hailed as the Third World's saviour; it has been vilified as the peasant's principal enemy. Since 1980 the World Bank has financed numerous eucalypt planting projects, ostensibly to counter the present or looming fuel crisis in the Third World. Yet peasants in Karnataka (where the World Bank is financing half the cost – around US$40 million – of a grandiose social forestry project) rip up eucalypt seedlings in the tree nurseries. Why has the eucalypt become such a contentious issue? How can one tree genus arouse such passions?

Australia is an odd continent: in fact it is the driest inhabited continent. Three-quarters of its land area is either desert or land suited only to very low intensity grazing, and virtually unpopulated. The oddity of those indigenous Australian fauna and flora which have survived is the consequence of millions of years of separate development since the continent broke away from the earth's southern land mass, Gondwanaland. But that oddity also rests on the fact that the Australian landscape and its inhabitants have been largely shaped by fire.

There is good reason to believe that before humans reached Australia, a large part of the continent was frequently subject to catastrophic fires. So fire-conditioned is the flora of Australia that the seeds of many woody species will not germinate until they have been exposed to fire. The first Australians, the Aborigines, arrived from the north, from what is now New Guinea. This was at least 40 000 years ago, but it may have been very much earlier. Within a few thousand years of arriving the successors of these first Australians had occupied the whole continent. Some made their way round the coasts, others penetrated inland. Certainly they reached the Murray–Darling river system, and the inland lakes found in that depression up to some millennia ago. They spread through the land, the different clans and tribes learning very different ways of living from the land, moving about, hunting and gathering. Though they never developed settled agriculture, permanent settlements, or hierarchical societies, they did produce art, music and religion, of quite startling subtlety and complexity. In the course of time their stone tool technology became simpler and lighter, thus better adapted to a mobile life. Undoubtedly they influenced their environment, but it was through fire-stick farming – the technique of setting fires to encourage the regrowth of species preferred as food plants, and for hunting.

Even so, the influence of many millennia of Aboriginals on the

Australian landscape was nothing like as profound as that of two centuries of white settlement. The first Europeans to land on Australian soil saw it as a land of 'sand, flies, and the miserablest people on earth'. Even James Cook, one of the few to foresee Australia's potential, acknowledged that in its state of nature the land was indifferently watered and indifferently fertile. Certainly the first settlers, convict or free, had a hard struggle to survive, and many did not.

The British were not the first Europeans to see the continent: the Dutchman Tasman was there in 1642 and his name was subsequently honoured through Tasmania, the name given to the island previously called Van Diemen's Land. James Cook raised the British flag in Botany Bay in 1770. In 1788 the first fleet of convict ships arrived in the spot which had been chosen as Britain's new penal colony, New South Wales. This was because the British government could no longer dump its undesirables in America or hold them indefinitely in convict ships on the Thames. Freed convicts were joined by other settlers, some of them marine officers deserting the sea to build up estates using convict labour. Other settlements and penal colonies were established elsewhere. The remote subsidiary settlements – Macquarie Harbour and Port Arthur in Van Diemen's Land, Newcastle and Port Macquarie on the north coast of New South Wales – were set up to punish secondary offenders under very severe conditions. The hard labour involved, it is interesting to note, was in each case logging. It was not until 1829 that the British, fearing French intrusion, laid claim to the whole continent. After a stuttering start, the several colonies expanded and prospered, but it was not until 1901 that they united to become Australia.

Cook had pointed unerringly to the two factors which made Australia more foul than fair to so many of the early European settlers. As a land from which a decent livelihood can be won, Australia starts out with two of the worst handicaps imaginable: a paucity of decent soils, with many of its soils highly vulnerable to wind and water erosion; and rainfall which, over most of the continent, is sparse and erratic, with disastrous droughts by no means uncommon. It has been estimated that at the time of the arrival of Europeans something like 40 per cent of the land carried forest, mallee (eucalyptus scrub) or tall shrubs, that is, some form of woody cover. In some of the better watered areas the Europeans on their arrival encountered some of the world's finest and most impressive forests, fit to rival the redwoods of California; for example, *Eucalyptus regnans* (mountain ash) in Victoria, *Eucalyptus diversicolor* (karri; see figure 15.1) and *Eucalyptus marginata* (jarrah; see figure 15.2) in Western Australia.

It was the forests that helped the early settlers to survive. Jarrah was exported to Britain and to all parts of Asia where the British were consolidating their empire; it served as railway ties and constructional wood. At one stage, exports of sandalwood saved Western Australia from bankruptcy. Exports of red cedar were important for Queensland in its

Figure 15.1   A mature, tall eucalypt forest in south-western Australia. Karri (*Eucalyptus diversicolor*), the species shown here, is the world's tallest flowering plant (photo courtesy D. Cullity)

early days. Eucalyptus oil proved a great success on the world market, and by the middle of the nineteenth century Australia had a world monopoly and a thriving oil industry. Another important export was wattle bark for tannin manufacture, but this faded out when plantations of Australian wattle were established in Africa.

Today, Australia exports little timber and holds only a small percentage of the world market in eucalyptus oil. For its domestic needs it relies heavily, and in the future will rely even more heavily, on its plantations of exotic species rather than on its native timbers. This is because the first hundred years of white occupation witnessed a reckless double assault on Australia's forests. The finest timber stands were exploited, for home use or for export, as if they were limitless. Many areas of rainforest (known as 'big scrub') were cleared because rainforest was an indicator of good soils. Where the forests were less valuable and trees sparser, the trees were cleared to permit cultivation and the grazing of domestic stock.

Among what are today recognized as significant Australian agricultural exports – wool, wheat, wine, meat and dairy products – none is indigenous. They were brought to Australia, and adapted to thrive there, by Europeans. This is a remarkable achievement given that, of the less than a quarter of the land area with apparently adequate rainfall, much is mountainous, barren, or has very poor soils. Thus only one tenth of the land area is suited to cultivation or intensive stock raising. Moreover, so limited are water resources that the maximum irrigable area that could ever be developed would represent less than a quarter of one per cent of the land area.

Nevertheless a thriving agriculture, including animal husbandry, capable of feeding 15 million Australians and millions of overseas customers, has been built up. But in clearing land for cropping and for creating pasture and in running stock on the existing vegetation, about two thirds of the original woody cover has gone.

This transformation has its debit side. There has been excessive recourse to unsuitable or unsustainable land management practices: overgrazing, misconceived irrigation schemes, misuse of herbicides and pesticides. Considerable areas of land which have been put under the plough for irrigable farming have been deserted as a result of salinization, a phenomenon analogous to that which arose from British imperial irrigation schemes in the Punjab. Water taken out of the upper reaches of the Murray River finds its way back to the river lower down, heavily salt-laden. There are also areas where the clearance of unregarded eucalypts has brought about a rise in the water table, again bringing salt to the surface.

Animals can and do graze some of Australia's empty spaces – mile upon mile of semi-arid land with scanty vegetation. But unless that grazing is controlled and of very low intensity the land speedily becomes desert. Because the number of introduced stock carried was excessive, and

---

Figure 15.2 (page 101) Mature jarrah (Eucalyptus marginata), about 200 years old, in Western Australia. Jarrah produces a hard, heavy wood, originally used for railway sleepers (much of London's Underground rides on it); now it is peeled to produce high-quality veneers (photo courtesy D. Cullity)

because watering points were developed, grazing continued during drought: a recipe for land degradation. Today Australia faces land rehabilitation problems, requiring agriculture-supportive forestry, as acute as in many underdeveloped countries.

It was only well into the second half of the nineteenth century that the voices calling attention to the dangers were listened to. South Australia was the first colony to set up a forest department. By the time of World War I every State had enacted forest legislation and set up a forest service. Though the primary task allotted to each was to ensure a maintained wood supply, they did not neglect other functions of the forest, including their role in water management. The fact that some parts at least of the best indigenous forests have been preserved and managed is the consequence of the sharp struggles of the first professional foresters. Forestry was at first a Colony, later a State, concern. Only gradually, in the course of the twentieth century, did recognition of the national interest, and Federal influence on State action, grow. Fears of a timber shortage for domestic industries led to Federal support for State planting programmes.

By the 1960s the environmentalist concerns blossoming in Europe and North America had their echoes in Australia. The rapidly extending blocks of exotic pines were much harder to stomach than had been the no less exotic fields of wheat or flocks of sheep. What particularly aroused environmentalist wrath was the decision to clear areas of native forest, exporting the wood as chips, to make way for pine plantations. Foresters also came under stern attack when politicians, succumbing to local pressures, authorized logging in the temperate rainforests of Tasmania and the warmer rainforests of Queensland. Both these are forest types which, if not unique, are sufficiently rare to warrant the reservation of areas adequate for scientific purposes.

The press, radio and television hastened to join the environmentalists' attack on the foresters, overlooking the fact that politicians, not foresters, make policy, and that foresters are not always successful in restraining politicians. There had long been widespread agreement, even shared by many environmentalists, that the resource of exotic pines had to be expanded to safeguard the forest industries. However, unwilling to risk forfeiting the 'green' vote, the Federal government decided that Federal support to State planting should henceforth be conditional upon a satisfactory Environmental Impact Report.

Two States, Victoria and Western Australia, sought to appease environmentalists by departmental reorganizations, curbing the remits of foresters, and leaving responsibilities for managing reserved forests and promoting agriculture-supportive forestry very much in the air. However important it may be to assure future wood supplies, the key tasks in Australian forestry are water management and fire control; both require a high degree of forestry professionalism. Time will probably demonstrate that no reorganization will for long hide confusion about policy and lack of clarity concerning priorities.

Some of Australia's finest timbers come from species which are relatively slow growing and costly to manage sustainably. For a long time Australians had assumed that there was plenty more to come, just as there was land *ad infinitum* in the outback. Foresters have estimated that the remaining native forests could yield at least twice what they do at present provided appropriate management measures were taken. But that would be costly, and would certainly mean higher timber prices. No Australian state has as yet agreed to the required level of investment in and management of the native forests, nor to proper pricing of the wood they yield. This may yet come. The irony of the woodchip export fracas was that the proceeds were supposed to have contributed to better management of the native forest. Meanwhile the resource of exotic pine species continues to be built up to serve the future expansion of the forest industries.

Eucalypts

If Australian forestry, like Australian farming, has come to depend heavily on introduced species, global forestry owes much more to species originating in Australia. The most important of these are eucalypts but they also include the acacias (wattles), casuarinas, araucarias and others. Today, outside Australia, the world has over 6 million ha of eucalypt plantations and close on half a million ha of acacia plantations. Unlike rubber and cinchona, the seeds of which had to be secretly smuggled out of Brazil and Peru respectively, to subsequently furnish plantations which commercially eclipsed their forebears in the native forests, eucalypts and other seed have been freely donated and freely sold. Today fifty tons of seed of Australian species are exported annually, at a value of over five million dollars. The Commonwealth Scientific Industrial Research Organization's Tree Seed Centre, in collaboration with development assistance agencies, annually sends 6000 seed lots of Australian tree species to about 85 countries.

The country boasting most eucalypts today – Brazil, with an estimated 2 billion trees – first received seed, perhaps via Portugal, about 1830. But the first major boom in eucalypt planting there came early in the twentieth century, when the São Paolo railway, having denuded the native forest on either side of the line, opted after trials for three eucalypt species for extensive plantations to fuel its wood-burning locomotives. These

---

Figure 15.3 (opposite) A tall forest of *Eucalyptus saligna* in temperate south-eastern Australia, near Sydney. This species is one of the eucalypts widely planted outside Australia (photo M. Westoby)

Figure 15.4   Coastal eucalypt woodland in a high rainfall area but on very poor soil, in south-eastern Australia; the understorey is composed of cycads, plants related to conifers but resembling ferns and palms (photo R. C. Carolin)

plantations survived for many years, since coal soon replaced wood for fuel. But it was the existence of the plantations and the known productivity of eucalypts that made possible an indigenous iron and steel industry, since charcoal could take the place of coke and Brazil did not possess suitable coking coal.

The great boom in eucalypt planting in Brazil came four decades later, when fiscal incentives made it possible for rich landowners, business men and even professionals to become owners of forest plantations instead of paying income tax. By 1970 Brazil had eucalyptus plantations (along with the simultaneously planted subtropical pines) in far greater quantities than could ever be needed for domestic purposes. By now, however, it had not only been established that eucalypt pulp, with its high alpha cellulose content, was specially suitable for rayon, tyre cord, transparent cellulose wrappings and associated industries; but that hardwood (short fibre) pulp could replace more expensive softwood (long fibre) pulp to a greater extent than had previously been thought possible in several grades of paper. Thus foreign pulp and paper industries hastened to join Brazilian capital in establishing new pulp export plants based on this plentiful unused resource.

France, Portugal, Spain and Sicily all have important forest industries based on eucalypt plantations, as has Argentina. Countries as different as

Figure 15.5 Open eucalypt woodland in semi-arid grazing land in temperate inland New South Wales, in an area where the average rainfall is about 400 mm per year. The grassland under the trees is being invaded by shrubs in the absence of fires (photo B. L. Rice, 1979)

China and New Zealand are planting eucalypts for industry. It was progeny of the seeds of five eucalypt species sent by the Bishop of Melbourne to the Three Fountains Abbey outside Rome which enabled Mussolini to drain the Pontine marshes. The Emperor Menelik II of Abyssinia is supposed to have settled on Addis Ababa as his permanent capital because eucalypts thrived there; successive preceding imperial sites had in turn become incapable of supporting court needs as they were speedily deforested for firewood. However, the global boom in Third World eucalypt planting was given impetus by the World Bank (and others) when the extent of the looming energy crisis in about 100 Third World countries was revealed by an FAO study of fuelwood consumption and future fuelwood needs.

The many eucalypt species in Australia are adapted to a very wide variety of soils and climate, ranging from temperate to tropical, although only a few are frost resistant. Their great value, for industry and for meeting urban and rural energy needs, is that they grow fast, coppice freely, and many species thrive on relatively poor soils. Planted on vacant patches, they can provide the small farmer with poles for building and wood for fuel in three to five years. Because they grow fast, they consume a good deal of water. Their roots can penetrate deeply in their search for

Figure 15.6 Eucalypt grassy woodland in monsoonal tropical Australia, with a dry season of 7 – 10 months. This vegetation is subject to fire almost every year (photo B. L. Rice, 1981)

water and nutrients, drawing on the water table, or alternatively spread laterally near the surface, impoverishing the soil surrounding the tree. Their leaf canopy is relatively sparse, intercepting or checking the speed of falling rain to a lesser extent than that of other species. This means that they are of less use than other species in controlling run-off and soil erosion. Rarely can eucalypt plantations be grazed, but there are cases where some species, closely planted on adequate soils, can be safely grazed in the first few years after establishment.

Koalas thrive on some species; domestic livestock on none. Eucalypts provide neither fodder nor browse. Nor is the leaf litter suitable as fertilizer. Micro-organisms break down the leaf litter only slowly, so that there is a considerable build-up of litter as potential fuel for ground fires. Though the leaves of many species yield valuable extractives, medicinal as well as essential oils, those same extractives make for easy igniting and high flammability. In high winds fire can leap from crown to crown with lightning rapidity. Planted eucalypts are no less fire-prone than those in the native forests. The enthusiasm evinced in recent decades by Australian suburbia for indigenous flora, switching from English-type gardens, has significantly raised fire risk in the urban fringes.

This is far from an adequate summation of the pros and cons of eucalypts. But perhaps it is sufficient to indicate some of the issues under contention. Eucalypts *have* taken pride of place to date in so-called social forestry. But this is because most social forestry projects have failed to study, or chosen to ignore, the political and socio-economic context within which they must operate. In the vast majority of cases, the small farmer looks to trees to provide him not simply with poles and fuel, but also with fodder, fertilizer and food. Moreover, his trees should help his other crops thrive, not steal water and nutrients from them.

The better-off farmer, eager to take advantage of a ready market for eucalypts as raw material for industry or as fuel, often finds it pays better to grow eucalypts than to grow grain. The Karnataka social forestry scheme mentioned above realized after a few years that adjustments were necessary; by 1988 only 15 per cent of the trees being planted were eucalypts, as compared with 80 per cent at the scheme's outset.

The blame for eucalypt-addiction in social forestry projects is sometimes laid at the door of Australian advisers: unfairly, since Australian foresters are at least as aware of the social implications as their professional fellows, while being more conscious of both the potential and the constraints of the many eucalypt species. Studies now underway in Australia are likely to enlarge the range of eucalypts in use abroad. There are at least eight salt tolerant eucalypt species (*camaldulensis, calycogana, gracilis* and others) which may help to make productive use of saline soils. Selection and breeding for frost resistance may permit the introduction of species into new areas. And there are still very many Third World situations where presently available eucalypts can be planted to the advantage of the small farmer and the landless. Appropriately selected, and planned with due regard to the social and economic impact, the Wizard of Oz has many people yet to serve.

16   Brazil

Brazil's tropical forests are today disappearing at the rate of 2.5 million ha a year. Brazil is perhaps the richest country on earth for natural resources: it is twice the size of Europe with less than a quarter of Europe's population. Obviously Brazil is not overpopulated. Nor does it lack sufficient resources to feed its people.

Up to the middle of the seventeenth century Brazil was the world's largest sugar producer and the biggest market for slaves. Then the Dutch, who had taken over both sugar producing and slave trafficking, decided to pull out of Brazil's north-east, where the soils were wearing out, to the

Caribbean, much closer to the European market. What did they leave behind them? Here is how Eduardo Galeano (1973) describes it.

Sugar had destroyed the north-east. The humid coastal fringe, well-watered by rains had a soil of great fertility rich in humus and mineral salts and covered by forests from Bahia to Ceara. This region of tropical forests was turned into a region of savannahs. Naturally fitted to produce food, it became a place of hunger. Where everything had bloomed exuberantly, the destructive and all-dominating latifundio left sterile rock, washed-out soil, eroded lands.

Brazil's north-east has never recovered. Millions of the world's poorest scratch a bare living from these degraded lands. The climate has been completely changed. When the rains fail, countless thousands vote with their feet, trekking hundreds of miles in search of less barren soils on which they may squat.

The threat of hunger has never left the north-east. What happens to people if generation after generation goes hungry? Listen to Nelson Chaves, of the Nutrition Institute at Recife University (quoted by Thierry Mabisiak, the *Guardian*, 2 November 1980).

Our studies have led us to conclude that people in the region are getting smaller because they're hungry. The average height, which ought to be 1.75 metres, is 1.60 metres for men and 1.58 metres for women. This is veritable nutritional dwarfism.

The north-east is not the only region of Brazil to have been already almost completely deforested. Over 500 000 km^2 of forest in south-eastern Brazil have disappeared, save for a few scattered patches. Their original inhabitants were Amerindian hunters and gatherers, who, though they may have used fire, had negligible impact on the forest. About 1500 years ago the indigenes were pushed inland by Tupi-Guarani shifting cultivators. Though they exercised greater pressure on the forests it was only to the extent that limited areas of primary forest cleared, planted, then abandoned, came up as secondary forest. With the arrival of the Portuguese settlers, the Tupi-Guaranis were hunted; some were enslaved, while many succumbed to settler-borne diseases.

The mestizo population, also practising slash-and-burn but armed with iron tools, cleared the forests more effectively. But it was the whites, especially those with money and connections, who obtained title to the cleared lands. The peasant cultivators, like many of their predecessors elsewhere and millions of their successors, were acting as land-clearers for planters and ranchers who followed. Gold and diamonds, sugar, coffee, railroads: each in turn brought waves of immigrants, more forest destruction, urbanization, land speculation. Where this forest once stood, one-third of Brazil's population now lives. Some have argued that the liquidation of that forest capital was a necessary prerequisite for capitalist agriculture, industrialization, and their attendant blessings. But the long-term costs of the thousands of fortunes which were made there are hard to quantify and are borne by someone else: indigenous peoples exterminated; thousands of species of both flora and fauna rendered extinct; rural people made landless and driven to the shanty towns; denuded watersheds leading to dried up rivers and more frequent floods, jeopardizing both water and power supplies to the towns.

The Amazon

The north-east, the south-east: but Brazil has the Amazon. When tropical forests are mentioned to most people their thoughts immediately speed to the Amazon. Often they will summon up a mental picture of loggers mowing down the Amazon forests with chain saws. However, this is a myth, given currency by those who would like a readily identifiable villain.

In fact, Brazil's humid forests in the Amazon region contain about 50 000 million m^3 of timber. The loggers take out each year only four million m^3 – that is, less than a hundredth of one per cent. The reason is that the Amazon forests are not rich in species presently considered commercial. The cost of getting timber out and transporting it to the industrialized parts of Brazil is high. This is why loggers in Brazil's Amazon operate only in easily accessible places, on a small scale, using very simple equipment, and taking out just a few selected species. Nor is this situation likely to change very much. The intention is that more and more of Brazil's industrial wood needs will be met from plantations – artificial forests. Only China, the USA, and the USSR have created larger areas of man-made forest than has Brazil.

Nearly all the deforestation in the Brazilian Amazon takes place either round the network of trans-Amazonian highways, with accompanying colonization schemes or spontaneous settlement, or through large-scale ranching projects (see figure 16.1), both in the southern Amazon forests and in the proximate open savannah woodlands (*cerrado*). Trans-nationals are to the fore in these developments, the aim being cheap beef, mainly for the domestic Brazilian market. Further north, in several of the countries of Central America, exactly the same process is at work, with peasants being displaced by ranching and pushed into the forests. There the beef is exported to the insatiable North American market: the 'hamburger connection'.

What actually lies behind the absurd Amazon 'dream' of marrying the 'men with no land' (from the north-east) to the 'land with no men' is that *shifted* cultivators are once again acting as land-clearers for big business. It has suited successive Brazilian governments to jeopardize the tropical forests rather than carry out the land reforms they have so often promised.

Figure 16.1 Forest cleared for large-scale ranching in Brazil (photo copyright T. Gross/OXFAM)

With Brazil on the edge of economic collapse, civilian rule returned in 1985 and Brazil has a government which won power pledged to land reform. Half of Brazil's people are landless peasants with their families. One per cent of its landowners occupy 42 per cent of its cultivated land, while the 52 per cent who own less than 10 ha each occupy less than 3 per cent of the cultivated land. These figures make it clear that the Amazon forests are not shrinking because Brazil is overpopulated: the pressures that bear on the forest are the consequence of a political system which denies well over half the population access to land and other resources.

The Bishop of São Paolo, Alfredo Ernest Novak, describing what was happening in the interior of Brazil, pointed out that it mirrored what was happening in all Latin American countries:

Peasant economies and peasant cultures are often totally destroyed with the expansion of commercial agriculture in these rural areas, frequently involving even violence and physical confrontation. Peasants are expelled without any recognition of their rights to the land and to the benefits of their labour in clearing virgin areas. (Novak 1981)

Successive reports of the Brazilian Church's Commission on Lands have for years been a litany of murders of priests, peasant leaders and trade union organizers, the suppression of peasant organizations, and so on.

But surely, if Brazil stands so high in the table of countries establishing artificial forests, hasn't this helped the rural poor? The answer is no. Practically all the 4 million and more ha of plantations established in the last two decades are in the southern states, half of them in the state of São Paolo. The fiscal incentives which led to their creation represented a free gift of valuable resource assets to companies, rich landowners, and well-off professionals. Hardly a single hectare went into the north-east where they could have provided employment for some of the famine-ridden millions and laid the basis for new, permanent forest industries.

Has Brazil's civilian government the will and the power to carry out its pledges? Only if it is prepared to mobilize the rural millions to break the power of the landlords and thus carry out its pledges for land reform, will the steady disappearance of the Amazonian forests be stemmed.

The prospects are not encouraging. As yet the persecution of rural organizers has not ceased, nor have the private armies of the biggest landowners been disbanded. The pressure of the influential landowners' lobby brought the resignation of the first appointment as Minister for Agrarian Reform and Development. Supported by the Roman Catholic Church and the agricultural unions, he had sought to settle 7 million landless families on some of Brazil's 200 million ha of unused arable land. The third Land Reform Minister died in an air crash in the eastern Amazon where he had been investigating land disputes in which hundreds had died.

One tragic aspect of the manner in which the Amazonian forests are being destroyed is that it involves the genocide of the indigenous Indians. It is not only that by destroying their habitat the people themselves are destroyed. Landless peasants who are pushed into the forest on which the Indians depend come into armed conflict with them, and add to the threat posed by mineral prospectors, transnational ranching projects and huge electrification schemes. The future of Brazil's remaining 200 000 Indians remains bleak. Jucas Filho, the head of Funai, the National Indian Bureau, has declared that 'Indian communities have no money to improve conditions, but they are sitting on treasures'. The intention to contract reserved lands to sawmills and mining companies is clear. Simultaneously, Funai has ordered the evacuation of Catholic missionaries who have taken up the cause of the Indians. One Jesuit, Vicente Canas, was murdered when attempting to protect the fragile Enauene tribe in Mato Grosso.

Brazil is fortunate in having many lively intellectuals and vigorous conservationists who are aware of the threat to the Indians and the squandering of Brazil's natural resources. Their brave campaigning can meet with success if it is accompanied by sufficient external pressure. The withdrawal of World Bank support from the huge Polo-Nordeste electrification project, the consequence of US conservationist pressure on the Bank via the US government, led to the abandonment of the project. This is the only signal victory scored by conservationists in Brazil to date.

> To illustrate my meaning and intention more plainly, I would compare the relationship existing between Forestry and Agriculture to that which exists in ordinary life between husband and wife. Forestry stands in the place of the husband, dark, stern and strong, but protecting and cherishing; Agriculture, bland, benignant and bountiful, may, in my parable, be described as the wife. Deprived of the aid and resources derived from the forests, agriculture pines and languishes, and becomes barren and unfruitful.
>
> 'G. K. B.', *Indian Forester*, XV, 330, Sept. 1889

No forest history outside Europe and North America is better documented than that of the Indian subcontinent. Though well documented, it is far from being completely written. The ample documentation continues to be explored, and in the course of that exploration some pages have been rewritten several times.

The approaches of those presently writing are far from uniform. Some castigate the British invaders as timber pirates, land thieves and soil wreckers, sometimes implying that there had been no significant deforestation until the British came on the scene. Others extol the British for pacifying and unifying the subcontinent, implanting forest science there, ensuring that at least some forests were reserved and managed, and leaving behind them the largest and best-trained corps of foresters in what has come to be known as the underdeveloped world.

Neither of these views is correct. India had an important history before the European 'assault'. The motivation of the British, when they succeeded in expelling their rivals and establishing their domination over the whole subcontinent, was never altruistic. Though they did leave behind them a relatively well staffed forest department, the reason for setting it up in the first place was to keep alive at least some of the geese that were laying them such golden eggs.

The highly prized commodities – silk, spices, jewels and the like – which found their way to Europe and eventually triggered off the European assault were only a spill-over from an intricate and highly developed inter-Asiatic trade conducted, mostly by sea, between states ranging from petty kingdoms to giant empires. The original objectives of all the European East India companies were first, to acquire part of this lucrative trade; next, to monopolize it if possible; then to expand it by adding other export commodities in demand; finally, to develop all imaginable means of raising revenue. Every Company had the blessing of its government, a blessing translated into military help when needed. Because it always was needed, the Companies were eventually absorbed into the imperial powers.

Thus the squeezing of wealth out of peasant cultivators, with concomitant deforestation to get more land tilled, neither began with the British nor, sadly, did it end with the British withdrawal. Nearly three millennia ago it was deforestation of the north which shifted power from the earliest civilizations of the Indus to the fertile Ganges plain. Nevertheless, it is reported that when Alexander the Great extended his campaign to the Punjab, reaching the river Indus (326 BC), he was able to hide his armies in dense forest. Most of the millennium before Christ was a period of continuous strife, during which some of the world's most important religions were born. Not until Asoka (273–236 BC) was the subcontinent brought under a single ruler. With his death the first Indian Empire broke up under the impact of invasions from the north. Five centuries later the Guptas again established empire over most of the subcontinent, only for it to collapse in its turn with the barbarian invasions of the fifth century. The nomad invaders, like their successors many centuries later, burned forests to create pasture. The political disaggregation after the barbarian invasion was longlasting, and not until Muslim expansion following on the Islamic revival did a unified India again appear. Northern India was under Muslim domination by 1500, but the Mughal Empire was only consolidated by Akbar, Babur's grandson, in the second half of the sixteenth century.

By then, the European maritime powers, after rounding the Cape, were pursuing the lucrative spice trade hitherto conducted partly overland and controlled by Venice. Portuguese, Dutch, French and British competed with no holds barred. French hopes in India were extinguished when they were defeated at the battle of Plassey (1757).

The rise of British rule

Britain proceeded to swallow the subcontinent by stages, making treaties where appropriate, fighting wars when necessary, annexing outright when other measures proved insufficient. The spice trade was small beer compared with the revenues entering the pockets of local rulers. Means had to be devised of acquiring some of these revenues and expanding them.

Mughal India, weakened by its internal contradictions, disintegrated under the impact of the policies pursued by the East India Company, its death signalled by Clive's victory in 1751. But by this time India was far from being a uniform mass of subsistence cultivators, organized in simple village communities. The tributary system in force varied from region to region, with differing social structures corresponding to the several ways in which wealth was extracted. Responsibility for collection of land revenues lay with village headmen, with large landlords (zemindars), or with appointed government officials. Under the Mughals land ownership rested on an unstable and tenuous foundation. At the bottom of the pile, the peasant producer had the right and the duty to cultivate the land. Failure to till it meant loss of occupancy right. Ultimate title might rest with the sovereign, and land transfers were prohibited or required approval. But both zemindars and government-appointed revenue collectors were frequently greedy and corrupt.

Already by the time of Akbar a cash-based system of revenue collection was in force. This tributary system meant that in many areas there was already substantial regional and interregional trade, including exports, long before the Europeans had any pronounced impact. Thus it is reported that Patna, in 1660, had no fewer than 600 brokers engaged in the insurance of cargoes and goods in transit. Indeed, the population of Agra at the beginning of the seventeenth century was half a million, bigger than either London or Paris.

In the Bombay hinterland, for example, small cultivators were growing cotton, wheat, indigo, opium, oil seeds and tobacco for cash sale. Before the British arrived, they paid the government a fixed share (a third to a half) of the harvest, in cash or kind. The tax was collected by village headmen, the bottom stratum in the rural power structure. The villages, settled communities of cultivators, were separated from each other by large areas of jungle, waste and forest. To the British, all this was deplorable waste – waste in a literal sense, because it did not produce revenue. The most important task, therefore, was to put it under the plough, preferably for cash-yielding export crops. This was encouraged by offering legal title to anyone who would clear and plant 'waste'. No matter that peasant cultivators relied on recourse to the forest and waste, for grazing their animals, for fuel and building materials, even for supplementary food in hard years. No matter that much of the forest was the home of shifting cultivators, whose mode of existence was threatened as their living space was restricted. No matter that many tribal peoples lived by collecting and selling, in the villages and towns, a vast range of minor forest products. No matter that some upland deforestation accelerated erosion and flooding.

The quotation which heads this chapter manifests an awareness of the delicate agriculture–forest interdependence. But that, of course, came after a forest department had been set up. And the setting up came only with renewed fears about the availability of good timber. The first anxieties, in the first decade of the nineteenth century, had been for timber for the British Navy as well as for export. Thus it was that India's first Conservator of Forests was not a forester, but a Captain Watson of the police, appointed in 1806 to supervise a monopoly of timber in Malabar and Travancore and the consequent extinction of all private rights. Opposition from private traders led to the abolition of this post in 1823, with a consequent free-for-all. Nevertheless, similar appointments to the same end were made in Bombay in 1847 and Madras in 1850. Again, the concern was with earmarking the best timber for the Company or the British Crown, not with managing the forests. Warnings about the adverse ecological impact of deforestation – by observant Company officers in the first half of the century, by professional foresters later – fell on deaf ears. Always, before and after the Crown superseded the Company, it was the Revenue Officers who counted.

It was the depletion of the teak forests along the Malabar coast that first turned British attention to Burma. Burmese teak and ironwood were known and traded all over Asia. These timbers were traditionally the exclusive property of Burmese kings, and forest areas were farmed out to merchants and traders. In 1824, after border friction, the British extorted a treaty which, while leaving Pegu Burmese, annexed Arakan to the north and Tenasserim to the south, as well as establishing a protectorate over Assam. Two years later the director of the Calcutta botanic gardens was sent to assess the forests. However, these continued to be ravaged by European contractors and their Burmese agents. In 1852 the Irrawaddy delta was annexed to the Indian Empire. Quarrels between Burman officials and agents of the Bombay–Burma Timber Company led to the final Anglo-Burman war, bringing about British annexation of the rest of Burma. A turn came with the Dalhousie Memorandum in 1855. The Governor General of India thereby declared all teak and similar timbers to be the property of the Government of India and made cutting without government authorization a criminal offence. The German Dietrich Brandeis was charged with setting up a forest department in Burma. This department, from 1860, had the task of leasing forest areas to private contractors, demarcating permanent forest reserves, and curbing shifting cultivation in the forest. These activities concerned only the valuable timber-bearing dry deciduous forests of Upper Burma. There was no attempt to conserve the fascinating heterogeneous evergreen forest of the Irrawaddy Delta. The rich delta lands were cleared, settled and transformed, in the course of the second half of the nineteenth century, and especially after the opening of the Suez canal, into the world's greatest rice exporting area. Thus, though scientific forestry came to Burma before it reached India, its concern was only with the few species deemed marketable.

In 1853 Parliament in London wrangled over the renewal of the East India Company charter. The debates included some first misgivings about the 'unacceptable face' of imperialism. Even so, no-one – not even the percipient political journalist writing on Indian events for a New York paper, Karl Marx – foresaw the unthinkable: the mutiny of the Sepoys in 1857.

The Indian mutiny, which shocked every Briton, came just after British rule seemed to be becoming a shade more enlightened: there was less emphasis on immediate loot, more looking forward towards a peaceful permanent revenue-yielding possession. The annexation of Sind in 1843 and the conquest of Punjab in 1849 had completed the expansion of British power (and closed the north-west gate to the Russians). A peculiar amalgam of agrarian unrest and nascent nationalism had given rise to the mutiny. The sepoys had close ties with the peasants and with petty landowning classes. Discontent was widespread, if not exactly national; it affected mainly the upper Ganges valley, homeland of the Bengal army. It was the first time that a native army, trained and led by Europeans, had risen against its masters. The mutiny may have been unforeseen, but it had to be countered. First, of course, exemplary punishment for all concerned. Next came the abolition of the Company and the creation of a single, reliable army, ensuring that all artillery and arsenals stayed in British hands. But it also meant drawing local rulers into closer alliance, spreading the communications network so that troops might be moved speedily where needed, and bonding a British-Indian administration.

Though not all of India was affected by the mutiny, there were few areas where British rule had not created some disquiet, even unrest. Already some of this had its roots in deforestation and its consequences, in the clearance and settlement of jungle and waste and the theft of the 'poor man's overcoat'. But it was the railway age which was to start the most significant havoc in the Indian forests, and which made the establishment of a forest department obligatory. Timber was needed for spreading the railways that would bring more potential revenue-producing land within reach of markets. This railway expansion would also facilitate troop movements, thereby avoiding a repetition of the 'unthinkable'. These were the needs that brought an Indian forest department into being. Although the British can take some credit for creating an Indian forest service, it was under the British Raj that the most catastrophic ecological degradation, the deforestation of the western and central Himalayas, started and gathered pace. Its bitter consequences for the river systems are today experienced annually as far downstream as Bangladesh.

Even such a major critic of the Raj as Marx exaggerated the 'progressive' aspect of British conquest. As Kiernan (1974) has pointed out, the picture Marx carried in his mind of India, based as it was on officers reporting from areas which were quite unrepresentative, led him to the notion that the advent of capitalism would set in motion the forces that would propel a slumbering, changeless Asia into the modern age. But the subcontinent was far more heterogeneous and complex than Marx supposed. Not only had much happened before the British got there; British objectives had to be pursued in an immense variety of socio-political (as well as ecological) contexts.

The creation of an Indian forest service

In 1864 the government brought Brandeis from Burma and appointed him

Inspector General of Forests, thus founding the Indian Forest Department. Its upper levels were staffed by Britons who had received a three-year training at the Royal Indian Engineering College at Cooper's Hill. Indian subordinate officers were trained at the Indian Forestry School established in 1878 at Dehra Dun. Forest guards and other staff were recruited locally. A Forest Act of 1878 (replacing an inadequate Act of 1865) gave the Forest Department control and management of reserved forests. They were charged with harvesting systematically; putting an end to shifting cultivation; and limiting or halting grazing and the taking of wood and other products. Guards had police powers and could levy fines and impound cattle.

From its inception, and still today, that Department has had problems with the formulation in the Dalhousie Memorandum: 'The sole object with which State Forests are administered is the public benefit . . . the rights and privileges of individuals must be limited otherwise than for their own benefit, only in such degree as is absolutely necessary to secure that advantage.' Dalhousie probably had little idea what eventually would be involved in defining and securing that advantage, the public benefit.

By 1890 a *Times of India* editorial could report that 60 000 square miles of forest reserves had been created, that every province now had a permanent forest administration, and that the Department, with a gross revenue of 13.5 million rupees, provided a net annual surplus of 5.5 million rupees. Forest offences, however, remained at a high level. For example, in 1885–6 a total of 23 000 were reported, of which over 6000 went to court; the remainder were compounded by forest officers by the levy of fines or fees. Of the cases which went to court, 72 per cent resulted in convictions. In Punjab alone, 40 000 cattle were impounded for forest trespass; evidently pound fees were not a sufficient deterrent. Five provinces accounted for all but a thousand of the cases, and the report complacently observed: 'the numbers in the other Provinces being comparatively small, showing that the relations between the Department and the people are excellent'.

'G. K. B.', whose words head this chapter, went on:

But now the pressure is far greater. Agriculture is turning impatient, grasping and ungrateful, forgetful of past benefits: 'Make room for fields, your appointed task is done, we can do without you, you are obsolete,' is the cry with regard to the forests. But Nature's laws are immutable, and where forests are removed without just and due reason, drought, pestilence, famine and flood appear, and call attention to the fact.

G. K. B.'s words were written in 1889. Time was to show that they were to apply with equal force almost a century later. Foresters, both British officers and their Indian subordinates, lost no opportunity of expressing their concern. In 1880 the *Indian Forester* commented favourably on a checkerboard plan advanced by Colonel Corbett: that for every 6 square miles put under the plough, 1 square mile of forest should be reserved as protection, and to supply fuel and small timber needs. The checkerboard plan never got anywhere.

G. K. B. failed to mention, and perhaps did not recognize, another and different kind of disaster which was being prepared by the large-scale irrigation schemes undertaken to extend cultivation in the Indus valley. Deforestation and large irrigation canals during the second half of the nineteenth century brought about widespread salinization of the soils in north-west India.

Yet for all their concern, both with the devastating environmental effects of deforestation and with the plight of rural people, there was little the Forest Department could do. The tasks thrust upon them, justified by Dalhousie's original words, brought them increasingly into conflict with the peasants, who from time to time resisted fiercely. But the worst was yet to come.

Deforestation in the Himalayas

The opening up of India (by 1890, 16 000 miles of railway had been built; by 1920, 57 000) needed wood for sleepers (ties), fuel and public buildings. Deforestation climbed steadily up the Himalayan foothills. Sal, an acceptable and durable timber in the Terai, was speedily overcut (although after 1900 sal plantations established by the Forest Department began to bear). Further up, deodar, ideal but slow growing, fell under the axe. At still greater elevations, softwoods such as blue pine, spruce and silver fir remained intact until the building of high mountain roads after independence in 1947.

The attempts of Brandeis and his successors to control logging in the Himalayas met with scant success. The pressures on the Forest Department to satisfy mounting and changing timber demands were just too great. Wartime military demands produced new pressures from 1914. Relations between the Department and hill dwellers became ever more strained. Throughout the interwar period forest use was a highly political issue.

Some writers have argued that 'forest *satragraya*', non-cooperation and non-violent resistance on the part of hill dwellers, emanated from Indian Congress political strategy as influenced by Gandhi. But Ramachandra (1985), who has traced peasant resistance in the Kumaon since the turn of the century, has made it clear that this interpretation seriously underestimates peasant autonomy. It echoes, in an odd fashion, historians and politicians who ascribe peasant protest not to worsening conditions but to the inflammatory intervention of outside agitators. Peasant resistance in the Kumaon has a long history. This is of particular interest since that area is now the centre of the Chipko movement, which involves 'tree-hugging', to prevent contractors felling the trees that protect the soils the locals work and that provide products they depend on – a movement which has captured the imagination of conservationists world-wide. Chipko in the Kumaon is but the latest in a long series of protests since commercial forestry, and state intervention, reached the region.

When the warlike Gurkhas from Nepal conquered the isolated hill tracts, their incursions endangered British authority. The treaty of 1815, which ended the Anglo-Gurkhan wars, annexed Kumaon and Garhwal to the Company. Thereafter both the Company and the British army relied heavily on the sturdy, courageous Gurkhas, for whom army life meant escape from a precarious poverty.

The central Himalayas are composed of two distinct ecological zones: monsoon-affected low and middle altitudes, and high, steep valleys to the north. Here there were no sharp inequalities in land ownership, but rather scattered, solid village communities, with well over half the hill land occupied by owner-cultivators – a very different land tenure system from that which the British had encountered on the plains. The villagers had fertile fields in the valleys, good forest and grazing on the hills. The oak forests were valued for fodder and fertilizer and the pine forests periodically burned for fresh grass. The villagers had enjoyed joint rights for fuel and grazing in the commonly held forest and waste from time out of mind. British admiration for the Gurkhas' fighting qualities meant that soldiers were generously settled on retirement and land revenue taxes were light.

Though the demand for timber rose steadily through the nineteenth century, and brought heavy depletion of the sal forests to the south, Kumaon remained unaffected up to the last quarter of the century. The 1878 Forest Act permitted the designation of 'protected' and 'reserved' forests, placing the burden of proving 'legally established rights' on illiterate peasants, incapable of understanding how a distant State could establish proprietorship of communally owned and managed woods and pasture lands. By now, the chir pine forests were becoming important to the British: means had been discovered of chemically treating this wood for sleepers (by 1880 the railway system needed a million sleepers annually); and tapping for resin was becoming a highly profitable industry.

The peasants had another grievance. British administrators operated forced labour systems, known as *utar* and *begar*, taken over from former petty hill chiefs. In difficult country, with neither hotels, guest houses nor transport systems, all officials and white travellers required considerable labour levies. For most of the century this burden had been relatively light, but it rose sharply in the last quarter, with the establishment of the Forest Department, and provoked outbursts, especially when villagers were called away from seasonal agricultural tasks. By 1893 the Deputy Commissioner for Garwhal reported that 'Forest administration consists for the most part in a running fight with the villagers.' That was the year in which all waste land was declared protected forest, while even in those forests to which access was still permitted, eight tree species were reserved for the Department.

Rural protest took many forms, but was almost always non-violent. Some peasants moved away; officials were provided with misleading information; malicious fires were set. By 1916 there were reports of deliberate and organized incendiarism. But it was the pine forests which were set alight; the broadleaved forests – of far more use to peasants – were left intact. Indeed, those few forests which were left in communal ownership continued to be well managed and maintained. Forest *satyagraha* and the anti-*begar* movement received an impetus from returning soldiers. Women joined in too. In 1921 the Conservator of Forests was refused coolies.

Independence and beyond

The Indian Forest Act of 1878 still effectively controlled the fate of India's forests. When the British Parliament passed the Government of India Act in 1935, it set up provincial legislatures, and devolved responsibility for forest matters to the provinces. Thereafter, up to and after Independence and right up to 1976, forestry remained on the State list. State forest services found it much harder than had a centralized forest service to resist pressures from local politicians: these included pressures to surrender lands for conversion to agriculture, and to grant cutting rights for timber to feed new industries. There was little semblance of a truly national forest policy and the Inspectorate General in Delhi became little more than a post office. Promotion remained strictly by seniority, damping down any innovation. The palatial Forest Research Institute at Dehra Dun continued to publish papers, but few of them were relevant to India's real needs, and those few were scarcely read. The School continued to turn out the most highly trained professional foresters in the Third World – trained, however, for tasks of the past rather than of the ever-changing present. They knew how to manage the reserved slow-growing sal–teak forests; they were quick to learn how to establish fast-growing plantations of industrial wood; but they had little understanding of the small farmer's dependence on the forest and waste, and they had few ideas of how to encourage hill dwellers to manage community forests.

Meanwhile, the Green Revolution came to India; between 1951 and 1973 3.4 million ha of forest went under the plough or were destroyed for river valley projects to provide irrigation for agriculture. This had a double impact. The deforestation had both serious ecological effects (such as floods and soil erosion) and social effects (undermining the life support

Figure 17.1 Cowpats drying on a wall prior to their eventual sale as fuel

of millions more rural dwellers wholly or partly dependent on the forests). And the polarization of the rural social structure consequent on the Green Revolution (which mainly benefited the better-educated and larger land-holders, able to utilize credit, fertilizers, selected seed, and so on) added to the numbers of rural landless. In fact, deforestation was now proceeding faster than under the British, with even greater ecological damage and social misery. Some estimates suggest that forest cover in the three decades after Independence shrank from 40 to 20 per cent, and even of that 20 per cent nearly half was sadly depleted. However, firm and comparable figures are hard to come by.

Finally, in 1976, recognizing that the national forestry situation was rapidly deteriorating, India's National Commission on Agriculture (NCA) recommended the adoption of a revised national forest policy based on the most important national needs. All forest lands were to be classified as either protection forests, production forests, or social forests. The policy laid great emphasis on fast growing artificial forests to feed industry. 'Each hectare of forest land should be managed to yield a net income many times more than at present.' Meanwhile social forests were to be established on waste lands, village commons, and beside railways, roads and canals. Forest plantations, shelter belts, and mixed farm-forestry were to be encouraged. Social forestry, in the NCA context, was not forestry to serve urgent social needs (though these were recognized in several passages of the report) but rather forestry practised on land not belonging to the Forest Department.

By this time, the world's development establishment had decided to espouse 'social forestry'. State after State in India found itself offered substantial financial support from the World Bank or other agencies, and a wide variety of projects purporting to benefit the rural poor and carrying the 'social forestry' label were begun. Indeed, the biggest World Bank investment in social forestry to date is in the state of Karnataka. However, as will be seen from chapter 26, only very few of these projects have succeeded in bringing relief to the categories of people in most need of help.

Fortunately, a new and more socially conscious generation of Indian foresters is now finding its voice. It is extremely critical of some of the policies presently being pursued and of many of the projects being sponsored. It understands that there is no hope whatever of finding continuing employment in afforestation, forest management and timber harvesting for the 40 million *adhivasis* (tribal hill dwellers, displaced shifting cultivators, small farmers dependent on the forests, collectors and sellers of minor forest products). It realizes that even if funds can be found to re-establish the immense tracts of forest cover required to repair some of the ecological devastation, those forests will not long survive if the hungry landless have nowhere else to go.

Nevertheless, India today is in one sense a crucible, a test case, of forestry's ability to make trees serve people. It is also a display centre for social forestry projects – some good, some bad, a few utterly disastrous. Most have disregarded the socio-economic context within which the projects have to be executed. Moreover, there is still over a century of enmity between Forest Department officials and the rural poor to be overcome. It may well be that the reafforestation, both protective and agriculture-supportive, which alone can ensure that India's future generations will be fed can only come about by abolishing or completely restructuring the existing Forest Departments. The heart of the problem has been succinctly expressed by Sharad Kulkarni (1983):

The forest can never be protected by forest guards or police. They will be protected only when the need for their preservation coincides with the interests of the rural poor.

18 China

Because the most important function of forests, woodlands and trees in the world today is to contribute to raising the welfare and improving the quality of life of millions of rural poor, it is of particular interest to see how far success has been achieved in China, the country which accounts for about a third of the world peasant population. No country in the world has ever encountered a need for afforestation as great as that which confronted China when the People's Republic was established in 1949. China's efforts since then to 'make green the motherland' eclipse by far the afforestation efforts of any other country in any time. The magnitude of the forestry problem which the new government faced stemmed not only from the sheer size of the country, with its extremes of climate. It was determined by the changes wrought in the landscape by continuous human occupation and cultivation over a longer period than anywhere else in the world.

Only 5 per cent of China's land area remained under forest, and this was mainly in the south-west, much of which was inaccessible, and in the inhospitable north-east. The most important consequence of deforestation was that many of China's soils had been eroded by wind and water. Down the centuries, the principal rivers, silted by eroded soil, and dyked again and again, flowed well above the surrounding cultivated countryside. Scarcely a year passed without breached dykes, disastrous floods, lost crops, immense loss of life. Over most of China, too, there was a chronic shortage of both industrial timber and fuelwood. The ruthless exploitation of the timber resources of the north-east, started by Japanese concessionaires early in the twentieth century, accelerated during the Japanese occupation from 1931 on.

So the forestry problems which confronted the Chinese people and their government when the People's Liberation Army conquered the mainland in 1949 could hardly have been more serious. The Chinese Communist Party had shown itself aware of these problems, and had in fact encouraged afforestation efforts well before 1949 in the 'liberated areas'. Tree-planting was an integral part of the Programme of Ten Small Points mounted in the Border Region in 1944.

The communist armies triumphed because they had the support of the peasants. The conditions which the rural population had endured for centuries were so wretched that the Red Armies and their policies of land redistribution were greeted with open arms. Step by step, peasants were urged to establish mutual aid teams, then cooperatives, leading finally to the setting up of communes. Party activists mobilized the rural population to raise the production of staple grains and to carry out the related giant tasks of 'making green the Motherland' and taming China's rivers.

The achievements have been immense – miraculous, in the eyes of some foreign observers. But the cost has been immense too; indeed, often unnecessarily high. It has been borne by hundreds of millions of hard working peasants, supported by the labour, voluntary or involuntary, of townspeople and 'intellectuals'. Much of that labour was enthusiastically volunteered; but much of it resulted from irresistible social pressure.

The wastage of the early years sprang from lack of professional expertise and experience. China had few trained foresters, and many of these fled the country in 1949. Most forestry experience had been built up in the forested areas of China; little was known about the afforestation of more difficult sites. Hence species were selected that were ill adapted to sites. Much of the seed used was of poor provenance. All the emphasis was on the number of trees planted; subsequent tending was almost universally neglected. The upshot was that survival rates were inevitably low. Richardson (1966), while acknowledging the scale of the effort, catalogued innumerable errors and shortcomings.

In interpreting what is happening in China, it is unwise to rely only on what the Chinese say about themselves. The tangle of ideological differences and factional rivalries which, time and again since 1949, have led to yesterday's heroes becoming today's villains and tomorrow's rehabilitees, continues to obscure official utterances and statistics. However, forestry is in some ways easier to assess than other economic sectors. Trees can neither hide nor be put in place overnight. Thus any experienced and observant forester who has the opportunity of travelling widely, by plane, rail and road, can arrive at an informed judgement. Thus a more informative picture of the people – tree relationship in China in the decades since 1949 emerges from piecing together the observations of the many individuals and delegations of professional foresters who have by now visited and travelled widely in China, than from the fluctuating and contradictory statements of the Chinese themselves.

Mao's Great Leap Forward (1958–60) nearly put some of the communes on their back, and it took time to recover. Some of the ideas had been positive in principle, for example the setting up of small industries at commune level to make use of locally available materials and mop up under-employed rural labour. But for the most part it led to unrealistic targets, confused objectives, technical inefficiency, and a serious setback in production. One example was the encouragement of local communes to establish small pulp and paper plants, based on whatever pulpable materials were at hand: rags, waste paper, agricultural residues and the like. Within a year or two most of these had been abandoned, the problem of controlling polluting effluent proving insoluble on that scale. The afforestation target set at this time – 20 per cent forest cover by 1968 – proved nonsense: indeed, it is not yet in sight.

By the early 1960s, the folly of some of the earlier megalomaniac afforestation claims was recognized, and a critical re-examination in professional and party journals brought about greatly improved practice. Afforestation continued, and suffered relatively little interruption during the upheavals of the Cultural Revolution after 1965. The peasants were still with the party, though communes, like factories, were now led and managed by 'revolutionary committees'. They may have been bemused by some aspects of the Cultural Revolution (why it was more important to be red than expert), as they were puzzled by the exhortations to anathematize Liu Shaoqui and Deng Xiaoping, then Lin Biao and Beethoven, and later on the Gang of Four. But trees continued to be planted, with special emphasis on protection forestry and on creating locally available wood supplies, for both fuel and building purposes, in the agricultural communes, while amenity planting in the towns was encouraged. I myself, after a month's tour in 1974, concluded that 'China has succeeded in something which very few other countries have achieved, in establishing a truly effective and fruitful integration between agriculture and forestry.' China's afforestation successes were subsequently endorsed by many official delegations and scientific exchange visits. So much so that the 'Chinese model' was eventually deemed sufficiently important for it to be demonstrated, and China became a place of pilgrimage, hosting seminars and study tours for Third World officials, professionals and students.

How had the peasants' commitment to forestry been won originally? They trusted a government which had redistributed land, helped them set up schools, trained their bare-foot doctors. The 'round the house' tree planting programme they were asked to undertake comprised quick-growing species, with a harvest date in sight; the trees thus represented tangible accruing personal income just as much as the pigs they were raising in their back yard for eventual sale to the State purchasing office. Furthermore, forestry encompassed not only timber and fuel trees but also orchard trees and economic crops: tea oil, tung oil, nut and fruit trees, bamboo groves – each had its place where soil and climate were appropriate. Nor were peasants blind to the benefits of protection forestry. The increased yield behind shelter belts was measurable: they could see new land under crops after dune fixation, and could recognize the lower incidence of flood and erosion after protective afforestation.

The four modernizations

The Cultural Revolution lingered on through a bewildering variety of political changes, and was only finally declared at an end in August 1977. The Gang of Four was arrested after Mao's death in 1976, and Deng Xiaoping reassumed power in 1978–9. He was now free to set the 'four modernizations' in motion. Systems of contract responsibility by peasant families were established, allowing them to sell or use their produce as they wished, after specified sales to the state. Agricultural prices were raised. Economic criteria for management decisions were emphasized, China joined the World Bank and the International Monetary Fund, and the Special Economic Zones were set up. In other words in order to build 'the primary phase of socialism' some elements more associated with capitalism, and notably market forces, were henceforth to be invoked.

The results were spectacular, not all of them foreseen. Peasants' response to the responsibility system coupled with higher prices was intensified effort, a sharp increase in output, with supplementary crops like fruit and vegetables flowing into the free markets which sprang up. Individuals who had sufficient land mobilized all the labour they could to step up yields. Those rural areas with adequate soils and climate and sufficient market outlets prospered. Within a few years peasants in such areas were enjoying a life style well above that of their urban compatriots. But meanwhile the commune system collapsed and enthusiasm for cooperative effort to maintain and expand social capital inevitably waned; among other things, rural afforestation declined in both quantity and quality.

Quite early on in the 'four modernizations' there was awareness that all was not well on the forestry front. The Minister of Forests, speaking in October 1981, on 'The Situation in Forestry and Our Tasks', spelled out four major points:

1   Future forestry work to concentrate on afforestation and forest protection. Hitherto undue concentration on timber production had resulted in severe ecological disasters.
2   Have regard, both economically and ecologically, to the multiple functions and multiple benefits of the forest.
3   The influence of mistaken 'left' ideology in the past had dampened the enthusiasm of the peasants; hence low survival rates in afforestation. It was now necessary to emancipate the minds of the peasants and bring out their initiative.
4   Backwardness in forest science and technology must be overcome. The technical level must be raised, scientific management applied, forestry education popularized.

As Deng's reforms gathered force, the ability or willingness to heed the Minister's four points receded. As the economy grew in the 1980s the rising needs for industrial timber were not being met. Between 1980 and 1985 timber imports into China rose to 10 million m³. This was in spite of heavy exploitation of the north-east forests. Harbin radio, at the end of October 1982, reported the findings of a symposium of eighty scientists and technicians held in Yichun, Heilungkiang. In the key forests of the Greater and Lesser Kinghan mountains, where annual net growth was estimated at 16.7 million m³, fellings had reached 25 million m³. Even more serious than this continued overcutting in China's best (though slow-growing) forest resource, was the fact that the effective timber utilization rate was no more than 23 per cent.

How had this come about? Richardson, revisiting Dailing in 1986 after an interval of over twenty years, was shocked by the changes he saw. What had once been a model of close utilization, albeit with primitive machinery, transport and organization, had now become an aggregation of technologically advanced forest extraction and wood processing units, in no way integrated, and badly and wastefully managed. In the meantime, the virgin forest had receded; it now took two days by road to reach the margin of the coniferous forests. The Research Institute had been turned into a hotel, and an exhibition hall of forest culture was being prepared for tourists. 'Soviet and North American models of forest industry development which the Chinese have adopted,' he observed, 'may be sensible in countries with vast forest resources . . . but they are sadly inappropriate in wood-starved China.' Clearly, the four modernizations had gone badly astray.

The reason why the points made by the Minister in 1981 and the concern expressed by the scientists in 1982 have gone unheeded is obvious; the need for operations to demonstrate economic profitability has over-ridden ecological considerations. It may be that the intention is to speedily clear the remaining primary forest, because of its slow growth, and replace it by plantations. But the planting rate in the north-east falls far, far short of replacement needs.

The environmental consequences of the current direction of China's development path are also likely to be serious. Nearly twenty years ago Norman Myers, for long consultant to the United Nations Environmental Programme (UNEP), wrote with admiration of China's efforts to make use of all available materials, recycling, eliminating waste. That positive judgement was based on the fact that China then was a 'thrift' economy, rather than a fully environmentally conscious country. But there was even then plenty of evidence of serious atmospheric pollution in the industrial centres, and China's rivers, though flowing more evenly, thanks to afforestation and water conservancy works, were far from clean.

Those who have read of and applauded China's efforts, in collaboration with the International Union for the Conservation of Nature and the Worldwide Fund for Nature, to save the disappearing giant panda may be alarmed by one manifestation of the new reforms. In the quest for foreign exchange a company has been set up in the forested north-east to exploit the local game potential. Tourists are invited to a new luxury camp and permitted to hunt both protected and unprotected species, each trophy priced according to the quarry's rarity.

The reforms may have some positive aspects. Bare mountain land is now made available to individual households, for tree planting and management, on long-term (thirty- to fifty-year) renewable, heritable leases. This may do something to revive rural afforestation. But most of

China's achievements in creating social capital sprang – indeed, could only have sprung – from collective effort based on an awareness of the degree to which family benefit is indissolubly linked with collective benefit. Individual effort will not maintain and extend water conservancy work, nor will it complete the Great Green Wall. One-tenth of China's land surface, roughly 100 million ha in the north and northwest, is desert. It has been estimated that 13 million ha of this could be reclaimed and turned into farmland. It is hard to imagine that this can be accomplished without a revival of the collective enthusiasm and social pressures that went into creating the social capital which China has acquired since 1949.

Though dismayed by much of what he saw, Richardson (1986) nevertheless still felt able to endorse my own view in 1974: 'The most striking features are still the integration of forestry with agriculture and urban land use.' The changes presently underway, he believes, are irreversible. But China may yet surprise him, as it has surprised so many experts over the last half-century. Ever since the 1930s, Western business men have had their eyes on the huge potential market represented by China ('Oil for the lamps of China'). The recent opening up has rekindled their hopes. But the Chinese, even the sexagenarians who have replaced some of the octogenarians at the political power centre, are pragmatists above all. In their quest for Western technology, they are unlikely to let the Chinese economy run riot.

19   Cuba

Before the European assault described in chapter 12 almost the whole of Central America and the Caribbean countries were as green, well-wooded and fertile as a few parts of that area remain today. The few Amerindians who occupied the Caribbean islands when Europeans first set foot in the New World were hunter–gatherers whose impact on the forest cover was negligible. They were speedily exterminated as island after island fell to Europe's civilizing mission. Since those first forest clearances, afforestation has proceeded at different rates in the various countries. There are some countries where disaster situations have already arisen. Prospects are perhaps most grim for the peoples of Haiti, El Salvador, and the Dominican Republic. In these three countries forest cover related to total land area has fallen to 2, 7 and 14 per cent respectively. In all three the concentration of land, wealth and power in the hands of a few, with a growing army of rural landless, means that the few remaining forests are under continuing pressure. Most piteous is the situation in Haiti, where the disappearance of the forests has carried most of the soil on the hills to the sea. Of all the countries in the Caribbean area, Cuba has made the greatest effort to check and reverse the march of deforestation.

It has been observed that, historically, clearance for sugar plantations has perhaps been the greatest single factor in tropical deforestation. It was sugar which swept away the Caribbean forests in turn: Barbados, the Leeward Islands, Jamaica and Haiti. Sugar reached Cuba relatively late. It was the slave rebellion in Haiti after 1791, mentioned in chapter 12, which left that country in ruins and sparked the sugar boom in Cuba.

When Cristobal Colon, the Genovese navigator, reached the north-east coast of Cuba in 1492 he was very impressed by the island's rich forests. A few years later, the priest Fray Bartolome wrote that it was possible to walk from one end of the island to the other without leaving the shade of trees. Towards the end of the next century, Havana had become the leading shipbuilding centre in the Antilles, its output having included 128 warships for the Spanish navy. Though Spain had long dominated the seas, Spain itself, as we saw in Part II, was running out of forest. After the deforestation provoked by the Romans, further forest destruction took place during the struggles against the Moors, and the wood demand for the enormous navy required to conquer and maintain the Spanish empire heavily taxed the remaining forests. (In the sixteenth century the ships of the Spanish Armada amounted to some 300,000 registered tons, and for each ton about 20 m^3 of high quality timber was needed. Wooden ships lasted no more than 15 to 20 years.) Thus already, by 1500, Spain needed to import timber. That is why Havana became an important shipbuilding centre.

Nevertheless, Cuba's forests recovered from these incursions, and at the beginning of the nineteenth century still covered 9.9 million ha, about 90 per cent of the land area. But the sugar boom was beginning and sugar-cane began to eat the forests. Fire and the axe were also used to clear forests for ranching, so that by the end of the century forest cover had shrunk to 5.5 million ha. With the declaration of the Republic in 1902, and the subsequent heavy penetration of the Cuban economy by US capital, the forests continued to shrink. Smallholders' lands were swallowed up by the latifundia and they were driven to eke out a living in the hills. Their struggle for survival there, along with the insatiable demand of the sugar mills for fuel, took heavy toll of the upland forests. Thus by 1946, forest cover was down to 1.3 million ha (or 11 per cent of the land area): a loss of nearly 5 million ha in less than half a century. Such forests as then remained were of mediocre quality, since the progressive removal of the best trees down the centuries was in effect a process of anti-selection. Not until the overthrow of Batista in 1959 was there any serious attempt to protect or manage the forests or to replant. Many upland areas were seriously eroded. The fertility of some of the soils which had long carried sugar was declining.

In 1959, when Fidel Castro's movement overthrew the Batista regime, the Cuban economy was almost entirely dependent on sugar and tourism, the latter based largely on gambling, drugs and prostitution and centred on Havana. The loss of tourism, and the US blockade, meant even heavier dependence on sugar, with the main export market for that sugar cut off. The inevitable consequence was an even more radical shift in domestic policies and increasing dependence on the socialist countries. While land reform and the rapid expansion of health and education facilities ensured popular support, many intellectuals and professionals who earlier on had welcomed the overthrow of the Batista regime now left Cuba.

The task facing the revolutionary government, of restoring forest cover in Cuba to the level needed to protect the watersheds and provide domestic wood resources, was far from easy, given the depleted state of the forests, the degree of erosion, and the considerable areas where the soil had already lost much of its fertility. It was hampered by the paucity of trained staff and the lack of relevant research.

However, the new government, unlike all its predecessors, recognized the significance for agriculture of adequate forest cover; but it was also obliged by the US blockade to lean more heavily on indigenous resources for meeting its timber needs. It embarked on an ambitious forestry programme, initiated the training of staff at both professional and technical level, and established forest research with a network of experimental stations in the field. Its planting programme was expanded by harnessing voluntary labour. However, as in China, much of the early effort was wasted as the result of elementary errors: seed of poor provenance, species ill-adapted to sites, over-emphasis on the number of trees planted and neglect of subsequent tending.

Moreover in the years immediately after 1959 there was no proper understanding of either the limited capacity of Cuba's remaining forests, or of the way in which wood requirements would grow as the Cuban economy changed direction. In the early 1960s forest production (150 000 m^3), while meeting only half of wood needs, still involved overcutting. This prompted an increasing emphasis on achieving economies in the ways in which wood was used, a decision to reduce the annual cut to 45 000 m^3 (corresponding to about a quarter of planned needs), and an expanded planting programme.

At the time of writing most of the upland areas in dire need of protective planting have been covered, though the forest resource is still far from being adequate to meet future wood needs. By the early 1980s the forest area had been stepped up to over 3 million ha, or 26 per cent of the land area. This means that in the three decades which have elapsed since the Castro government took power, the annual net addition to the forest area has averaged about 10 000 ha. At the same time, a number of representative areas of native forest have been set aside as national parks. The lessons, positive and negative, which Cuba has learned in recent decades may prove valuable in due course for those countries in Central

America and the Caribbean which today find their hills deforested and their soils exhausted, in much worse plight than was Cuba in 1959.

20   Indonesia

Chapter 12 described how the several European powers reached out across the oceans to exact colonial tribute in various forms. Holland, at the height of its power, dominated the seas and had the most far-flung imperial connections. Even after it had been dislodged from many of its trading posts, it hung on to its most important possession, the Dutch East Indies, until after World War II.

Indonesia, which still contains the greatest area of tropical forest outside the Amazon, is of great interest because it exhibits the way in which different forms of exploitation have brought about deforestation in different ways through history. It consists of about 3000 islands, spread across 5000 km of ocean from west to east. All were once heavily forested, and some still are – including the most recent acquisitions, West Papua and East Timor, where the Indonesian government is currently trying to impose its sovereignty by military occupation and army-assisted migration. The islands have been peopled by successive migrations of Malay stock from the Asian mainland. Each new wave pressed on earlier arrivals and drove them inland, the main migrations taking place 3000 years ago and earlier.

However, the islands were by no means similar. Java and Bali, with heavy rainfall and rich volcanic soils, made possible the development of complex irrigation systems on terraced hillsides, allowing two crops per year in many areas. This wet rice cultivation was very different from the shifting cultivation practised in Sumatra, Borneo and the Eastern Islands, which were heavily wooded but with less fertile soils, and hence sparsely populated.

Thus, from the beginning, Java dominated. An intensive agriculture developed which required cooperation between villages to ensure that irrigation systems were maintained. Hierarchical societies evolved, with kings, courts, priests, warriors and bureaucracies, sustained by the agricultural surplus extracted from the peasants. Various principalities rose, warred against each other, and declined. Wealth at the top was sustained and expanded by exacting war tribute and by carving more tillable land from the forest. Muslim penetration, which occurred from the seventh century on, was based largely on sea power and trade, but the village, while embodying some peasant communal values, remained the firm base of the hierarchical structure of society. Java and Bali, rich and fertile, fed a considerable inter-Asian trade for centuries. It was this trade, and particularly that in spices, which attracted first the Portuguese (who established a string of forts in the sixteenth century) and, later in the seventeenth century, the rival British and Dutch East India Companies. The Dutch had greater success with their eastern than with their western empire. They occupied Batavia (now Jakarta) in 1619, and massacred the British at Amboyna in 1624. Steadily their imperial interests spread beyond a monopoly of the trade in spices to the installation of a plantation economy, beginning with sugar. As the eighteenth century wore on they became dissatisfied with the Chinese, who had come to play the part of trading go-betweens, and farmed land which the Dutch now wanted. So much so that, after progressively restricting Chinese legal rights in Java, a wholesale massacre of Chinese was carried out in 1740, in the course of which it is estimated that all but 3000 of the 80 000 or more Chinese in the Batavia area were killed. Thus the Dutch supplied the precedent for the politically motivated massacres in 1965 that established the power of General Suharto and the generals who came to rule Indonesia after him.

At first the Dutch, like the Portuguese and the British whom they had squeezed out, were primarily concerned with the profits to be made from a trading monopoly: collecting and exporting cloves, nutmeg, pepper, coffee and sugar for the European market. In the course of the eighteenth century the Dutch East India Company (soon to be taken over by the Dutch state) added to collection the principle of forced deliveries, thereby wresting from local rulers the right to tribute. After the Napoleonic Wars a more highly organized system of forced deliveries obliged an increase in the area under export crops and called forth an expanding population as had similar systems in the Americas. Throughout this period Java's labour was being more intensively exploited, more of its land was being brought under cultivation, and the population increased. But the Dutch government monopoly had brought about no technological change. From about 1870 on, however, the character of exploitation changed. With the penetration of private capital, exports multiplied and industrial raw materials – oil, tin, copra – were added to the traditional items and eventually eclipsed them in importance. Dutch government efforts to restrain the excesses of private capital were in vain. Although after the turn of the century the metropolitan power recognized some obligation to Indonesians, and made some efforts both to extend health and education facilities and to develop agricultural extension work, the distortion of the traditional village system continued: indentured labour returning to the villages found no place, and towns grew, along with overcrowded urban kampongs. Every step in this process brought extra pressure on such forest resources as remained in Java.

Export plantations extended to Northern Sumatra, but by and large the outer islands were left untouched. There were, however, limitations to the extent to which traditional agriculture could absorb more labour, especially as village patterns were changing, land distribution was becoming more skewed, and the numbers of landless were growing. At the same time, since the Dutch monopolized administrative and clerical posts, an unemployed intellectual younger generation arose to feed nationalist aspirations.

Thus when the nationalist leader Sukarno declared Indonesian independence on the collapse of Japanese rule in August 1945 he was cashing in on a very wide variety of often conflicting discontents. He adroitly controlled the warring factions, successfully linked the islands together, and gave them a common language and a sense of nationality. Dutch capital had lost its power, and Sukarno's government took a series of steps to win control of the decaying colonial economy. It eased the tax load on the rural population, but did not carry out large-scale land redistribution. Like many radical nationalist leaders in the Third World Sukarno rested on very diverse bases of support, and by the sixties he was dependent both on the large, pro-Chinese Indonesian Communist Party (PKI), the largest communist party outside the USSR and China, and the powerful and independent senior officer corps of the military machine, many of whom had been trained in the USA. He failed, however, to satisfy either the basic demands of the rural poor or the hopes of the rising national bourgeoisie.

In 1965 the political balance on which Sukarno rested collapsed in the supposed 'coup' of 1 October, which was immediately followed by General Suharto's takeover and the ensuing massacre of hundreds of thousands of communists (or those suspected of being communists) and members of the Chinese minority. Much of the killing was carried out by military units, aided by Muslim extremists. The terror was a turning point in the wider history of south-east Asia; one of its effects was to encourage the USA to step up its involvement in Vietnam. But, as well as being a tragedy for the people of Indonesia, it spelled disaster for their forests. How did this come about?

Despoiling the forests

The political overturn and the terror following October 1965 paved the way for a marriage between foreign capital and the generals, who commandeered, among other things, Indonesia's natural resources. The new rulers crushed agitation in the countryside, accelerated industrial production, both for import substitution and export, and enriched themselves through a military and bureaucratic oligarchy which in many respects resembles the 'kleptocracies' dislodged in the Philippines and in Haiti during the 1980s.

There had been a small export of logs from Indonesia in the early 1960s but at the time of the military takeover this was still a trickle, with an export value of only US$3 million. But as concession after concession was granted, the logs started to pour out to such an extent that Indonesia became the world's dominant tropical hardwood exporter. From 1972 to 1978 exports hovered between 15 and 20 million m³, reaching their volume (but not value) peak in 1978. Most of this exploitation has been carried out by specially created joint companies, the foreign partner furnishing the capital, the generals or their nominees contributing the forest resource: a resource which belongs by right to the Indonesian people.

Eventually it dawned on the military government that the export of raw logs was limiting earnings and they put pressure on their foreign partners to set up wood processing plants; some obliged, others pulled out. It became clear that the government was intent on rapidly damping the flow of logs to the world market and setting up domestic processing facilities instead of feeding logs to competitors. These latter (which included in-transit processors like the Philippines, South Korea, and Taiwan) carried both capital and know-how to Indonesia. By 1985 log exports had fallen to less than a million m³. But by then well over 2 million m³ of sawnwood was being exported, while plywood exports had soared from zero in 1974 to US$800 million.

Indonesia has thousands of intelligent and dedicated foresters. But to a large extent they have been obliged to serve as accessories to the ruthless pillage of Indonesia's forest heritage. This has taken place mainly in Kalimantan, but logging operations have also been extended to West Papua (Irian Jaya) and East Timor. The people of East Timor, evacuated by the Portuguese when the Salazar dictatorship fell, are also fighting a relentless, and probably hopeless, battle against the Indonesian army and migrants from Java to win political independence. In both of these areas, as in Kalimantan and Sumatra, logging operations and forced transmigration schemes are clearing forests from lands incapable of sustainable agriculture. What is happening today to the Dyaks of Kalimantan and the Asmats of West Papua amounts to genocide.

Of the billions of dollars which have flowed into Indonesia during the post-war boom in tropical woods, practically nothing has been spent on finding out how to manage these forests on a sustainable basis, or how to replace them.

The Indonesian government hosted the Eighth World Forestry Congress in Jakarta in 1978, and the first-ever World National Parks Congress in Bali in 1982; its official delegation adhered to both the Jakarta and Bali Declarations. The Twenty Year Long-Term Plan prepared by its Ministry of Forests in the mid-1980s made it quite clear that the current ruthless despoliation of the vulnerable forests of the outer islands was to continue, that hundreds of thousands of hectares of land presently forested are targeted for transmigration schemes, though demonstrably unsuited for permanent agriculture, that logging would continue to be uncontrolled, and that though millions of hectares were slated for the establishment of national parks, nature reserves and the like, there was no coherent plan for delineating, still less managing, these reserves. The whole Plan, riddled with internal inconsistencies, was but window-dressing designed to mollify those international conservationists who had expressed concern about the rate of shrinkage of these important tropical forests. Most Indonesian foresters, and especially those indigenous conservationist groups which are fighting a desperate and sometimes almost clandestine battle to save some of the country's resource heritage, know that the Plan was a shabby hoax.

Subsequently, with the assistance of the International Institute for Environment and Development, alternative forest policies for the sustainable development of forest lands have been worked out and given the nod of endorsement by the Indonesian government. To receive this nod, the analysis supporting the alternative policies has necessarily had to skip the political realities which have brought the present situation about, and which still obtain. The proposals nevertheless contain much of value. The chances that they will be implemented by those in power at the time of writing are remote.

Much the same applies to the new guidelines for transmigration settlements in forest areas which in 1988 were being worked out by Indonesia's Ministry of Population and Environment in cooperation with the International Union for the Conservation of Nature and the United Nations Environmental Programme. Doubtless these guidelines will seek to ensure that forest clearance for transmigration settlement will take place only on lands which lend themselves to a sustainable agriculture. But the implementation of such guidelines presupposes prior research and experimentation, followed by demonstration and adequate support for the settlers in the first years. None of this has been forthcoming in the past. Transmigrants have fled, made their way home, or resorted to precarious shifting cultivation.

The contrasts within Indonesia demonstrate very clearly that it is not population pressure as such which destroys forests. In spite of the fact that Java, Bali and Madura are heavily populated, with land far from evenly distributed, peasants have developed complex and highly successful agroforestry systems which enable them to obtain high yields continuously from surprisingly small parcels of land. In this respect they have more to teach expatriate agricultural experts than to learn from them.

As will become clearer in Part IV, there is a sense in which Indonesia epitomizes the history, including the contemporary history, of tropical forests. Those standing on fertile soils were cleared for agriculture, slowly at first, then with increasing rapidity as hierarchical systems developed and a growing agricultural surplus had to be extracted to support the court, the nobility, the priesthood, the army and the bureaucracy. When European colonialism arrived, it at first contented itself with the profits from trade. Step by step, it amplified its interests by exacting tribute, transforming local village headmen into tax collectors, and it extended the plantation system devoted to agricultural export crops. This required tighter political control, an expanding labour force, an intensified rate of exploitation, and the further clearance of forests. In due course, it called for forest clearance on inferior soils, and pushed rural labour, excessive or no longer needed, into clearing the more remote forests.

21   Nepal

Some recent writers on forest history have heaped all the blame for deforestation on the imperial power. As was pointed out in Part II, forest clearance, mainly as a step towards piling up an agricultural surplus, has characterized all hierarchical societies. The colonial powers, especially during the nineteenth century, perhaps exercised more imagination and more efficiency as exploiters. But they were not the first to deforest.

Nepal is characterized not only by scenic beauty, but by environmental fragility. Nowhere is the balance between forestry and agriculture more delicate. But the pressure on its forests – at least until the second half of the twentieth century – was entirely home-made. The story of this pressure and of attempts to alleviate it, especially since World War II, holds many lessons.

Nepal extends from the Himalayan mountains down to the Terai, the warm, humid lands of the Ganges plain, and a region which, as in Bangladesh, carries jute plantations. Much of the population is concentrated in and around the central valley, lying between the high Himalayas and the Siwalik foothills, which is also the location of the capital Katmandu. The importance of trees for maintaining soil fertility was recognized by Sidhartha Gautam, the founder of Buddhism, half a millennium before Christ, when he ordained that every family should plant a tree every five years.

Nepali kings have indulged in large-scale logging since at least the ninth century, for the building of temples and palaces and the like. Deforestation of the middle hills was already well under way in the eighteenth century as rulers sought to increase their income by converting forests to agriculture, exacting a 50 per cent tax on the value of produce. The country was not unified until 1743, and even after that local warring continued into the nineteenth century. Soldiers were paid with land grants, and large forest areas were given to the nobility as favours by rulers.

After a century as a British protectorate, Nepal was accorded its independence as a feudal monarchy in 1923. The dominant ethnic group, the Gurkhas, provided elite troops for the British and Indian armies from the early nineteenth century onwards. Again, land grants to retiring soldiers speeded forest clearance. The hardwood forests of the Terai remained relatively untouched until the 1950s and 1960s, when land hunger led to settlement of part of this area and the forests were heavily logged, mostly by Indian entrepreneurs, for the avid Indian market.

Fifteen million of Nepal's sixteen million people live by subsistence agriculture. They all rely on the forest for fuel, fodder, timber, fibres for weaving, as well as for dyes, glues, resins and the like. In spite of exploitation by autocratic rulers and a greedy nobility, Nepali peasant communities had worked out and applied traditional systems of forest management, with community checks on misuse. The significance of the forest was quantified by Wyatt-Smith (1982), who demonstrated that, under present forest management practices, a family farm of 1.25 ha needed 3.5 ha of forest for fodder, 0.3 to 0.6 ha for fuel, and 0.4 ha for timber. Fodder is important, since animals are the only source of fertilizer.

After World War II, the wind of change reached Nepal. The new government which came to power in 1947 sought to curb the autocratic elite which treated forests as their private property. A series of measures culminated in the Forest Nationalization Act of 1956. This was followed in 1964 by a land reform which set limits to the size of holdings. However, these measures, which were intended to limit the power of the rich few and establish an effective forest administration, failed on both counts. There were insufficient trained staff to carry out the work of mapping and demarcation; the powerful upper classes manipulated the laws to their own advantage. The peasants saw no reason to exercise control while the rich were able to do as they pleased. The traditional community management system had completely broken down. Even so, it is interesting to note that the forest plots which surround shrines were never touched.

It was some years before the error of ill-advised and uncontrolled nationalization was recognized. New regulations in 1978 turned over lands and forests to community ownership. But by then the peasants had grown mistrustful. They had come to believe that the government forests belonged to nobody. Though they still needed trees, especially for fodder, they had serious doubts about security of tenure. Damage continued. It proved impossible to rebuild overnight the traditional community forest management system which had collapsed under the impact of well-intentioned legislation. Steadily the situation deteriorated, with pressure most intense on the middle hills where half the population lives. Narrow terraces on the higher, steeper slopes carry maize and millet (which do not require irrigation) and rainwater sinks to the lower, flat, more fertile terraces which carry irrigated rice and wheat. The people of the middle hills need 5 million ha of forest: they have 4 million. Though the forest area remains stable, forest quality is steadily deteriorating (figure 21.1).

Figure 21.1   Erosion, deforestation and terracing on a Nepal hillside; there is some reafforestation in the foreground (copyright Jeremy Hartley/OXFAM)

Nepal does not lack sympathy or help in facing its forest problems. In the 1970s the streets of Katmandu teemed with destitute hippies scrounging from tourists. A decade later the hippies had gone, and the tourist was more likely to encounter expatriate project staff. About 30 different forestry projects are receiving external aid at the time of writing. The World Bank estimated in 1984 that overcoming the forest shortfall required the planting of 50 000 ha annually to 1990 and 10 000 ha annually thereafter. Planting is well underway, but protection is insufficient, while most of the plantations consist of pines, which yield good timber but fail to satisfy other needs. It has become evident that the only solution is to revive local management systems. But it is much easier to destroy than to rebuild. Although each *panchayat* (village council) has, since 1977, set up a local forest committee, these committees are dominated by the more wealthy and influential. Moreover, distances are great and communications difficult.

The obstacles to restoring and maintaining adequate forest cover in Nepal are not technical, but socio-political: how to make rural people aware of their rights, and how to encourage them to exercise those rights and to make their own decisions. This is particularly difficult after two decades of top-down advice and administration, which have weakened community curbs on the more wealthy. By 1988 one small project perhaps provided a pointer. After discussion in the wards (each *panchayat* consists of about nine wards of 300 to 500 people) and a village assembly, one particular *panchayat* agreed that women were the main users of forest material. It thereupon elected a forest committee entirely of women. Within half a year they had decided and started to implement a series of measures which, in aggregate, constituted an effective and just management system. Private cutting for sale was banned; all pine was to be pruned; grass cutting was controlled; firewood was subject to joint sale and accounting; all seedlings were fenced. In other words, the peasants became not simply forest guards or forest labourers, but deciders. The external support to this project has yet to face up to the problem of how many non-forest demands it should try to meet; for example, this forest committee has already requested an adult literacy class.

It may prove possible to counter undue influence at the *panchayat* level by carrying information to, and seeking decisions at, the ward level. Certainly, wholehearted cooperation from the peasants can only be forthcoming when rural people are convinced that the forest is theirs and the decisions about the forest are theirs too.

The inordinate emphasis by external agencies on pine for planting (it grows well even on impoverished soils, and provides good timber) will, it is hoped, be countered by a current research project designed to determine which indigenous species best satisfy the special mix of local needs. This is perhaps the only technical issue of significance that Nepal's reafforestation needs to resolve. Even that stems from an intimate understanding of social needs. All the other problems, including problems of organization and administration, are essentially socio-political problems.

Conditions in the Terai, to which some of Nepal's peasants have been driven by land scarcity, are very different from those in the central valley and middle hills. But here too the nanny-knows-best attitude of some external advisers and agencies can lead to the distortion of a well-conceived project. In one case of an Asian Development Bank project the original proposal was to help villagers by planting native hardwoods capable of coppicing, and thus able to yield usable fuelwood in the early years and valuable timber in the stems left to grow. Meanwhile, peasants were to be encouraged to fight forest fires by the distribution of 500 bicycles to the labour force on the condition that they made themselves available for fire fighting when needed. (It should be mentioned that this is an area of few roads and no vehicle maintenance facilities.) But by the time this project had become operational, the bicycles had been eliminated and been replaced by landrovers for the management, while instead of indigenous hardwoods to serve the peasants, eucalypts were to be planted to fuel tobacco curing.

22   The Philippines

A beautiful short television film of the 1980s described the life and forest habitat of the majestic Philippine monkey-eating eagle. The film told how one of the principal logging companies in the Philippines had been persuaded to halt operations over a small area of its vast concession, thereby leaving undisturbed one of the last breeding sites of this rare species. This noble gesture, it was hoped, would help to save this rapidly disappearing species from extinction. It was a film to gladden the eyes and warm the hearts of wildlife lovers and conservationists everywhere. But there was much about the Philippines' disappearing forests, and the species thereby threatened, that the film left unsaid. To understand what has been happening – and what is still happening – it is necessary to look further back.

When the Spaniards conquered the Philippines in the middle of the sixteenth century, forests covered about 90 per cent of the islands, judging from contemporary accounts. A scant population of tribal societies lived along the coasts and along the river valleys. By 1900 forest cover had dropped to 70 per cent, and about fifty years later it was down to 55 per cent. By the late 1980s it was well below 50 per cent. Moreover, what this shrinking figure fails to reveal is the serious depletion in the forest which remains.

But what is interesting about these figures is the sharp contraction before the end of the nineteenth century. This was long before the tremendous boom in the export of tropical logs from south-east Asia which occurred in the decades after World War II. The Philippines shared in that boom and was one of the principal log exporters until 1972, when concern about the diminishing forest, and about log supplies for domestic industries, led the government to impose controls on log exports – controls which were not difficult to evade.

The main loss of forests occurred in the nineteenth century, when forests were cleared to establish plantations of export crops: sugar, abaca, coffee, indigo and tobacco. It was the commercialization of agriculture which turned land into a commodity, just as in other times and on other continents. As always, plantations commandeered the flat lands, the gentle slopes. Other cultivators, including those who laboured on the plantations, were pushed into the uplands, onto lands harder to clear and till, onto more vulnerable soils. More people had to carve a living from less and worse land. Thus it was not simply that part of the forest cleared for plantations disappeared. Nor that surrounding hills were bared for fuel, though sugar-cane displaced more forest through the use of fuelwood for processing than in the provision of growing area. But a new pressure on the forest started which could only increase as the decades wore on. Moreover, in those forests where indigenous shifting cultivators practised slash and burn agriculture – a mode of production carried out for centuries in harmonious balance with nature – the shrinking of the forest area available to them obliged a shortening of the forest fallow. This lowered fertility, setting in motion the downward spiral of forest depletion and destruction.

The Philippines has not always been, as it has been described in recent years, the United States' best friend. During the nineteenth century, American and other foreign enterprises shared with Spanish firms the Philippines' rapidly growing export trade. Two American firms, for example, controlled the export of abaca, in response to the US navy's need for cordage. When, in 1898, Spanish colonialism, foundering under rising nationalist armed resistance, ceded the islands to the USA by the Treaty of Paris, the stage was set for the further penetration of American capital. Nationalist resistance to the new domination was not easy to subdue. Estimates of Filipinos killed in the Filipino-American War range from 250 000 to 600 000. But once resistance had been overcome, the process started under the Spanish *hacienda* system continued, with a slight pause during the Japanese occupation of 1942–5 and until the declaration of Philippine independence in 1946. It accelerated under the Marcos regime: for example, in the single year 1978, the area devoted to the commercial production of sugar-cane, coconut and fruit expanded by 494 000 ha, while that given over to the production of rice and corn staples fell by 120 000 ha.

Only now are some of the most outrageous excesses of the Marcos regime being admitted. It was a regime underpinned by the US government until the very last minute, when it became clear that unless the United States withdrew support, and quickly, the wave of popular anger might sweep away not only the Marcos family but also the giant US economic and strategic interests which still dominate the Philippine economy.

The Philippine population is scattered across more than 2000 islands and includes more than 50 national minorities, each with its indigenous cultural heritage. Many of the minorities live in, and are dependent on, the forest. These people have been steadily losing their ancestral lands. They have been dispossessed, legally or illegally, by commercial agriculture, by logging and by mining. US-based transnationals have a heavy stake in all three. The logging roads open up an avenue of entry into the forest for rural landless and for small farmers thrown off their land by the extension of export-oriented commercial agriculture. The Marcos regime was repeatedly condemned for violation of human rights, and it was one which savagely used military force against peasants and tribal minorities who stood in the way of agribusiness and mining interests. Thus in one area of Mindanao, where thousands of hectares have been turned over to plantation agriculture owned by Goodyear and Firestone (rubber), Guthrie (coffee and palm oil), Del Monte (fruit) and other large corporations, the government used the notorious 'Lost Patrol' security guards to help clear the small farmers out.

The Philippine government has always been one of the World Bank's favourite clients, and the thousands of pages of World Bank documents leaked make fascinating reading. They do not, of course, reveal any derailment of World Bank funds into the pockets of Marcos, his wife Imelda and their close associates. This is now coming to light as the Committee established by President Aquino gradually traces the 'missing billions'. It is frankly incredible that hard-boiled bankers should have had no inkling of what was going on.

In recent years the World Bank has financed a number of projects, including tree farming, which have ostensibly endeavoured to help the small farmer. In fact, few small holders, and even fewer landless have benefited. The principal beneficiaries have been large 'smallholders', including absentee and company landowners, together with the pulp company which enjoys a monopoly position as purchaser.

The new government has attempted to control commercial logging more effectively, by enforcing the (very generous) contracts the Marcos regime made with foreign and national concessionaires, and by signing new ones only on much stricter terms. But the staff of forest guards available to police logging operations is pathetically insufficient, and where army units are given responsibility for controlling the trucking out of logs along forest roads they are frequently bribed to turn a blind eye. The government has also taken some steps to encourage shifting cultivators in upland forest areas to switch to forms of settled agriculture. But such efforts have received too few resources to have a significant effect.

Marcos has gone: but at the time of writing many of his former friends still hold high office, both military and civilian. The long-promised agrarian reform has made little progress (it has not yet touched the family estates of the new President, the largest sugar estate in the Philippines). Insurgent forces are disinclined to lay down their arms without surer guarantees that popular demands will be met. Unless Aquino changes existing power relationships and ensures more equal access to land and other resources, then the needs of the people who swept her into power will remain unsatisfied, and the tropical forests of the Philippines will continue to disappear.

Part IV The main forest issues

23 The tropical forests

Forest cover is disappearing at a rate of more than 200 000 ha per year in each of Brazil, Colombia, Indonesia, Mexico, Thailand, Ivory Coast, Ecuador, Nigeria, Peru and Malaysia. All these countries lie wholly or mainly in the tropics. The impression conveyed by the media in recent years, that the world's tropical forests are shrinking fast, is thus correct. There is room for argument about how fast they are disappearing. This, as explained in chapter 14, lies in the nature of the data presently available to us. But this database will steadily improve. Within a few years there will become available a much more precise picture of what is happening – more precise, but not necessarily more encouraging. In the case of the few countries for which we have comparable data over a sufficiently long period, the most recent data have shown that deforestation has been proceeding at a faster rate than had previously been estimated.

So varied are the forests which lie in the tropics that it is impossible to classify them in a manner which will satisfy all scientists. They differ according to altitude, latitude, amount and incidence of rainfall, nature of the underlying soil, past climatic history, and the degree of human intervention.

Because of the constant references to tropical rainforests and to evergreen tropical forests there is a widespread belief that all forests in the tropics are rainforests and are highly heterogeneous, consisting of extremely complex webs of both flora and fauna. They are thus seen as fragile and vulnerable, so that the slightest intervention from outside can put the whole system in peril. This is not true. Not all moist tropical forests are evergreen, nor are all tropical forests moist. Indeed, the drier and more open tropical forest formations, together with the shrubland into which they merge (and which still falls under the definition of forest) are not only almost as extensive; many more people live in or near them and are dependent upon them. The drier tropical forests are even more acutely threatened, and their shrinkage should give us equal cause for concern. The problems encountered there are if anything more serious than those in the tropical moist forest, on which we concentrate in this chapter.

Tropical moist forest

Tropical moist forest (TMF) is not a very satisfactory term, but it is one which has now won widespread acceptance. It includes the closed high forests lying in the tropical belt where there is either year-round rainfall, or only a short dry season of not more than four months. (The word 'closed', it will be recalled from chapter 14, means that the canopy covers at least 20 per cent of the land surface, not that it is complete.) TMF includes both wet rainforest and dryland forest formations, monsoon forests, mountain rain and cloud forests, and mangroves. Nearly all these forests consist of broadleaved species, coniferous forests accounting for less than 3 per cent.

Thus the broad category TMF comprehends hundreds of different ecosystems, many of which are today under threat. It represents 1.6 billion ha out of the world's total of 3 billion ha of tropical forest. But a quarter of this area (410 million ha) is forest fallow, either under crops or recovering from shifting cultivation. Of the balance, over 200 million ha have already been logged, with rather less than a billion ha still virgin. Of the TMF not yet logged, about two-thirds is believed to hold commercial timber prospects, the other third being considered non-productive or inaccessible.

At least that was how things were in 1980, according to such evidence as was available to international experts. Those familiar with the evolution of events in countries possessing the largest areas of TMF suspect that as new data become available and are analysed, a more serious rate of shrinkage will be revealed.

Concern about the disappearance of the TMF has spread rapidly since the 1960s. One of the reasons for this is that these forests contain most of the many millions of species of flora and fauna as yet unidentified, and therefore not assessed from the standpoint of their potential value to us: as foods, as pharmaceuticals, as raw materials for industry. These forests contain 90 per cent of all primates, and on present estimates, 60 per cent of all plant species and 80 per cent of all insect species. Many of what are today the world's staple foods originated in the TMF, and modern pharmaceutical industries are based largely on plant materials extracted from these forests. These forests contain the wild cousins of important and long-domesticated food and industrial plants. These wild cousins are crucial for the continuous plant breeding which alone can ensure vigour and resistance to disease in the domesticated plants on which the world has come to depend.

This argument, forcefully presented by Norman Myers in his books *The Sinking Ark* (1979) and *The Primary Resource* (1984), cannot be contested. But it is possible to overstate it. One hectare of Peruvian rainforest may have revealed a count of 41 000 insect species but it does not necessarily follow that preserving all these should be a first priority. It is in the nature of evolution that hundreds, and more probably thousands, of species become extinct every year. Moreover, the earth is not a clock which can be stopped until all its parts have been examined. The past has generated present pressures which limit the scope for determining the future. Whether we like it or not, there are substantial areas of TMF which will inevitably disappear in the coming decades. But that does not absolve us from the responsibility for determining how much, and which, ought to be preserved, and how best to preserve it.

Another argument is that the disappearance of the TMF will bring about changes in the composition of the earth's atmosphere which could have serious, even catastrophic, consequences for the configuration of the continents, the climate, and the earth's food-producing capacity. This argument has focused mainly on what has been described as the greenhouse effect. The burning of the forests, it is argued, drives up the amount of atmospheric carbon, diminishing heat radiation from the earth's surface, bringing about a gradual rise in temperature, the melting of the polar ice caps, and a steady rise in the sea level. The consequence would be massive, and probably disastrous, changes in local climates.

How far forest shrinkage contributes to the rise in atmospheric carbon is as yet far from clear. It is known that the amount of carbon in the atmosphere is going up year by year, by roughly half the amount which is being pumped into it annually by the burning of fossil fuels. Undoubtedly, the rise in atmospheric carbon is a serious matter and warrants more intensive research than has so far been undertaken.

But the most important and immediate reason for attempting to stem the shrinkage of the TMFs is the devastating effect their disappearance has on the lives of those who live in and near them, on those who depend on them, directly or indirectly. These latter include millions who may live a thousand or more kilometres away from the forests, even in different countries. The periodic floods in Bangladesh have their root cause in deforestation which extends as far as the distant Himalayas.

More directly, contemporary deforestation in the tropics does not merely involve the erosion of rights in the forest; it involves genocide – the deliberate destruction of the habitat of forest-dwelling peoples, with the hunting down of such as dare resist.

So it does matter that the TMFs are disappearing. But those who want to help save them need to understand which ones are disappearing, and why. The reader will already have glimpsed, from the country profiles presented in Part III, that the issues involved are more complex than they appear at first sight. The problem is not simply that the numbers of people living in the tropical forested countries are increasing. Nor is it simply that the appetite of the affluent countries for tropical woods has become more avid. If measures are to be devised to halt contemporary tropical deforestation, it is necessary to examine more closely the processes which underlie the shrinkage.

Is the TMF a renewable resource?

While most tropical forests are highly heterogeneous, not all are. There are several types of tropical forest which are relatively simple in their composition, and which present no insuperable technical problems to their exploitation on a sustainable basis.

There are different kinds of heterogeneity. We can have a tropical forest in which hundreds of different species are found in a given square kilometre, yet with that same kind of mix persisting over thousands of square kilometres. Or we can have a given mix in one place, and a completely different mix just a few kilometres away. Much depends on the topography and the underlying soils. The latter type of heterogeneity presents greater problems than the former. The TMF is not one single ecosystem, but many hundreds of different ecosystems. And the lamentable fact is that, as was pointed out in chapter 6, little or nothing is known about how to renew or replace most of them. The reason less is known about many tropical forests than about the surface of the moon is that so few resources have so far been devoted to learning about them and finding out how to manage them.

Some scientists have argued that the TMF is not a renewable resource, as are most other forests; that science has failed to provide us with any clear ideas on how to manage these forests; and that therefore they should be left intact and guarded from any human intervention. This is not a view shared by the two international foresters with the widest experience of the technical and economic aspects of managing TMF: an Englishman John Wyatt-Smith, and an Australian, Alf Leslie. Both, however, recognize the conditions which must be satisfied if sustained management is to succeed; similarly, both are fully aware that these conditions are rarely satisfied in practice. The former has observed that 'It is virtually impossible to manage forest effectively, least of all TMF, without a declared and firmly committed national forest policy. The production cycle of TMF goods and services is too long to endure either vacillation or sudden change in policy.' This is one reason why less than 3 per cent of TMF is even claimed to be under management.

It may be true that, in many types of tropical moist forests, there is no conceivable kind of intervention or manipulation which would ensure that the forest would renew itself exactly as it was before. But intervention can be so controlled that the forest does renew itself, though perhaps with changed composition. Indeed, it can be 'improved', that is, its value can be enhanced for human use, by appropriate intervention. Species deemed valuable can be encouraged, and unwanted species discouraged. Manipulations of this kind may not be easy and they are unlikely to be cheap. The unhappy fact is that for many tropical forest ecosystems no effort has yet been made to discover what manipulations would be appropriate, and how much they would cost.

But what is incontestable is that there are certain practices, especially in the methods used for getting timber out, which everyone knows perfectly well are destructive of the forest, which ruin the forest's capacity to renew itself, and which should be banned. It may not yet always be clear exactly what should be done; but both experience and common sense have provided sound notions of what should not be done. In practice this knowledge is rarely applied. Not only are few attempts made to renew or replace the forest, the logging methods used almost everywhere in the tropics are such as to destroy or degrade the forest. The available knowledge is not applied, for the same reason that 'manageable' tropical forests are not managed. That reason has to do with the way in which tropical woods are marketed and priced. For there are several types of forests in the tropics which are 'manageable', in the sense that they could be harvested regularly without destroying the forest's capacity to renew itself.

Tropical forests we could manage

Some of the forests in south-east Asia which first attracted timber traders and foreign governments consist largely of shorea species, or of dipterocarp species which are closely related and have similar wood properties, so that a high proportion of trees in the forest are marketable. Similarly, there are considerable areas of okoume forests in Gabon which are uniform and easily exploitable. For obvious reasons it is these less heterogeneous kinds of forest, with a high proportion of marketable species, which are first exploited. That is why Thailand is on the verge of becoming a net forest products importer. For the same reasons many of the forests of peninsular Malaysia are also disappearing. Methods of managing these relatively simple forests in a sustainable way have been devised. All too rarely have they been applied.

There are other forest types in the tropics which present no major problems for sustainable management. Some tropical and subtropical forests consist mainly of conifers. They are mostly at higher altitudes, and they occur in both Asia and Central America. Though enough is known about most of these to make it possible to manage them on a sustainable basis, in practice very few are. Most of the more accessible of the forests have already been cleared or have been badly depleted. This process continues today over most of Central America, so much so that there is a serious danger that some rare pine species which might have proved brilliant exotics in other environments will become extinct before their potential has been tested. This is no flight of fancy. The large, expanding and successful forest product export industries of Chile and New Zealand are entirely based on artificial forests of Monterey pine, a tree of poor form and only moderate growth in its very restricted native habitat, the Monterey Peninsula in California.

Mangroves under threat

There is justification for considering as 'manageable' the mangrove forests, those dense low-growing forests that border many tropical and subtropical coastlines and tidal rivers. Mangroves root in river-borne silt and can withstand saline water, and can be regarded as arbiters of land and sea. Though there are many hundreds of species their form and habitat are closely similar. Their wood is used as fuel, for charcoal, for tanning, and for innumerable native crafts. The trees are usually too small or of too poor form for conversion into sawnwood or plywood, although they can be chipped and used for various kinds of reconstituted wood. But by far their most important function is as a food source and breeding ground for fish. Many riverain peoples in south-east Asia depend on mangrove forests and use them in a sustainable way. If they are overexploited, the consequences may be dire indeed. This is clearly demonstrated by what has happened in Vietnam, where US forces destroyed hundreds of thousands of hectares of mangrove forest with Agent Orange and napalm. Efforts to regenerate or replant have met with scant success. It had been hoped that the forests would recover within decades, but it seems that the lasting effects of poisoned soil had been underestimated; scientists now believe it may take centuries.

'Arbiters between land and sea': it is still not clear whether mangroves are land-reclaimers, colonizing newly deposited silt, or erosion-retarders, resisting the inroads of river and sea currents. It could even be that they play whichever role local circumstances dictate. Certain it is, however, that massive uncontrolled inroads into mangrove forests for wood chipping could have untold adverse consequences. Already wood-hungry pulp industries have started chipping some Asian mangrove forests. This is a practice which should be immediately halted. Though mangroves attract little attention from the media, they have a significant ecological role to play and many indigenous peoples depend on them.

So there are some kinds of tropical forest which are relatively simple – from the standpoint of sustainable management, that is. Why, then, are almost none sustainably managed? The answer has to do with the ways in which timber is taken out of the tropical forests, and how that timber is priced.

Loggers, past and present

FAO has estimated that over two-thirds of the destruction in the tropical *moist* forest stems from the activities of loggers, either directly or indirectly. This is only a very crude estimate, since it is not easy to distinguish the indirect consequences of logging from other socio-economic factors. The popular view is that the timber barons are principally to blame for the disappearance of the tropical forests, a view strengthened by television scenes of chain saws mowing down vast swathes of tropical forest like a harvester passing through a field of corn. The clear-felling of tropical forests by loggers has happened on occasion, but it has happened very rarely. Such scenes certainly are not, and never have been, typical.

Most exploitation for timber in the tropics in the early days was for highly prized species unobtainable elsewhere. The mahogany hunters and the cedar-getters have already been mentioned. Other important tropical woods which became the target of logging for export were the greenheart of what then was British Guiana (resistant to marine borers, and thus valued for marine piling until the invention of salt-resistant cement), and teak and similar species from south and south-east Asia for ship timber, railway sleepers and furniture.

So long as the loggers concentrated on highly prized species scattered sparsely through the forest, their activities had relatively little impact on the forest as a whole, even though they depleted the hunted species and damaged other trees while felling and hauling out the logs. When, however, they turned their attention to those forests rich in species for which there was a growing market, their depredations became more serious.

But the important thing which has to be understood is that never, since tropical forests were first exploited for timber, has the price of that wood been determined by what it cost to renew or replace it; it has been determined only by the profit which could be made in selling it on the market after allowance for getting it out of the forest and to the market.

The same was true of the temperate and boreal forests until relatively recent times. The shift to management came about only when wood became scarcer and therefore dearer, and when forestry science had advanced sufficiently to enable the forests to be managed as a renewable resource. Even today there are some temperate and boreal forests which are not managed.

To explain the intensified assault on the tropical forests after World War II, some have argued that the giant timber industry interests, having exhausted the temperate forests, thereupon moved on into the tropics. In fact, as we saw in chapter 14, the temperate forests have not been exhausted. Europe's forests, until the relatively recent impact of such factors as acid rain, were in better shape than they have been for a century: more extensive, better managed, more productive. North American forests, too, have been steadily brought under more effective management, and are still supplying less than their potential sustainable capacity. The timber barons moved decisively into the tropics after World War II not because timber supplies in the temperate zones were exhausted, but because it was possible to obtain in the tropics either wood which they could not obtain elsewhere or wood which, for the purposes for which they intended to use it, was cheaper than wood they could obtain from elsewhere. No longer is the logger's interest in the tropical forests confined to precious hardwoods. Today those forests are exploited not simply for rare and precious woods, but for woods which might fairly be described as run-of-the-mill.

The boom in tropical wood exports after World War II certainly owed much to rising affluence in Europe, North America and Japan, with the consequent rise in demand for furniture and similar durable goods. But it also rested in part on advances in wood technology which broadened the raw material base of the wood industries. Thus, much of the wood exported was not particularly precious wood, but rather utility hardwoods used for joinery manufacture, or as the face or even core veneer in plywood. It became profitable to import non-'precious' woods from the tropics for the very simple reason that their price continued to be related not to the cost of renewing or replacing them, but only to the cost of getting them to market. With wood prices rising relative to prices generally, and with the market willing to take species and dimensions it formerly despised, greater volumes of timber could be taken out of each hectare. Thus the impact of infrastructural costs (such as road building) on each cubic metre was reduced. The growing market and technological advance combined to make more of the tropical forest usable and saleable.

This does not mean that mixed tropical forests were clear felled for industrial use, although more could be taken out of each hectare. This has occurred only when there has been a market available for mixed tropical hardwood chips for the manufacturer of paper, board or reconstituted wood. In spite of developments in specialized ocean transporters and wood chip handling equipment, it 'pays' to clear-fell and chip mixed tropical forests only if the timber standing in the forest is virtually given away. In the few cases where this has happened, it has been because the government concerned has wanted the forest cleared: either to convert it to agricultural use or to replace it by tree plantations. Thus the JANT operation in Papua New Guinea (PNG), sad as it was, was atypical. Here a company jointly owned by the PNG government and a Japanese transnational cleared and chipped TMF, exporting the wood chips to Japan in ships owned by the transnational parent company (figures 23.1 and 23.2). The only measure of chip volume was the ship captain's declaration. The operation continued for more than ten years without the

Figure 23.1 Clearfelling operations by Japanese New Guinea Timbers (JANT) in the Gogol valley, Madang Province, PNG, in 1983 (photo Anthony Fraser, Oxford Forestry Institute)

jointly owned subsidiary ever declaring a profit. Unsurprisingly, the replanting that was to be conducted was never undertaken, on the grounds that the land title was not clear. This, of course, was known from the outset; the dislodged tribes have appeared on Western television screens. The final irony is that the indigenous peoples are now being allowed back into what was their forest to establish their gardens on the understanding that they simultaneously plant trees and move on once these are established.

The clear-felling of tropical forests may be atypical, but the loggers' assault on them has undoubtedly intensified. How did it happen that the tropical forests were exploited for timber at an accelerating rate in the post-war decades, with so little regard for the actions necessary to ensure that the forests were renewed or replaced?

Partners in pillage

As the demand for tropical wood soared the governments of many countries possessing tropical forests rushed to cash in on this new

Figure 23.2 Stockpiled mixed hardwood woodchips awaiting bulk carrier transport to Japan, JANT mill, Madang, PNG (photo Anthony Fraser, Oxford Forestry Institute)

bonanza. The right to exploit millions upon millions of hectares of forests was handed over to concessionaires. The terms of the concessions left much to be desired since the parties negotiating them were unequal. The clauses which governed the operator's responsibility towards the forest were often so vague as to be meaningless; the governmental forest services were too small, often badly trained, always badly paid, and utterly incapable of controlling the operator and ensuring that the terms of the concession were observed. Thus the damage inflicted on the forests was much greater than it need have been, while the sums which did reach the national exchequer represented only a fraction of the benefit which should have flowed from the disposal of the national heritage.

The tropical hardwood trade has always been one which lent itself to deception and dubious practices. It requires a good deal of experience and expertise to discern, either in the standing tree, or in the cut log, whether on the forest floor or piled at the quay, the ultimate value of the timber it contains. Royalties – the amounts paid by the concessionaire to the forest owner (normally the central or local government) – are usually based on the volume, species and log quality of the timber taken out. Thus profits can be piled up if logs are undermeasured, undergraded, or recorded in an inferior species category. These malpractices flourish where forest services lack staff who are qualified and who can afford to be honest. The prices paid for logs as they come out of the forest in no way reflect the great disparities between the final values of those logs when they reach the hands of those who will finally process them. A great deal of the 'cake' to be found in the forest changes hands at the price of 'bread'.

Because in many underdeveloped countries there is a shortage of national enterprises with the requisite financial resources, technical background and marketing expertise, operations are frequently confided to joint ventures, partnerships between transnationals (the *de facto* controllers of the operations) and often dishonest local figures wielding political influence. Even in cases where the local partner in a joint venture is honest, the country with the forest resource can find itself cheated: the joint venture can go on showing little or no profit year after year, while the overseas parent transnational thrives on underpriced wood purchased from its subsidiary.

It would be possible to fill a book with examples of these unsavoury aspects of the tropical timber trade. The reason for mentioning them here is to emphasize that there is no point in pillorying only the transnationals, the global timber barons, for the pillage of the tropical forest resources in the underdeveloped world. They are able to inflict damage only where they can win or buy the consent and collaboration of people of influence inside the forested tropical countries. Whatever the intentions of the latter, however, they are always subjected by the unequal world economic order to tremendous pressures to produce foreign exchange.

Damage from logging operations

The most serious damage occurs where the logging operation destroys the water-holding capacity of the soil; on steep slopes this can be disastrous. In most tropical countries there are areas of upland cloud forest and rainforest which ought to be permanently reserved because any disturbance can bring about erosion, floods and landslides on the lower slopes and in the valleys – sometimes of a magnitude to sweep away or bury whole villages. To admit logging operators into these areas makes the conceding authority guilty of being an accessory before the fact of manslaughter. The mud avalanches on the Andean slopes which were reported by Western television were not natural disasters: they were man-made. They were the consequences of reckless deforestation; they could have been avoided.

Even in those forest areas that are not so vulnerable that logging should be rigorously excluded, there are still a number of precautions that should always be observed when forests are exploited. Open areas should be of limited size and duration, damage to regrowth kept as low as possible, soil compaction avoided, interference with the natural forest drainage kept to a minimum. After logging, any measures necessary to ensure regrowth, including replanting, should be undertaken without delay. It is what happens during and after logging that determines whether and how the forest will be renewed, and its future composition. These measures are costly. Even if they are set out in the terms of the concession they are rarely carried out by the concessionaire. The national forest services lack the means, the power or the support to impose any control. Still less do they possess the resources to ensure forest renewal themselves. But, resources apart, the root cause of these abuses is that in most Third World countries political power rests in the hands of people more interested in facilitating exploitation than in controlling it. The corrupt involvement of the Indonesian military in forestry is notorious; but Indonesia is not alone. A substantial part of the world's tropical forest has already been converted into money in Swiss bank accounts.

Perhaps the most destructive aspect of 'cut and run' in the tropical forests is that the roads opened up by the loggers provide avenues of penetration for the rural landless. The expulsion, by fair means or foul, of small farmers from the better soils in order to make way for plantation-type and usually export-oriented agriculture, generates armies of landless people. These peasants are augmented by changes in crops grown and techniques employed, and by switches to ranching, all of which add unemployed rural wage labour to the ranks of the dispossessed. Their numbers are on the increase in almost all tropical countries, and the landless poor already constitute the majority of the rural population in some. They represent the principal instruments of tropical forest destruction today, an indirect impact of the loggers' activities which is even more destructive of the TMF than the logging itself.

Thus the domestic partners in the pillage of the tropical forest consist not only of those who facilitate, join in, or condone the ruthless and reckless exploitation of the forests for timber; they also include all those forces in society which, by denying access to land and water resources to the many, retaining it in the hands of the few, oblige the growing army of landless people to press further into the forest.

From forests to farms

There are those who argue that all the TMFs stand on soils which are fragile, so that the conversion of the forests to agricultural purposes, even if possible in the short run, will be catastrophic in the long run. They are mistaken. There are many parts of the tropical world where permanent and sustainable agriculture is today being practised on land which was once covered by tropical forest. It is therefore quite likely that there are still some forested areas which can be safely converted. But all depends on the kind of agriculture and how it is practised. There have already been many cases where disaster has followed on clearance, and these cases are today multiplying. Precisely because most of the better soils have already been converted, any further transfers of TMF to agriculture require that specific precautions be taken if that conversion is to succeed. These precautions are not being taken. Forests are being converted to farmland more rapidly than ever, and in nearly all cases to agricultural systems which are not sustainable.

The fragility and vulnerability of many tropical forests does not lie in the complexity of the ecosystem. Complexity is not necessarily a weakness: it may even increase the ecosystem's capacity for self-adjustment. The vulnerability stems from the rapidity of nutrient cycling and the nature of the underlying soils. Where temperatures are high and moisture is adequate, biological activity is also high. This means that decaying nutrients are quickly recycled, so that a very high proportion of the total biomass is above ground in the growing vegetation, while the soil itself contains little humus. The apparent luxuriance of the above-ground vegetation often belies the poverty of the underlying soil. If for any reason a clearing appears in the forest, there is little ground protection; heavy rains can leach out essential minerals as well as erode soils. The hot sun can dry thin bare soils to a brick-like consistency.

Even so, down the centuries, peasants have worked out ways and means of gardening unpromising tropical forest soils: either by forms of itinerant agriculture, or by careful attention to retaining shade, maintaining soil cover, and renewing fertility. Today these systems are breaking down. Shifting cultivators find themselves cut off from areas of forest they were wont to use, and compressed into ever more limited areas; forest fallows are shortened, and the land must be cultivated again before it has had time to recover its fertility. Settled peasant cultivators find themselves obliged to discard traditional cropping systems in order to grow cash crops. More ominously, as we have seen, a new and growing army of dispossessed and landless families is invading the forest. Faced with the alternative of flocking to the shanty towns around the main cities where they may pick up some parasitic means of existence, or of moving further into the forest to clear a patch of ground from which they may scratch a living, they opt for the latter. They are not shifting cultivators in the traditional sense: forest dwellers who down the ages have learned how to clear, till, harvest and move on, leaving the forest a long enough period of fallow to recover before returning to clear and work that patch again. The new army is of shifted cultivators. Unlike the shifting cultivators, the shifted cultivators find themselves on soils very different from those they knew, and frequently of low fertility. Their experience and traditions are not adapted to the new environment in which they find themselves, so their impact on the soil is more destructive. Their hopes of establishing themselves are vain. Within a year or two they are obliged to leave the patch they have laboriously cleared, and push further into the forest.

Hardly better is the plight of those families who find themselves transferred under official settlement or transmigration programmes. Schemes designed to clear substantial areas of tropical forest for permanent agriculture often overlook the lessons which peasants have learned in the course of centuries, with the disastrous consequence that agriculture cannot be sustained nor can the forest recover.

However, the fact that most of the conversion of tropical forest to farmland which is taking place today is unsuccessful does not mean that all such conversions must necessarily fail. To date there has been all too little research into the composition and structure of tropical forest soils, and the possibilities they hold for varying types of agriculture. Most of the investigations carried out under colonial regimes were concerned only with locating soils which might support plantations of export crops. Very seldom were they directed to ascertaining the best ways of growing staple foods on which the indigenous peoples depended. By way of example, when Mozambique gained its independence, virtually the only usable information about Mozambican forests available to the new government after centuries of Portuguese rule was indirect information included in the report of a team of botanists sent out from Lisbon to locate areas suitable for growing cotton for export.

Until recently most scientists believed that only very limited areas in the Amazon basin would eventually prove capable of supporting sustainable agriculture. Recent research provides hope of a more optimistic assessment. Certain soil types have been shown to suffer from particular mineral deficiencies which can be put right both easily and cheaply. Laboratory work, followed by experimental and then demonstration plots, has led to the successful installation of small-scale farming on some areas formerly regarded as useless. Although the breakthrough is a very limited one (applicable to only a tiny percentage of the Amazon basin soils), it is significant in pointing to the prospects that may be opened up by more intensive and better directed research.

The spread of agriculture over the earth's surface is closely bound up with forest clearance. Even in the temperate zones, it took centuries for farmers to learn that trees were not their implacable enemy, that some measure of tree cover was absolutely necessary for crop cultivation and animal husbandry. There are substantial areas in both the north and south temperate zones which bear witness to past errors and which are still incapable of supporting either crops or animals. But the errors which are being committed today in the tropical forested countries are occurring much more rapidly and will have more devastating consequences. As yet the effort being put into devising and disseminating sustainable agricultural systems adapted to tropical forest soils is negligible. Meanwhile, the available good land already cleared is in the hands of the rich and powerful few, and is largely devoted to growing plantation export crops or to ranching – growing the wrong crops for the wrong people.

A highly skewed distribution of wealth and land is characteristic of nearly all the tropical forested countries, and is often a central factor in the destruction of their forests. Rich and powerful landowners in Brazil, for example, continue to extend their estates by legal trickery and often aided by their own private armies. Those whom they dipossess have served their purpose. They have carried out the back-breaking task of clearing the forest. It is now ready for takeover by ranching interests. The dislodged peasants are obliged to move deeper into the forest and start clearing once again. Thus aspects of the history of the temperate forests in Europe are today repeating themselves in accelerated forms in the tropical forests. The dispossessed may still have their own folk heroes, outlaws who have formed bands and sought to mete out rudimentary justice: the modern counterparts of Robin Hood and Eustache li Moine (see chapter 11). But, to date, neither peasant associations nor rural trade unions – even with the backing of country priests – have succeeded in halting the theft of land.

Population pressure and the tropical forest

The spectacle of tropical forests being invaded by the landless has led many to believe that sheer population pressure is the principal cause of tropical deforestation. But the most rapid clearance of tropical forests today is taking place in Brazil, a country twice the size of Europe, immensely rich in natural resources, and with a population only one quarter that of Europe. Thus to attribute tropical deforestation to population pressure alone is to argue that spots cause measles. It is useless to blame the peasant for haplessly multiplying. Paradoxically, they must multiply to survive. The tropical forest cannot be saved by distributing IUDs and condoms.

This is not to say that there is no population problem. But real population problems are not simply the result of a ratio between numbers of people and quantity of resources, but come from much more complex interactions. These include the terms on which people have access to the available resources and the way in which the rapid *growth* of population (as opposed to its actual size) produces pressures for more consumption and less investment, thus reducing the society's ability to protect its forest and other resources. A number of the countries with tropical forests do have a serious population problem. But the contemporary clearance of tropical forest does not solve those problems. At best it postpones them for a little while; at worst it amplifies them and greatly complicates the search for solutions. Thus the policy of transferring hundreds of thousands from the Brazilian north-east to the Amazon was conceived not to relieve the situation of the poverty-stricken landless, but to avoid the redistribution of resources through land reform and the investment in support services that would have been required to help them where they were. The north-east was and is overpopulated in the sense that, under the existing land ownership, distribution and cropping systems, and with many of its soils badly degraded, it cannot feed the people who live there. The opening up of the Amazon has done nothing to solve the problems of the north-east; and it has generated new problems in the Amazon which in the long term will be even more difficult to resolve.

Similarly, Indonesia's grandiose transmigration programmes are always presented as schemes to relieve the intense pressure on the land in overpopulated Java and Bali by developing the thinly populated outer islands and the underdeveloped parts of Sumatra. The outer islands include West Papua (formerly Dutch, then occupied by Indonesia whose sovereignty was confirmed by a dubious UN plebiscite) and Timor (unlawfully occupied when the Portuguese regime collapsed). The transmigration schemes (heavily dependent on World Bank support) have in fact a multiple aim. They seek to evade land reform in the main islands, where there is uneven distribution of landownership and growing numbers of landless; they seek to relieve overcrowded prisons by shipping out of harm's way thousands of criminals, petty delinquents, and people deemed potentially subversive; they seek to extend Indonesian settlement and assure political and military domination of territories newly acquired or conquered; and they seek to stamp out any resistance or impediment to this last objective.

So far as most of the lands on which the migrants are dumped are concerned, the very fact that they have not been commandeered in earlier times by the colonial powers is already an indication that they are inferior for most forms of agriculture. The sparse population, the scattered settlements, and the 'primitive' cultures of the indigenes (for example, of the Dayaks in Kalimantan and of the Asmats in West Papua) represent adaptations to the poverty of the soils. Only rarely are the transmigrants provided with means to live other than simple tools for land clearance, food to sustain them to the first harvest, and a minimum allocation of seed. And rarely is there prior effort to ascertain whether the land to be cleared lends itself to sustainable agriculture, or how traditional practices of cropping and working the land need to be modified. Most often the migrants are left without support services of any kind. Where the soils are particularly low in fertility, some migrants fail to survive, some carve their way deeper into the forest, and some flee the land and congregate around the urban settlements, while a few succeed in making their way back to the main islands.

Should the land carry any sizeable amount of marketable timber, that may already, in some cases, have been extracted by the loggers. Both loggers and migrants impinge upon, then collide with, the indigenes' interests and means of life. The genocide now proceeding in Indonesia's outer islands and occupied territories is both direct and indirect: direct by military repression, indirect through destruction of habitat.

In most of the countries where substantial areas of TMF remain, the problem is not simply one of too many people: it is that too many people are being obliged to wrest a living from poor soils while elsewhere large areas of land lie unused, underused, or wrongly used. The pressure on the forests stems from the unwillingness of those holding power to pursue policies which accord a more equal access to land and water resources and accord priority to crops which ensure that their own people are fed.

Governments which treat the tropical forest as a land bank, and which sponsor transmigration or settlement schemes as a means of evading the demands of the landless for a more equitable distribution of resources, are responsible for contemporary tropical forest destruction. In the longer term, some existing tropical forest should and must be converted to farm land. Until such governments carry out the land reforms to which so many of them are pledged, that conversion will be grossly excessive, irresponsible, irrational and piecemeal. But in the process the tropical forests will disappear. Land reform would win the time needed to conduct the research, experimentation and demonstration that will enable sustainable agricultural and agroforestry systems to be established on soils presently carrying tropical forest.

Meanwhile, there are millions now living on the edge of famine in tropical countries that once were well forested but from which the forests have now virtually disappeared: in south Asia, for example, and in some of the countries of Central America and the Caribbean. Bangladesh typifies the former, Haiti the latter. Though climatically very different, in both forest depletion has led to declining fertility, either through heavy soil erosion or failure to retain river-borne silt. In both, the process has been accelerated by the heavily skewed distribution of land. In both, any hope of rendering the land capable of growing enough food to support its people at a minimum level will require much more than agrarian reform and family planning campaigns. In these countries, as in so many of the drier tropical forested countries, the most urgent 'development' task is to stop matters getting worse. Haiti will continue to lose its surplus population by starvation or by boat until programmes aimed at land rehabilitation and countering soil erosion are well advanced; tree planting will form an essential part of these schemes. But no land rehabilitation programmes can succeed without land redistribution. Similarly, famines will recur in Bangladesh without tree planting for flood control, for fuelwood supply, and for integrating food and fodder trees into small-scale cultivation farming. But a precondition of these measures being effective is that the rural landless and the small peasants have an enduring stake in the land.

Deforestation and genocide

We have seen that it is social relations, not simply the pressure of numbers, which is destroying the tropical forests. These same processes are bringing about the genocide of indigenous forest dwellers.

Today there are few remaining areas of tropical forest without some human presence. Where humans exist as scattered groups of palaeolithic hunter–gatherers or primitive societies of itinerant gardeners, they can be regarded as part and parcel of the ecosystem within which they live. If they are left alone, if they are given sufficient space, their impact on the forest is negligible. It would be nonsense to demand that they should be swept out of the forest, even from the standpoint of ensuring that tropical forest genetic resources be preserved.

But cases where indigenous forest dwellers have remained immune from exogenous influences are now very rare indeed. The examples given in Part III showed that the numbers of these peoples are now in rapid decline because of new pressures on the space they occupy, pressures which are the consequence of government policies. In countries where large areas of cultivable land lie unused or underused, it would seem reasonable to earmark and reserve to them sufficient tropical forest for their needs. But it is in those same countries that the rural landless are pushed into the forest and into direct collision with more primitive forest dwellers.

Several organizations, including Survival International, have campaigned on behalf of these people in recent years, and some tribes have discovered their own voices. But it is as difficult for sympathetic outsiders to formulate their demands as it is for them to reach a consensus among themselves. Obviously, there are certain aspects of their present way of life which many forest dwellers want to retain. But few of them wish to remain as living museums or field stations for anthropologists, still less to reject all material benefits which come from outside. Most of those who still survive accept that in the long run they will have to adapt to new ways of living. Meanwhile, they object to being chased from what they regard as their land.

A genuine land reform may assuage land hunger; it will not necessarily eradicate it. But if priority is given to satisfying domestic food needs, if methods of increasing yields from the land are worked out and demonstrated, if peasants are given sufficient incentives in terms of crop prices and goods available for purchase, the urgency of bringing more land under the plough can be deferred. That means that more time is available for indigenous hunter–gatherers or shifting cultivators to be won to a more settled existence.

Can international action save the tropical forests?

The history of efforts to halt the shrinkage of the tropical forest by intergovernmental action goes back nearly two decades. Though each step has been hailed by conservationists as marking a positive response to their widening campaign, that history can more fairly be described as a series of loudly trumpeted non-events. Some of the problems involved are illustrated by two of the most recent initiatives – the formation of the International Tropical Timber Organization (ITTO) and the launching of the World Tropical Forest Action Plan.

The latter, drawn up by the World Resources Institute in collaboration with a number of international agencies including the World Bank, has been described by Catherine Caufield, writing in the *New Scientist*, as a 'jet set' environmentalist's solution to the tropical forest problem which fails to take account of the interests of those who live in and near the forests. The plan seeks to double current spending on creating timber and fuelwood plantations, planting trees to bind eroded hillsides and encouraging local people in the tropics to farm in a way that does not destroy their environment. Desirable objectives, it would seem. But current expenditure on anti-erosion planting and on helping local people is negligible. And the latter objective becomes meaningless unless the circumstances which oblige local people to destroy their environment are understood, and measures are taken to change them.

One of the ideas under discussion is that a fund should be set up to compensate governments which agree to set aside and maintain specific areas of tropical forest, the compensation being related to estimated revenues forgone. It would be irresponsible to allocate such funds without obtaining guarantees that the reserved forests would be open to full and free inspection at all times by members of an independent international panel. Without the controls, an offer of compensation against desisting from logging is, in most of these countries, more likely to get logging operations started in new areas (to increase compensation claims) than to leave presently unlogged forests intact.

As for the ITTO, the bickering and jockeying which marked its gestation are clear indications that neither the governments of countries possessing tropical forests nor the governments of rich countries with a stake in those forests are yet prepared to overrule short-term and sectional interests. Governments of the importing countries still sniff an OPEC-type conspiracy which might enable exporting countries, acting in concert, to raise prices. This fear is utterly misplaced, since the commodity – tropical hardwood – is far too heterogeneous in form, quality and use to lend itself to traditional commodity control measures.

Nor is there as yet any disposition on the part of the timber-growing countries to act in concert. Some are still desperate to lure foreign investors in order to get the logs rolling out, to earn foreign exchange, an imperative partly imposed by the debt crisis and the constant worsening of the terms of trade of the primary producers. Other countries now have wood processing plants, and are exporting tropical sawnwood, plywood and veneers. They want to restrict log supplies to competing foreign processors, including Third World in-transit processors: sawmills and plywood plants set up (often with the participation of Western capital) in such low-wage countries as South Korea and Taiwan. Thus, quite apart from the seedy background to the tropical hardwood trade described earlier, there persist conflicts of interest among the Third World countries.

But by far and away the greatest impediment to efforts to save the tropical forest is an unwillingness on the part of governments, both inside and outside the tropics, to recognize the socio-economic and political factors which are bringing about tropical forest destruction. The pity of it is that this unwillingness is shared by so many conservationists who are vigorously campaigning to save the forests. Inside the tropical forested countries those organizations and movements (some of them necessarily clandestine) which are battling with their governments to win sound natural resource policies do recognize the political implications of their struggle. Conservationists outside such countries should seriously consider whether the initiatives they take are likely to encourage and strengthen such movements. Some past initiatives have simply provided reactionary governments with window-dressing.

Conservationists should also ask themselves why their campaign has suddenly, in the last few years, aroused the interest of governments of some industrialized countries, in particular that of the USA. Is it because those governments fear the rise in atmospheric carbon? Is it because they dread the extinction of the monkey-eating eagle or some rare butterfly? Hardly. As their official reports make clear, they have woken up to the fact that shrinking forests mean shrinking tropical wood exports which in turn mean declining Third World economies which in turn mean shrinking markets for First World exports. The United States, for example, exports more to tropical forested countries than it does to the whole of Europe, East and West. They have also realized that their giant pharmaceutical industries depend heavily on materials emanating from the tropical forest.

The net effect has been to cause the US government to adopt a conservationist stance. But the detailed practice of US policy is most frequently to obstruct or torpedo measures which could have real effect. Exactly the same applies to the governments of other leading industrialized countries – Japan, for example. The lesson for conservationists is that it is not sufficient to bombard governments to the point at which they feel obliged to don conservationist clothes. It is necessary to observe closely their every action, examine the implications of those actions, and call the governments to account when (as has so frequently happened in the short history of the ITTO and the World Tropical Forest Action Plan) their deeds betray their words.

The very success of the conservationists in arousing governmental interest has brought about confusion, a lack of clarity about which tropical forests should be saved, how much, and for what reason.

Take, for example, the gene reservoir argument. It would be unreasonable to call for the preservation of a sufficient area of at least one example of each of the many different ecosystems which go to make up the tropical forests. Nor would that guarantee that none of the so far uninvestigated species of flora and fauna will disappear before it has been catalogued and its potential value appraised. Firstly, there are far too many different ecosystems, even though the differences between some of them may seem slight. Secondly, no ecosystem is static; each one is in a state of continuous evolution, with species becoming extinct and new species evolving all the time. Thirdly, the interdependence of species within any single ecosystem is so little understood that there are no generally accepted notions of the minimum size of reserve that would be needed to ensure the survival of particular species. Experts of the International Union for the Conservation of Nature (IUCN) have nominated a number of forest zones which should be considered as having priority for the establishment of forest reserves. Their listing represents a compromise between scientific best guesses and what they deem politically feasible.

First World government interest also reflects anxiety about future supplies of tropical timber. That is why plantations represent an important component of the World Tropical Forest Action Plan. But determining the areas needed to assure future supplies is an even more complex quantitative conundrum. How much the First World will need to import depends on price. Only a rise in the price of tropical hardwoods, together with a willingness to plough back into management a far higher proportion of income from timber, can make it possible to manage the forests on a sustainable basis. If a small proportion of existing forest were converted to artificial forest, to plantations of selected, faster-growing species, this would enable future timber needs to be met while avoiding the need to exploit the remaining unlogged forest. A few figures serve to illustrate this argument. Rational management and relatively simple silvicultural operations in TMF can treble the yield of merchantable timber, to about $6m^3$/ha per year. Enrichment planting (planting saplings of superior species in cleared spaces) can raise this figure to 10. Some dipterocarp forests, properly managed, can yield 15. On the same soils, however, plantations can provide yields of up to 35 for some hardwood species, 45 for tropical pines, and as much as $60m^3$/ha per year for some eucalypts.

These figures have persuaded many that the sensible thing to do would be to convert to plantations just enough tropical forest to cover future timber needs, and leave the rest alone. But this assumes that it is the demand for industrial wood which is the principal cause of deforestation–an assumption which we have shown to be false. The World Tropical Forest Action Plan plainly hopes that by sponsoring plantations in the tropics pressure on the remaining natural forest will be relieved. But such hopes are unlikely to be realized. Plantation-grown wood can replace that from the natural forest only within limits, even of the same species; the physical characteristics, and hence possible uses, are very different. Financial support for plantations is unlikely to guarantee either reservation of, or sustainable management in, the natural forest. In any case, plantations can never provide, to the same extent and for the same people, the wide range of goods and services other than merchantable timber which natural forests provide.

The history of what has happened in the tropical forests since World War II should have demonstrated to conservationists the futility of pressing on Third World countries the 'custodianship' argument. Governments which show utter contempt for either the short- or long-term interests of their own people will not respond to such exhortation. They will respond only to external pressures which threaten their political survival; only then will they conform to prescribed standards. The standards to which they are presently being asked to conform, as set by the richer 'donor' countries and by the international agencies which go to make up the development establishment, have the effect of deepening the rift between governments and the people they are supposed to represent. They seldom threaten the political survival of unrepresentative governments.

The battle to save the tropical forests lies not only in the tropical countries. In the First World too the battle must be engaged. It is the support of First World countries which keeps in existence those Third World regimes whose resource-destructive policies are responsible for contemporary tropical deforestation.

24   The road to famine

In the previous chapter we saw that in many parts of the tropics the moist forest shades off into somewhat drier, deciduous tropical forest, often with a substantial canopy, but subject to longer annual dry periods. Elsewhere in the tropics this gives way to more open forest, often interspersed with grass, sometimes known as savannah forest. It is possible to imagine a continuum along which the forest cover steadily changes under successively drier conditions. At the wet end are the evergreen tropical rainforests. Towards the drier end, there are dry open forests, shading off into scrubland, and finally quasi-desert. If it were possible to move along this continuum, it would be difficult to find the exact point at which, say, open forest ended and scrubland began. The destinction is as blurred on the ground as it is in the statistics. But the truly alarming thing is that throughout this continuum there is today, under the influence of a variety of pressures, a downward, degrading thrust. Chapter 23 explained the nature of these pressures in countries (mostly in the Third World) at the wetter end of the tropical forest spectrum. This chapter discusses the kind of pressures which have been operating, and which continue to operate, in other Third World countries, including those from which the dry open forest and scrubland is fast disappearing and which already have substantial areas which are completely treeless.

'As blurred as in the statistics': the definition of forest has changed from time to time and different countries are not consistent in compiling their statistics. There is now, however, a broad definition on which a number of experts have agreed, and this was discussed in chapter 14 and used to present an overview of the world's forest. (In brief, this definition regards forest as consisting of closed forest and other wooded land. Closed forest includes all land which is more than 20 per cent covered by tree crowns, and which is used primarily for forestry. Other wooded land 'has some forestry characteristics, but is not closed forest': it includes open woodland (with tree crowns covering 5–20 per cent of the area), windbreaks, shelter belts or small isolated groups of trees, together with scrub and brushland (land with shrubs or stunted trees covering more than about 20 per cent of the area).

Obviously the definition of closed forest is itself rather shadowy. In effect, it means all land which is mainly used for forestry purposes, where forestry is broadly defined as activities related to the production of wood and other goods and services of the forest. Even so, it is much better than some earlier definitions of forest, which focused only on the production of wood for industry. They failed to take account of the very different kinds of forest met with, and very different uses of trees made by people, in parts of the world other than Europe and North America. Some of these uses were discussed in the first part of this book.

There are in the tropics, apart from the drier closed forest, over 1500 million ha of open forest and scrubland. In these areas many people are dependent for their livelihood on such forest and scrub as remains; it is here that the forest is shrinking or being degraded most quickly; and it is here that famine is a constant threat. The dry end of the forest spectrum is the one most in danger. The dry open forests in the tropics are disappearing at the rate of 4 million ha/year. As the forests go, the other vegetative cover is reduced, the soils are exposed to erosion by wind and by water. Much of the arid and semi-arid land on which over 600 million people now live is already treeless; the rest – even that which still falls under the somewhat generous definition of forest cited above – is rapidly becoming so. Almost everywhere in the drier tropical forests a cumulative downward spiral of deforestation, devegetation and land degradation is at work.

In the countries at the drier end of the forest spectrum and in those which lie even further along it, consisting largely of marginal lands, the precarious balance that once existed between the uses of 'forest' land for fuel, for food crops, for grazing and for protection from wind and water erosion is today breaking down. Dozens of countries which only a few decades ago could produce enough food to feed all their own people (including their non-food-producing classes and urban populations) can no longer do so. This is not simply because numbers have multiplied, creating extra pressure on the land, but because exogenous factors have had the effect of suddenly disrupting those previous balances in land use – balances arrived at through a slow process of adjustment.

The lands with which this chapter is concerned are not synonymous with desert, or even simply with arid and semi-arid lands. Deserts have become newsworthy. In 1977 the United Nations organized the first-ever World Conference on Desertification. The Conference drew attention to the rate at which deserts are spreading, discussed some of the causes, and drew up a programme to halt the march of the deserts.

But though desertification is a graphic term, it is not a particularly useful one. The picture of the desert which most people carry in their minds is of a vast expanse of sand, stones, and rocky outcrops where little or nothing lives and grows: the Kalahari, the Gobi, the Sahara; they may also have seen pictures of the Sonora desert in Mexico, stretching across into the south-west United States, and the deserts of central Australia. Though the fact is not widely known, similar pictures have been taken in Antarctica. There are areas on the Antarctic continent which are arid; no ice or snow, simply dry rock and sand. What is now the Antarctic broke away from the rest of the earth's land mass before the human species evolved: the Antarctic desert is the consequence solely of climatic influences.

This chapter is instead concerned with a process now widespread: land degradation, not confined to, although most conspicuous in, areas where rainfall is very variable and unreliable. To understand the process we must consider what is actually involved when land is degraded by losing its vegetation cover. The capacity of land to support plant productivity can be reduced by several different processes.

1 More of that rain which does fall runs off the surface, and less infiltrates to join the store of soil water which plants use;
2 The soil on the surface may be eroded away, either by the flow of water across the surface or through being blown away by the increased wind speed near the ground;

3 The soil's ability to act as a warehouse for water and mineral nutrients may deteriorate, as its organic matter breaks down or is not replaced by continuing inputs of litter and dead roots from the vegetation;
4 Where vegetation is stripped, reduced transpiration can allow water tables to rise; and if the soil has salt at lower depths, the root zone can be salinized;
5 Increased reflectivity of the land surface may lead to fewer thunderstorms forming on humid afternoons;
6 Because there is no plant cover, the rain which does fall tends to be stored in rivers and lakes, rather than being quickly transpired back into the atmosphere by plants. Considered over large areas like the Amazon basin, vegetation clearance could lead to some reduction of rainfall because water is not cycled between atmosphere and earth quickly.

Of these different mechanisms, the ones which might actually lead to reduced rainfall, the last two, have modest effects at most. Stripping the vegetation may have some small effect on regional climate, but in no way can regions which were formerly forested acquire a desert climate, that is to say, have less than 200 mm/year of rain, by loss of trees. In this sense the word 'desertification' is misleading, and 'land degradation' or 'devegetation' are to be preferred.

How easily can degraded land be rehabilitated? The answer depends on the soil because even when vegetation has been stripped, the incoming sunlight and rain, the other factors of plant production besides the soil, remain in place. As soil varies so much from place to place, the question has to be answered by looking at the specifics of each particular case. Thus, on some lands a surface layer only a few centimetres thick holds most of the mineral nutrients. When this has been stripped by wind or water, seedlings can only be established on the exposed surface with great difficulty and intensive care. Other lands have fertile earth hundreds of metres thick. Erosion on these lands is certainly to be avoided, but revegetating their eroded surfaces is comparatively easy. Where salt has been brought into the root zone, removing it will be difficult and will depend on establishing plants which can tolerate the salinity. Similarly, where there is moving sand, the plants which are needed to stop the sands from moving at the beginning will be different from those which flourish best once the land surface has been stabilized.

The downward spiral

The reasons for land degradation are well enough known. They all involve mismanagement of land and water: wrong farming methods, wrong crops, misuse of water, overuse of land, overgrazing. The most advertised crisis is that in sub-Saharan Africa, where food production, not only per head but per hectare, has declined since about 1960. The process had started already in colonial times, and was akin to those triggered off by the British in British India. The better lands were turned over to export crops such as cotton and peanuts. Some export agriculture led to soil loss and soil degradation in so far as it left the soil exposed for longer periods than did indigenous agriculture. Meanwhile small farmers were pushed on to drier lands, to lands less fertile, lands capable of supporting the staple food crops (such as sorghum and millet) only if allowed to lie fallow long enough to let the soil recover and its humus content rebuild. As crop yields fall to near zero, peasant farmers inevitably invade the semi-arid pastures, the range lands of nomadic herdsmen, with their cattle, sheep, goats and camels. The pastoralists find their range restricted, and their situation has been rendered worse, not better, by development aid. The emphasis on sinking tube wells and promoting animal health has led to larger herds. The concentration of herds around wells, and more wells, means more and larger circles of destruction. Any shortage of rain intensifies overgrazing of the dry natural pasture, turning the land to dust.

There is a certain irony in the fact that, although human ancestors evolved in Africa, it is not African animals but animals domesticated elsewhere and brought in by Neolithic peoples entering Africa some 7000 years ago which are today turning soil to sand.

The numerous species of herbivores which today range the savannah lands of southern and eastern Africa once ranged the plains of north Africa. The Sahara is now desert, but parts of it were once sufficiently well watered to support crocodiles and hippopotamuses as well as giraffes, eland, and an immense variety of herbivores and their predators. Moreover, there were men and women around at the time; they have left drawings of these creatures in caves in the midst of the Sahara. Almost everywhere in the Sahara it is possible to come across pieces of petrified wood.

Animal husbandry, as well as crop cultivation, originated in and spread from the Fertile Crescent. The animals domesticated included sheep, horses, pigs, goats, cattle and dogs. These animals, and methods of managing them, spread from the Middle East to Egypt and to the Horn of Africa, and then across Africa westward through the belt of sub-Saharan countries which today compose the Sahel. It is possible that cattle also reached West Africa through a north–south corridor across the Sahara during a moister period 5000 years ago. But it was the Bantu peoples who subsequently carried farming and herding practices southward throughout Africa.

The Sahara had already largely dried up in historic times, but it was rendered passable by the camel, domesticated in Arabia and reaching Egypt about 600 BC. For centuries there were regular trade caravans of

Figure 24.1 Near a *manyatta* in Uganda. Goats are one of the main agents of overgrazing and soil erosion (photo R. A. Plumtre, Oxford Forestry Institute)

camels crossing the Sahara from north to south as well as east to west. Timbuctu was once one of the greatest trading centres in the world. There goods brought by camel caravans from the Mediterranean, the Near East, and even Asia, were traded for the gold and textiles of the early and rich African kingdoms. Today Timbuctu is a decayed desert town. The Sahara is extending in area by 15 000 km^2 every year.

The drought in the Sahelian belt of 1968 to 1973 was not the first of its kind. There had been at least two similar droughts earlier in the twentieth century, but in the most recent perhaps as many as 250 000 people died and another million were left without land or animals. Yet throughout this period the Sahelian countries, in aggregate, had an excess of agricultural exports over agricultural imports. It was not the drought which caused famine; it was misguided policies, embracing misuse of land and water resources and rendering poor peasants and herdsmen vulnerable, which turned drought into catastrophe.

After the crisis of the early 1970s the governments of the Sahelian countries and of the principal aid-giving countries, together with the international agencies, resolved to concentrate on attaining food self-sufficiency by improving rainfed agriculture. In fact more than a quarter of all official aid in recent years has gone into sub-Saharan Africa, although that region accounts for but a few per cent of the Third World population. But of the estimated US$7.5 billion pumped into this region as aid between 1975 and 1980, less than a quarter went into agriculture and forestry. Of the 8 per cent which went into rainfed cropping, most was devoted to promoting export cash crops.

It is not only in the Sahelian countries of Africa that famine has struck and is poised to strike again. Nor is it only colonialism and the continuation of its policies by newly independent governments which are responsible for the present state of affairs. When the feudal regime of Haile Selassie was overthrown in 1975, the new government of Ethiopia enforced land redistribution and encouraged peasant associations and production cooperatives. But so intense and ruthless was the exploitation of Ethiopian peasants by powerful landlords during preceding decades that the soils of the highland plateau were already largely ruined. Without security of tenure, and burdened by heavy taxation, farmers had little incentive to invest in land improvement or maintenance. Rapid deforestation had brought forest cover down to 7 per cent. Natural pastures were overgrazed by some 17 million head of livestock – the biggest herd of any African country.

The revolutionary government is aware of the technical measures required if the downward spiral is to be halted and reversed. But both its aims and its methods have fallen under suspicion. Its plans call for progressive resettlement of hundreds of thousands of families from the eroded lands of the north to the relatively unpopulated south and west. Some governments and organizations which provided relief at the height of the famine suspect that the death toll in Ethiopia would have been much lower had the government not blocked aid to Eritrea and Tigre, regions mainly controlled by those battling for independence or autonomy.

It is reported that some, at least, of the resettlement projects are succeeding: that they have sufficient material inputs and institutional support to enable new land to be brought under cultivation. But large-scale resettlement cannot solve Ethiopia's problems. Building and maintaining terraces to retain moisture, tree planting for soil holding, for fodder, for fuel, gradual restoration of the nutrient cycle; all these call for high labour inputs, not least from the women. These are forthcoming only if peasants are convinced that these efforts will bring quick and identifiable improvements in their own material situation. There is no reason to suppose that this will be the result of large-scale resettlement. Outside observers have not as yet noted any increase in productivity in the producer cooperatives, and we can assume that when peasants are described as lazy they have not yet been provided with sufficient incentive.

There are areas in countries of eastern and southern Africa which share with Ethiopia and the Sahelian countries the decline in output per hectare. It is African countries, more than countries in any other region, which will bear the brunt of the approaching fuel famine.

Figure 24.2 A charcoal wholesaler's yard in Mali. The impact of the urban demand for charcoal reaches as far as the distant countryside (copyright Jeremy Hartley/OXFAM)

In nearly all African countries, as in much of the Third World, all rural people and a considerable proportion of urban people depend on wood for energy: for heating, cooking, food processing, rural industries, and so on. FAO estimated that in 1980 in the world as a whole 100 million rural people suffered from acute scarcity of fuelwood: even with continued overcutting, minimum needs were not being met. Another 1000 million rural people were meeting minimum needs only by overcutting existing resources. By the year 2000, it was estimated, if nothing is done, 2250 million rural people will be 'involved in fuelwood deficit situations'. What this means is that most of them will have to reduce their already meagre food intake in order to purchase the fuelwood or charcoal they need to cook their food. Overexploitation for fuelwood concerns mainly the open and dry forests and scrubland, particularly along roads and within range of towns, but as in India and Thailand, it also cuts into the closed forests.

This dependence on wood for fuel, which characterizes so much of the Third World, means that wood and scrub are disappearing from an ever-increasing circle around each urban centre. It also means that animal dung and agricultural residues which should be restored to the land to maintain fertility are burned instead. Rural people, usually the women, spend more

Figure 24.3 Deforestation, here the result of burning trees to clear land and cutting them down for firewood; Yako to Koudougou, Burkino Faso, 1985 (copyright Jeremy Hartley/OXFAM)

and more time locating and carrying wood. Urban people have to spend more on wood and charcoal and therefore less on food.

Gone with the wind

Soil loss, land degradation and desertification are not confined to Africa, nor to the tropics. Top of the world tree-planting league today is China, the country which perhaps more than any other has experienced these phenomena in the past. Modern China's tree planting has a precedent. The greatest empire the world has ever known, that of Genghis Khan,

Figure 24.4 Nine-year-old eucalypt plantation in Lesotho, used as a woodlot for fuelwood (WFP photo by F. Mattioli, 1982/FAO)

extended from the China Sea across Asia to Moscow and the Mediterranean. His thirteenth-century dominion was controlled by a communications network of staging points marked out by trees. His capital, Karakhoram, now lies under the desert sand. The fate of vulnerable soils is well demonstrated by the contrast between the Peoples Republic of Mongolia (PRM), and Inner Mongolia, part of China. Both lie north of the Great Wall built to keep out invading Mongol nomadic herders, yet desertification has gone further in Inner Mongolia than in the PRM. Both have a continental climate with low precipitation, and both summer and winter grazing are available, though the land will carry far fewer animals in winter.

The cause of rapid land degradation in Inner Mongolia was the passage, from south of the Wall, of landless Hans, driven north by hunger and oppression. Today these outnumber Mongols six to one in Inner Mongolia's population of about 18 million. The lands on which the Han settled are not suitable for the kind of farming they were accustomed to: when the land is tilled and left bare, the thin light soils are blown away by the violent winds. Though grazing is possible, provided that it is strictly controlled, overgrazing brings bare soil and wind erosion. The process is rapid, and the topsoil can disappear in a couple of years. Until recently the better prices available for bigger animals encouraged overgrazing, so that many animals died in the winter.

The PRM is not yet under such pressures, with nearly 100 ha of land for each Outer Mongolian. However, similar problems lie on the horizon, and the PRM may well benefit from China's current experience, positive and negative. China is endeavouring to convert the nomads to settled farmers, growing fodder crops in the summer to eliminate winter grazing, erecting elaborate networks of shelter belts to check wind erosion, and fixing sand dunes with suitable shrubs followed by tree planting.

In China wind erosion is serious but far less significant than water erosion. The immense effort put into taming China's rivers, described in chapter 18, will need to be sustained for many decades yet.

Historically, wind erosion has probably been as important globally as water erosion in reducing the area of cultivable land. It is not limited to the countries classified as less developed. The 'dust bowl' in the USA, described graphically in Steinbeck's *Grapes of Wrath*, had its echo a few decades later in Krushchev's failure to reckon with the impact of wind on the thin, newly ploughed steppe lands of the USSR. There was something like a precedent on the American continent in the sixteenth century, when the Spaniards, eager to profit from the growing demand for wool in Europe, destroyed forest cover in order to introduce sheep on to the central Mexican plateau. The result was massive erosion.

China's successes – and there have undoubtedly been very significant successes – hold important lessons. One is that to use the term 'point of no return' when speaking of land degradation is unwise. Even in the direst situations, there are lands which can be in some measure rehabilitated – given the appropriate heavy investment, which consists essentially of labour. The problem of harnessing labour to create social capital will be discussed in a later chapter.

China is not alone in successfully rehabilitating degraded land, halting desert spread and reclaiming desert. Even the desert can be made to bloom providing sufficient labour is mobilized for that task or sufficient funds are available to buy the needed labour. Israel's forests are an example of the latter – perhaps the most expensive forests (largely in donated US dollars) ever created. Less well known, but perhaps of greater international significance, are the forests created in Algeria's 'Chantiers Populaires'.

A vast range of techniques are now available for improving and bringing back into use marginal lands in dry zones. All of them involve, at some stage, the deployment of suitable trees. Trees alone will not reclaim the desert, but the desert cannot be reclaimed without them. But in the drier and less forested countries of the Third World, farming itself is usually impossible unless trees in one form or another are an integral part of the farming system. More importantly, there are many lands not now farmed which could be farmed, as well as presently farmed land which could be rendered more productive, if appropriate trees were incorporated into the farming system. This requires, first, a marriage between what farmers have already learned for themselves and the new knowledge which properly directed research could bring them, second, social relations which ensure that the rural people have access to land and incentives to apply innovative methods. In these drier lands, as in the tropical moist forested Third World countries, forestry's most important objective is to support agriculture, to help those countries feed themselves as far as possible.

25   Forests in the rich countries

The two preceding chapters described the part which forests, woodlands and trees play and ought to play in the Third World, both in areas which still have fairly adequate tree cover, and in areas from which trees have already disappeared or are fast disappearing. Nowhere yet are trees making the contribution which they ought to make. As we have seen, one reason for this is that forestry research and teaching have been heavily concentrated on problems special to the First World. Another is that forestry has been unduly restricted to the management of land given over mainly to the growing of trees, with a special emphasis on those which are to provide wood for industry. Does this mean that forestry science copes satisfactorily with forestry problems arising in the rich countries? This chapter draws attention to the way in which these problems are presently changing and points to some new problems now looming.

   Chapter 14 pointed out that in most of the more developed countries of the world the forest area is presently increasing, cited some figures and mentioned some of the reservations which apply to those figures. The forests which survive in the world's more affluent countries – Europe, North America, Japan, Australia and the USSR – are mostly direct descendants of forests which already existed when humans first encountered them. But in nearly every case those forests have been heavily manipulated – that is, altered by people – down the centuries. Examples of 'virgin' forest are extremely rare. In the northern hemisphere there remain some boreal forests in northern Canada, Alaska and the USSR, plus a small area of mixed temperate forest on the Russian-Polish border. All other forests have been not only manipulated; most of them have also been brought under conscious management (not necessarily intensive) for one or more specific purposes. Most often the principal purpose has been for industrial wood production.

Europe

Not all forest has been set aside for industrial wood. Since the relationship between tree cover and the water regime became more clearly understood, larger areas have been designated as protection forests, in which either no felling (save of sick or dying trees) is allowed, or in which the felling of trees for commercial purposes is very rigorously controlled. Similarly, in alpine regions, such as Austria and Switzerland, certain forest areas are reserved as a protection against avalanches. Of Europe's forests today, no less than 26 per cent are classified as primarily protective: their protective role has been deemed to outweigh their function as wood producers. However, this does not mean that all Europe is adequately protected by forests. Even where the protective role of the forest is well understood, the authorities have not always been able to do what is necessary. It is true that the reckless depletion of forests on watersheds and in areas where deforestation could pose a serious threat is now rare. But there are still considerable areas which down the years have been badly eroded as a result of loss of tree cover and overgrazing and which cry out for reafforestation. This is particularly the case in southern Europe, but the governments concerned have not yet succeeded in setting aside the very considerable sums that would be required to assure tree cover (along with other works) adequate to avoid disastrous floods.

To some extent the spread and greater intensity of forest management since the middle of the twentieth century are responses to the acceleration of economic growth in the decades immediately following World War II. The production and consumption of wood and its products rose faster during the 1950s and 1960s than ever before in history. This was not simply the consequence of reconstruction needs consequent upon the war; it was the result of deliberate interventions by the governments of industrialized countries to promote economic growth, expand social welfare, and assure a high level of employment. Growth continued at a slower rate through the 1970s, and slowed down further in the 1980s, concomitantly with the reversal of earlier government policies in some of the principal industrial and trading countries.

The increased consumption of forest products from 1950 to 1980 was made possible by three factors: a rise of 16 per cent in the output of industrial wood from Europe's own forests, from 294 to 341 million m³, a rise in net imports, which in 1980 amounted to the equivalent of 58 million m³; and wood savings on a scale undreamed of in 1950. By 1980 44 million m³ of wood residues were being used industrially (this was wood previously burned or wasted); and waste paper collected and recycled corresponded to the saving of 40 million m³ of pulpwood.

The increase in forest output, and the greater use industrially of wood that was formerly used as fuel, has been brought about by better management and by other advances in forest science. Some of these advances were described in chapter 13. They cover seed selection, soil preparation, planting and tending practices, fertilization, pest control and harvesting methods: the precedents set by agricultural science led to qualitative and quantitative improvements in forest output. Because of the high labour content of wood delivered to the factory, a many-sided development of mechanization sharply reduced the numbers employed in the forests and made their daily work many times safer. In addition, throughout Europe the forest area has been increasing since World War II. Intensive farming has meant that agriculture has become more and more concentrated on the best lands, where such factors as mechanization, improved strains, and increased inputs of fertilizers have led to vast increases in yields. Millions of hectares of agriculturally marginal land in Europe have already gone out of production, and some of this has been planted to forest.

When petroleum prices rose sharply after the formation of OPEC, and with the prospect of extensive areas of unwanted farmland becoming available for forestry, interest was triggered in plantations of fuelwood for industrial energy. All the industrialized countries played with the idea, but Canada and Sweden carried out the most intensive research into the economics of various techniques. Only experimental schemes were launched as the slow-down in economic growth, along with other factors, reversed the trend in petroleum prices. But there are now plenty of blueprints ready on the shelf against the day when wood becomes economically feasible as an industrial energy source. It would be an ironic commentary on history if parts of southern England were once again to supply native hardwoods grown on the coppicing system to fuel industry as they did in Roman times.

Europe has so far been referred to as if it were a fairly uniform entity. It is not. The expanded output of recent decades has come about mainly in the well-forested Nordic countries, intent on maintaining their traditional exports of wood and its products, and in the countries of western and central Europe. There is still ample scope for raising output in southern Europe, both through improved management and afforestation.

In spite of the remarkable expansion in Europe's output of industrial wood, the growth in consumption has been such that Europe remains a timber deficit region, depending on imports of forest products from overseas more heavily than ever. Although a variety of scenarios have been advanced for the evolution of the European economy and its wood needs over the forthcoming decades, none of them suggests that its need for imports from other regions will diminish.

In the 1970s Europe's forests were in better shape than they had been for a century or so. Until recently most countries were optimistic in their predictions of future forest output. Now, there is some room for doubt whether the improvement so far registered can be maintained. The uncertainty stems from the widening impact of acid rain. Because this problem is not restricted to Europe it is discussed later in this chapter. But it is a phenomenon which to date has affected Europe more than any other region. Its full implications are not yet understood.

The USSR

The most extensive forest resource in the Northern hemisphere lies in the USSR, whose forests and other wooded land cover 930 million ha, or 42 per cent of its land area. Of these forests, 535 million ha are considered exploitable. For the most part, however, Russia's forests are slow growing and many of them are still difficult to reach. Furthermore, whereas 75 per cent of Russia's population lies west of the Urals, 80 per cent of its forest resources lie east of the Urals, in Siberia.

The USSR has always been an important supplier of wood to Europe, and exports have until quite recently mainly emanated from European Russia. Soviet exports are important on the world market, but they represent only a small fraction of the nation's total production: 7 per cent of sawnwood, panels and pulp output, and but 1 per cent of paper production. Because the USSR is itself a high wood consumer, and given the distribution of population, there is considerable pressure on the forests of the European part of the USSR and southern Siberia. Observers have long assumed that the European forests in Russia were being seriously overcut, and that the quantities available for export would diminish. So far exports have been maintained. It is very possible that earlier forest inventories underestimated the extent of European Russian resource; but there has been a marked movement of forest activities eastwards and northwards. However, this shift means opening up forests of lower quality, and involves longer transport distances and climatically harsher working conditions. It also involves, as experience to date has demonstrated, much heavier investment, direct and indirect, than had been foreseen. That is why Soviet forest policy is shifting towards reducing harvesting losses, improving wood utilization, and intensifying management in order to raise output in the more accessible areas. During the 1980s the forest resources of the Soviet Far East have been opened up for export, with technical and capital support from the prospective clients, especially Japan.

The Soviet forest resource is better described as plentiful rather than rich. Its distribution presents problems, given the great distances involved in transportation to the principal centres of consumption. On the whole the protective, recreation, amenity and scientific roles of the forest are well understood. However, with the emergence of independent environmental associations since Gorbachev assumed power in 1985 there have been collisions between forest production interests and environmentalists, for example over the effects of pulp and paper industries on Lake Baikal and its fragile ecosystems. Some forest damage from airborne pollutants has also been reported, but the scale of damage is apparently less serious than in Europe.

North America

Canada and the USA have approximately the same area of forest considered commercially exploitable: Canada just over 200 million ha, the USA just under. But whereas nearly all Canadian forests are publicly owned (91 per cent), and the forest industries largely export-oriented, 75 per cent of US forests are in private hands, and the forest industries are mainly directed to the vast domestic market. In fact, the United States is the world's largest producer of all wood products except sawn softwood, in which it ranks second to the USSR. US forests are both more varied and more productive than those of Canada. Although the forests of each country contain roughly the same volume of standing timber, the annual increment in the USA is about twice that north of the border: around 600 million m^3 against 300.

Both countries have considerable potential for raising output. However, the problems they face are very different. Of the US forests, 28 million ha already belong to forest industries, 47 million to farmers, and 66 million to other private owners. Thus the future of US forests depends to a large extent on how far federal and state governments are willing and able to persuade private owners to manage their forests properly. Generally speaking, to date there has been less disposition to put pressure on private owners than in European countries faced with the same problem. Some forest industries have taken vigorous steps to promote tree farming and forest improvement among small private owners in order to assure their future raw material supplies. Though the most impressive forests are the old-growth forests of the Pacific coast (mostly publicly owned), conditions for growing wood and extracting it cheaply are more favourable in the southern pine region, and it is here that US forest industries have expanded most rapidly in recent decades.

The richest of Canadian resources also lie in the west, in British Columbia; the immense and largely untapped reserves elsewhere are sparser and of lower quality. There is no reason why Canadian forests should not provide twice and possibly three times as much industrial wood as they do now without prejudicing future supplies. But this would require more intensive management: a reduction in losses from fire, pests and diseases, and in the course of harvesting; the adoption of the technology, already developed in Scandinavia, that will enable them to make best use of smaller dimensions; and the opening up of new areas. All these measures require enhanced investment. The road ahead is seemingly clear and well understood, but Canadian forestry is based on a major structural weakness: it is heavily dependent on exports, and in particular on exports

Figure 25.1 Second-growth deciduous forest in Maryland, eastern USA, in winter. In the second half of the nineteenth century, cheaper and more abundant cereals became available as the prairies were ploughed up; in consequence wide areas of the eastern seaboard previously cleared for farmland were abandoned. Regrowth forest on these abandoned farmlands occupies large areas of the eastern USA (photo B. L. Rice, 1968)

to its southern neighbour. Of Canadian wood products, 65 per cent of its sawnwood, nearly 60 per cent of its chemical wood pulp, and 90 per cent of its newsprint are exported. Of those exports 50 per cent of the pulp, 75 per cent of the sawnwood and 80 per cent of the newsprint go to the USA. Most of the rest goes to Europe and Japan. Any slump in these importing countries has a disproportionate impact on their imports of Canada's wood products. It should be observed also that a substantial proportion of the Canadian industries providing these exports are sections of transnationals in which policy control lies abroad.

These facts, together with the faltering state of the world economy in the 1980s and the problems linked to changing currency parities, tend to

Figure 25.2 The coniferous forest of western North America: ponderosa pine, sugar pine and douglas fir along the north fork of the American River, California (photo B. L. Rice, 1968)

inhibit the investment in improving forest resources that many Canadians deem necessary.

Japan

Japan has perhaps the longest continuous tradition of tree planting. All who have visited that country know that Japan is *par excellence* a 'wood culture'. Long before Japan became subject to Western influences, successive national and local rulers had not only encouraged but insisted on tree planting, variously making use of forced labour and offering commercial incentives. As early as the seventeenth century the Japanese forests were excessively exploited for construction material, fuelwood and monumental construction such as palaces, temples, and shrines. Overuse led to fuel and timber shortages, and also to soil erosion, silting, flooding, and the ruin of irrigation systems. It was these latter effects which led to afforestation and protection forestry early in the seventeenth century, based on earlier Chinese 'management of mountains and waters' policies. But from mid-century on, both timber harvesting and wood use were controlled, and afforestation addressed also to wood production. In the following centuries the rate of reafforestation waxed and waned, the lead being taken at different times by national and local authorities, by entrepreneurs, and by local cooperatives, but planting never ceased.

The consequence is that Japan is now easily the most wooded of all industrialized countries, with 68 per cent of its land area under tree cover. However, the fuel revolution of the 1950s, which brought a large-scale switch from charcoal to oil and petrol, meant that thousands of small mountain village communities were deprived of their livelihood; the consequence was rural depopulation and drift to the towns. Although the Japanese government spent the equivalent of over US$30 billion during the 1970s to support and stabilize the mountain communities, outmigration only started to fall with the slow-down in Japan's economic growth in the early 1980s. Today Japan, by virtue of its tradition and customs, and of its rapid growth in national wealth since World War II, is one of the world's highest per caput consumers of wood. Whereas in the mid-1960s 74 per cent of that wood came from Japan's own forests, at the time of writing this proportion has fallen to 31 per cent. Between 1965 and 1977, total annual consumption of industrial roundwood rose from 67 to 86 million m³. The imported wood came from various sources, and still does: the US west coast, Soviet Sakhalin, New Zealand, Brazil; the imports also included tropical wood – 22 million m³ in 1977. Ever since 1962, more than half of all wood exported from tropical countries has gone to Japan. Meanwhile, Japan's own forests are deteriorating. Foresters have been wringing their hands because low wood prices mean that they cannot profitably carry out the thinning now badly needed. It is price, not conservation, which is the issue. Japan's forest industries are not importing in order to conserve the native forests (in the way that Nazi Germany, for instance, plundered the forests of occupied countries to leave its own intact); they are intent on buying wood as cheaply as possible for its intended purpose, regardless of where it comes from.

Forest death: acid rain

Forststerben – forest death – was first seen on a significant scale in Germany and central Europe in the mid-1970s. The loss of leaves and needles, the withering of shoots, dieback of leaves, needles, twigs and branches, with eventual tree death, had often occurred, but not on this scale. Forest death continues to spread and intensify, and Europe is still the greatest sufferer; it is in Europe that the phenomenon has been most intensely studied. But forests lying close to industrial areas in the USSR, in North America, Australia and in Japan have also been affected in varying degrees, as have forests in China, Mexico and other Third World countries.

It was noted in Part I that trees, like people, get sick, grow old and die. Leaf loss and dieback can result from specific maladies or from various forms of stress: prolonged drought or undue cold, for example. Trees under stress, like weak or underfed people, are prone to pests and diseases. It was some time before German foresters, recognizing that the scale of forest death pointed to something other than natural causes, gave the alert. Some years earlier, Scandinavian foresters had noted excessive dieback in forests together with growing acidity in freshwater lakes. They suspected airborne pollutants, and specifically emissions of sulphur dioxide from electric power plants in Britain.

Their suspicions have proved correct. But Britain is far from being the worst offender in terms of tonnes of sulphur dioxide pumped into the atmosphere. Worst in this respect are Czechoslovakia and the German Democratic Republic, both heavily dependent for energy on surface-mined brown coal or lignite, with a high sulphur content. Both have been less successful than Britain in exporting their acid rain to other countries.

The London smog of 1952, held to be responsible for 4000 deaths, brought curbs on the burning of coal both for domestic use and for power in Britain. All new coal-burning electric stations had to be situated outside urban areas; their gaseous emissions had to be discharged from tall chimneys. The upshot was that thick fogs ended in London and Britain's air became cleaner, but most of the 5 million tonnes or so of sulphur dioxide discharged annually from Britain's power plants was now carried away by prevailing winds, part to be discharged on northern Europe's forests and lakes.

Acid rain is certainly responsible, directly or indirectly, for the blighted state of many areas of forest in Europe today. In 1985 it was estimated that in ten European countries with known damage attributable to air pollution, some 7 million ha of forest had been affected. A quarter of a million ha were already dead or dying and a further 1.7 million ha had suffered moderate damage. By far the worst sufferer was the Federal Republic of Germany, with half its forest area affected. There are, of course, other causes of damage to the forest besides airborne pollutants: insects, fire, frost, drought and so on. But the foregoing estimates exclude forest damage attributable to other causes. Current research is discovering which of the pollutants are mainly responsible and how they act: whether through direct impact on the needles and leaves, or through interactions in the soil–root system. It was because definitive answers to all these questions were not forthcoming that the British government argued, against all the weight of circumstantial evidence and the wide consensus among European scientists, that the case against acid rain was 'not proven'. Thus Britain became the exception in Europe, having refused until late 1986 to participate in the common effort to bring down sulphur dioxide emissions by 30 per cent by 1995. Even then the British government went only part way towards meeting the demands of other European nations. The British government's excuse, that factors other than air pollutants can cause tree damage, and that monitoring had not been conducted over a sufficiently long period to single out this as a dominant causal factor, was invalid. Long-term studies of the acidity of soils and lakes in northern Europe have demonstrated that, in the words of a report prepared for the European Forestry Commission: 'There is no doubt that the effort to reduce the exposure of forests to air pollutants must be intensified. Otherwise, European forest sectors, and European society in general, will face large problems in the future which it will be very difficult to solve.'

Besides the direct impact of acid rain (incorporating nitrogen oxides as well as sulphur dioxide) on tree foliage, and its consequent disruption of photosynthesis, chemical changes take place in the acidified soils. Aluminium is released, poisoning the tree, while important nutrients such as calcium and magnesium are washed away. The implication is that whole sites may become incapable of growing trees or certain species of trees.

Acid rain is only part of the story. Ozone is also dangerous to the forest: besides directly damaging plants, it hastens the formation of acid rain. A prime source of ozone is motor vehicle exhausts. It has been estimated that the amount of background ozone close to the ground doubled in Europe over the three decades from 1957. This is why measures to save Europe's forests require not only the suppression of industrial emissions but also control over motor vehicle exhausts.

The impact on soils and water of modern farming methods has already been mentioned. Recent observations suggest that in some parts of Europe nitrogen reaches the soils through fertilizers in such quantities as to saturate them. Nitrogen is essential for plant growth, but too much of it may lead to stress in trees, forcing them to grow when short of nutrients. This may account for some recent unexplained tree deaths observed on farms, while similar trees at roadsides, even though severely subject to exhaust gases, remained unaffected.

The shadow which hangs over the future of Europe's forests will take further research, followed by effective government action, to dispel. But Europe does now have an international agreement on transnational-boundary air pollutants, even if some governments have been laggardly in taking effective action. The problem of facing up to acid rain is likely to prove much more difficult in Third World countries bent on industrialization, given the extra investment necessary to reduce noxious emissions to the minimum. Moreover, the problem for them is

Figure 25.3   Poland: forest dieback caused by a nitrogen fertilizer factory (photo P. S. Savill)

exacerbated by the current trend of transnationals to transfer their polluting industries to Third World countries where industrial standards are lower and controls less effective.

Some idea of the high cost of fighting acid rain has been given by German scientists, who estimate that to clean up the air, to reduce soil and water acidity by vast quantities of limestone, and to add fertilizers and nutrients to forest soils, would cost their country US$25 000 million.

Is there enough wood?

In none of the industrialized areas so far reviewed do there exist insuperable difficulties in the way of raising forest output to meet further rises in wood needs. There is enough land available, and forest science has advanced to the point that enough is known to improve productivity in existing forests and to create new ones. It is true that airborne pollutants pose a new threat, but there is no reason why these should not in due course be identified and curbed.

How far and how fast will wood needs rise? This is anybody's guess. The exceptionally rapid economic growth of the post-war decades (with the concomitant rise in wood consumption) was largely the consequence of economic policies which have now fallen out of favour; no-one can say how soon and to what extent they will be resumed. In addition, these past decades have seen important changes in the pattern and structure of the forest industries, as well as technological advances that could affect wood consumption.

As GNP soared in the industrialized world in the first post-war decades, the consumption of pulp and paper soared even faster, almost invariably outpacing the highest estimates of long-term market trends. This was therefore the period of rapidly expanding capacity, of new technological developments, and of bigger and bigger installations. In chemical pulp making and newsprint manufacture there are huge economies of size. With investments in individual plants reaching hundreds of millions of dollars, capital charges weigh heavily in production costs. So much so that the difference in capital costs per tonne of finished product in a new large mill compared with those in a conventionally sized mill meant that the latter became uncompetitive even if it were to operate on free wood. In fact, many old mills closed down; others were able to keep going only because they had already written off their capital costs.

Because it can take up to five years between first planning a new large forest industry complex and the time the end product finally comes on the market, it was inevitable that there were times when world-wide installed capacity exceeded demand, even though demand was steadily rising. This is one reason why as much energy and ingenuity were spent on devising new products and new uses for pulp and its products as was spent on reducing production costs. This is what spurred the distribution revolution mentioned earlier. This is why those who live in the industrialized world flounder in a sea of paper which they do not want: junk mail, newspapers padded out by adverts and non-news; unnecessarily elaborate packaging. The 'paper plague' was made possible because technology, added to size economies, has kept the rise in the price of paper (alone among wood products) below that of the general level of prices.

Today, with television ubiquitous, with advances in microchip technology, and computers more common than bicycles, a new communications revolution is underway. This has already drastically transformed the economics of newspaper production. It could possibly lead to a decline in per caput paper consumption in the industrialized world – one reason why it is not easy to predict how fast wood needs will rise.

Forest industry complexes of the size which became dominant in the post-war decades require immense supplies of cheap wood. Some public forest owners, to attract industry, granted concessions on the condition that a mill was built and became operational by a specified date. Major North American, European and Japanese firms battled to secure rights to the remaining accessible areas of North American forests in the 1950s and 1960s, especially those in British Columbia and Alaska.

The scramble for cheap wood by forest industry giants has become global. The trend to make use of existing, or to create new, woodyards in the underdeveloped world is accelerating, especially in warm temperate and subtropical areas where wood fibre can be grown much faster. The technological advances which have broadened the raw material base for the pulp and reconstituted wood industries have encouraged the invasion of the tropical forests. It is no longer only those forests yielding a high proportion of high quality saw and veneer logs which are worth exploiting. Any forest which can be logged, chipped, and transported cheaply enough becomes attractive.

Hard on the heels of the global woodyard, forest industry too is becoming global. Though aware of the political and financial risks involved, metropolitan capital is ever more inclined to locate its new factory complexes in the woodyards, at the raw material source. Joint ventures, where possible, are preferred, as they offer a measure of political insurance.

Chapter 3 described some of the factors behind horizontal and vertical integration in the forest products industries: the security and optimum use of raw material, heavy capital investment, an extended range of marketable products and so on. These trends have also been facilitated by the periodic hiccups in the world pulp–paper supply–demand balance. Transnationals, with their readiness to transfer production, to close down existing plants and to build new ones elsewhere, in accordance with wage levels, labour docility, raw material and energy costs, and transport considerations, have expanded in power and size in the forest products industry as in other industrial sectors. This is why, when markets slow down, pulp and paper plants can be closed down overnight by faceless foreign corporations, as even Canada has discovered.

Governments in the rich countries have so far failed to work out and consistently pursue coherent forest policies, with clearly stated objectives. This is partly because, confronted by conflicting interests in the forests, they are hesitant to take decisions and even more hesitant to enter into commitments which, for obvious reasons, should be long term. For example, governments which have traditionally looked upon publicly owned forests as a source of revenue for the exchequer have difficulty in deciding how much should be ploughed back, or what new funds should be invested, in maintaining or building up the forest resource, to limit or reduce future dependence on wood and paper imports. The forest industries are strategic in the sense that many of their products are as essential in war as in peacetime. It may well be that the forest industry capacity deemed strategically minimal may be attracted and established only if sufficient supplies of cheap wood are available. If cheap wood is to be provided it may be necessary to forgo revenues, to subsidize state forestry, and to offer financial or fiscal incentives to private forest owners. Even if the forest is looked upon purely and simply as a woodyard for industry, forestry is a sector where national objectives are unlikely to be achieved if matters are left to the free play of market forces.

Not just a woodyard

Many of the values provided by the forest find inadequate expression or none at all in the market place. This is particularly true of the environmental services rendered by the forest; it was noted, for example, that as much as 25 per cent of Europe's forest was deemed to have protection rather than production as its primary purpose. This is also true of the amenity and recreation services which the forest can provide. The fastest growing demand on the forests in recent decades in nearly all the affluent countries has been for access to them for amenity and recreation purposes. This demand was at first fiercely resisted by many forest owners – in most cases national or provincial authorities – and by professional foresters acting for them. But the pressure has proved so strong that there is now much easier access to the forest even though it is tightly controlled.

People in forests can be a danger, unless they are aware and informed, to the forests and to themselves. At certain seasons in some types of forest the fire hazard is very high indeed. Some of the forests which holidaymakers most enjoy, with cloudless skies and near warm seas, are also unfortunately some of the most dangerous. There are now substantial stretches of the Mediterranean coast backed by dry maquis and scrub forest, or by salt resistant pines planted for dune fixation. Long periods of rainless heat make these wooded areas highly inflammable. Yet some of these areas are now so thickly populated by campers during the summer that they represent major accidents waiting to happen.

There are areas within the forest where the soil can become compacted and the root systems damaged if subject to exceptional pressure, with the result that trees sicken and die. There are, too, seasons when the wildlife of the forest should be subject to minimum disturbance. Yet people can learn these things about forests and trees, and enjoy the forest environment to the full, only if they are admitted and given the opportunity to see, learn and understand. Both public and private forest owners have made efforts, with varying degrees of enthusiasm and success, to allow entry to their forests under conditions which will minimize damage to the forest and maximize compensatory revenue for production forgone. Enlightened public forest authorities provide access and appropriate facilities for different categories of people seeking amenity or recreation in the forest.

Recreation needs differ widely. Some visitors are short-term, simply seeking time in the open air, with or without sophisticated supplementary entertainment. Others are longer-term, and require cabin facilities or spaced camping sites. And there are still others who crave the sensation of true wilderness and are prepared to backpack along indicated trails. 'Wilderness', of course, becomes a misnomer as soon as queues form and entries have to be severely limited.

Another problem is that the kind of forest which people most enjoy is not necessarily the kind which yields the forest owner the maximum profit. In the early years of the UK Forestry Commission, for example, the accent was very much on providing commercial timber as quickly as possible. Indeed, the Commission itself was established for this very purpose after World War I had revealed Britain's vulnerability during wartime through her heavy dependence on imported timber. This is the reason for the large black blocks of exotic conifers which, in the eyes of many nature lovers, now disfigure some of the less populated parts of the British landscape. In the decades since World War II, however, more careful landscape planning, and the discreet inclusion of areas of native broadleaved trees, have gone some way to improving the Commission's image. In addition, the Commission has developed a variety of sport, recreation and holiday facilities which find increasing favour.

In many of the rich countries a more enlightened public has begun to take an interest in surviving indigenous forests for their scientific and cultural value, and as possible repositories for material values as yet undiscovered. Thus a conservationist movement has grown up ready to counter any threat to log such forests or convert them to other use. This pressure has been particularly strong in those affluent countries where there remain areas of the original native forest in relatively undisturbed condition; for example, the rainforests of Queensland and Tasmania and the native beech forests in New Zealand. Conservationists have also resisted attempts to create new forests on lands where they may displace flora or fauna deemed sufficiently rare to be worth preserving; for example, wetlands in Scotland which serve as important staging grounds for rare migrating aquatic bird species. The fiscal incentives which made it possible for many British celebrities to acquire new forests instead of paying tax were revised only in 1988. Britain was perhaps the only country where environmentalists assailed government and foresters for planting new (rather than for destroying existing) forests.

Divided we fall

The consequence of all these new demands on the forest and of the changing values of society has been that in country after country in both the Second World and the First World, the public forest services and the forestry profession have come under fire from conservationists and environmentalists. Foresters have been accused of being the lackeys of forest industry; of having as their objective, and hence being trained for, only the most efficient way of producing wood for industry; of having recourse to dangerous chemicals in order to keep down costs; of ignoring, or paying insufficient heed to, the scientific, cultural, recreation and amenity values in the forest.

These are not proper charges to lay against the forestry profession. The real charge to be laid is that they have served their masters too conscientiously. They have sometimes failed to criticize in public actions by private forest owners which were contrary to the public interest, or government policies which failed to take account of either the long-term interests of the community or the changing values set on the forest by society. In most affluent countries the greater part of the national forest estate is publicly owned; in some entirely so. This means that most foresters are civil servants, and there is a long-established tradition that civil servants should refrain from public comment. They may have tried to exercise pressure on their political masters in the corridors of power, but once decisions have been taken they have been quietly obeyed. This has led to the spectacle of environmentalists arraigning the foresters, who have failed to answer back.

This is not to whitewash the forestry profession. It is true, as some old-time foresters have bitterly observed, that professional foresters were active in endeavouring to safeguard the long-term public interest before most contemporary environmental activists were born. Had it not been for the notions of sustained yield developed in forestry science, and the influence foresters were able to bring to bear upon politicians, there might well have been precious little forest left today in the affluent countries for environmentalists to get concerned about. But it is alas also true that foresters have far too often tamely done as they have been told, and have remained gagged. They have consented to be civic castrates.

Because foresters have not been sufficiently vocal in criticizing policy, environmentalists have sometimes succeeded in persuading politicians that the foresters' role in land use decisions should be curbed. This has happened, for example, in several Australian States and in New Zealand.

Environmentalists who concentrate their fire on the forestry profession instead of on the politicians who prescribe the objectives to be pursued by public forestry departments may discover such victories as they gain to be pyrrhic ones. In New Zealand they campaigned to save the remaining native beech forests. The upshot is that the important plantation forest resource of pine and eucalyptus, created by the Forest Service and today underpinning New Zealand's second most important industry, has become a state-owned corporation with a purely commercial orientation. Not only will the non-wood benefits (amenity, water protection, rural support) of this resource now take second place; it is tailor-made for privatization as soon as the political wind changes. Meanwhile, the surviving indigenous resources (podocarps, beech, kauri) are locked up and confided to a new Conservation Department; they thus become museums rather than managed forests. The Forest Service survives with limited research and regulatory functions. The likelihood is that in respect of both the native and the created forest resources the environmentalists will come to rue their victory.

In fact it has never been more important for foresters and conservationists to understand each other and see one another as allies. The environmentalist movement has grown in influence, and will continue to grow. It has spread an understanding of people's relationship with the natural world, and their responsibility towards it. As it has taken up and analysed successive issues, it has been obliged to face up to the political implications of those issues. Yet, it continues to suffer from certain weaknesses: one is that it remains largely drawn from, and reflects the values of, the middle class.

That is why the increased attention to the amenity and recreation values of the forest has been concerned largely with serving the leisure interests of the more advantaged sectors of society. The health and recreational needs of urbanites who are less wealthy and less mobile have received little attention, although trees and woodlands are needed both within urban conglomerations and within easy reach of cities. All cities need lungs, and for those who cannot venture far the need is greatest. The provision of recreation space for the city-bound is only one aspect. Trees should play an important part in city planning, providing shade, sound insulation, wind and storm barriers, play space, allaying dust, and so on. Trees to serve the urban poor are more important than wilderness areas which can only be reached by the urban well-to-do.

Environmentalists have been slow to formulate demands on behalf of the urban poor, but foresters have made a start. Although urban forestry is largely neglected in Europe, Canada has a research institute specifically devoted to it, and urban forestry is taught in a number of US forestry schools. In this matter, most of Europe trails behind North America, and surprisingly enough, even behind China. It can be argued that foresters have a particular obligation to press the needs of the urban poor. In the past, it was foresters, in battling for the principle of sustained yield, who sought to ensure that the needs of unborn and therefore unheard generations were safeguarded. Today's foresters need to ensure that trees and woodlands are created to serve those less-advantaged strata of society whose needs, though less vocal, are greater.

But trees outside the forest have an important job to do in the countryside, and here, too, the forester has been guilty of neglect. Most people in Britain are aware that the face of the countryside has undergone great changes in the post-war decades. There have been similar changes in continental Europe. Soon after World War II it was discovered (through the first-ever Census of Woodlands) that in Britain as much as 20 per cent of all growing timber was to be found not in areas classified as forest but in small copses, spinneys and hedgerows. The proportions in other countries are much less, but nevertheless of some significance. Since the war, under the onslaught of modern large-scale agriculture, these scattered woodlands and hedgerows have been steadily disappearing, and with them the varied flora and fauna they sustained. Until recently, protest has been sporadic and muted. The reasons are that foresters had no responsibility for trees outside the forest, while conservationists failed for some time to understand what was happening.

The principal concern of both foresters and environmentalists over the next decades will be to help society assess and secure what have come to be loosely categorized as 'the non-wood benefits of the forest'. This does not mean that timber needs will diminish; they will continue to increase, though less rapidly than in recent decades, and will necessarily loom large among foresters' objectives. Provided concerted action is taken to conquer 'acid rain' (using the term here as shorthand for a variety of ill-understood airborne pollutants), the rich countries should be able to continue pushing up their home-grown industrial wood supplies. If the shortfall between domestic supplies and needs continues to grow, there will be little difficulty in filling the gap from artificial plantations established or expanded in Third World countries favoured with suitable growing conditions. New wood processing industries will gravitate towards these overseas woodyards, a shift that will doubtless be favoured by fiscal incentives and less onerous environmental restraints.

Though the rich countries may look overseas to expand the woodyard for forest industries, it is hardly likely that they will do so for energy wood. Throughout the industrialized world, the domestic consumption of fuelwood continues to fall and the use of wood as energy for industry presently consists almost entirely of wood residues from the forest industries. The idea of deliberately growing wood for energy has been toyed with by many, but only a few countries have made a start. These are countries where public opinion has become increasingly disenchanted with nuclear power and its attendant risks. Thus Sweden foresees a definite role for wood energy, while Austria plans to devote 8 per cent of its arable land to growing fuelwood plantations.

This could change within a decade. In most affluent countries wood energy proposals have been shelved, allegedly on economic grounds. Meanwhile research into other renewable and non-conventional energy sources (solar, tidal, wind, wave, ocean temperature differential and the like) is desultory, lacking government encouragement and restrained by existing vested interests. But 'Green' pressure on governments to count the full social costs of fossil fuels and of nuclear energy will continue to grow. In many countries it may reach the point where governments will be obliged to sketch out long-term energy policies, with greater reliance on renewable resources.

'Non-wood benefits' are all too often seen narrowly as provision for amenity and recreation, including cosmetic landscaping. It needs stressing that in nearly every industrialized country, there are areas and locations where insufficient attention has so far been paid to protection forestry. The devastation caused in southern Britain by the 1987 hurricane raised tree-consciousness; an age-old landscape which millions had taken for granted was destroyed overnight. Though there was little loss of life, property damage was high. The likelihood of winds of this force recurring, with similar consequences, may be low. But the likelihood of floods and landslides, with a greater threat to life, in locations rendered vulnerable by lack of tree cover, is much higher. It is higher still in some other European countries which, with North America, USSR, Japan and Oceania, all still have areas in urgent need of afforestation or reafforestation to avert or reduce the impact of natural calamities.

Exceptional climatic conditions briefly arouse media attention, and serious damage to property or loss of life usually trigger relief measures. It is more difficult to get government or public attention focused on the long-term measures needed to avert repetition. There are also slower and more insidious processes at work which are undermining productivity. In the Common Market, modern industrialized farming, with cereals heavily subsidized, has led to larger fields, elimination of hedgerows, and extension to steeper gradients. Thus downslope, instead of contour, cultivation is bringing about heavy soil loss even in such areas as the South Downs in Britain.

Foresters and environmentalists need to publicize these issues until governments control land abuse and find funds for the afforestation that will help to maintain productivity and may save future lives. Their voices should sound in unison, and their professional associations should protect members with the courage to denounce antisocial resource policies.

Farmers, foresters and conservationists

Governments in the West are sensitive to lobbyists. The rich corporations can afford to spend most money on lobbying. The communications media, heavily dependent on advertising, are as sensitive as governments. Consequently, environmental issues which affect ordinary people are rarely debated in public in an objective manner. In many industrialized countries there is still a powerful farmers' lobby, which politicians dare not ignore. This is the reason for the butter mountains and wine lakes of the European Common Market. Consumers sustain European agriculture by paying prices which are held artificially high. This costs every Common Market European, man, woman and child, the equivalent of £100 sterling every year. All this is necessary, it is argued, in order to enable hard-working family farmers to win a decent living. This is a false image. All over Europe (as in the United States) the small independent farmer is disappearing as agribusiness takes over. The acreage of land owned and managed by corporations and syndicates grows annually, while that farmed by independent farmers diminishes. With the steady merging of chemical, fertilizer, pesticide, plant-breeding and seed production and marketing interests on the one hand, and the increasing monopolistic power of food processors, those small farmers who do survive find themselves ever more squeezed by the powerful transnationals. The progressive industrialization of agriculture has entailed the mechanization of planting, tilling, fertilizing, spraying, harvesting, and also standardization of crops and heavier inputs of both fertilizers and pesticides. Scattered woodlands, hedgerows, hedgerow trees became an impediment. This is why they, and the wild life they sustain, are fast disappearing. With their disappearance go many of the species that kept crop pests under control. Hence the need for more, and ever more powerful, pesticides. It used to be said that forestry was the handmaid of agriculture, that trees were the farmer's friend. The changing landscape of many European countries today suggests that trees have become the enemy of agribusiness.

Nevertheless, in spite of the political power wielded by the agribusiness transnationals and the heavy influence they are able to exercise on the media, there is in all the rich countries a growing public awareness of the adverse consequences of the industrialization of agriculture. They include the pollution of rivers, lakes and ponds by the run-off of excess chemical fertilizers; the parallel pollution of water sources by the liquid wastes of battery farming; the contamination of food by pesticides and fungicides; and the disappearance of varieties. There is also a restriction of consumer choice, as only those varieties best suited to mechanized cultivation, harvesting, packaging, transport and processing are grown.

This growing disquiet is beginning to generate a consumer revolt, and an understanding that the public interest and a healthy rural sector require more mixed and less specialized farming, more biological and fewer chemical controls, and more trees on farms, not fewer.

The consumer revolt is mounting just at the time when Europe (and possibly other affluent regions) is on the verge of further major rural land-use changes. The slow-down of economic growth has focused attention on the heavy price European consumers pay for agricultural produce which is destroyed, given away, or sold under cost. Cut-backs in subsidies to agriculture are inevitable, and this means that even more farming land will go out of production: first dairy, then beef, then cereal. And it is, of course, the smaller independent farmers who will be driven out of business first. The debate is now starting on how this land will be used. There is now an opportunity to extend the national forest estates, either by public afforestation or private planting. Many conservationists believe that the emphasis should be on creating new and varied woodlands with amenity and recreation as their primary purpose. But such forests offer little or no economic incentive, when compared with industrial forests, to the private landowner. There is a clear case for devoting some of the funds saved by cutting agricultural subsidies to supporting forest improvement and tree planting.

In North America there is not the same pressure as in Europe to extend the forest estate, although it too is likely to see a further diminution in land under the plough, and the continuing elimination of small farms. But there is a need on both sides of the Atlantic for agreement among and between foresters and conservationists as to how land coming out of farm production can best be used in the national interest, so that they may jointly campaign and press governments to adopt appropriate measures.

Part V Making trees serve people

Introduction

Our account has covered a large sweep in both time and space, and has drawn on very diverse examples and illustrations. We have seen that the relations between human populations and the forests on which they depend are complex, not simple. It follows that the practical conclusions which flow from studying the interactions between people and forests cannot be reduced to any simple set of prescriptions either. Yet the problems facing humanity today in using, preserving and restoring its forest resources are unprecedentedly severe, and demand of us that we search for solutions. In this final part of the book, therefore, rather than offer any neat resumé, I discuss where some solutions may be found.

More than the preceding parts, these final chapters reflect my own experience, first as an officer of FAO (from 1952 to 1974) dealing with forestry policy and aid in many parts of the world and subsequently as an individual continuing to think and write about forestry problems. Reflection and experience, together with the changing character of the problems themselves, have caused me to change my views over the years in some fundamental ways (some of the changes are recorded in Westoby 1987). In particular, I would now place more emphasis on the roles of ordinary people, and less on those of governments and international agencies, in securing sound relationships between people and their trees.

I have attempted to express my views pithily, but I should not wish them to be taken dogmatically. They are contributions to discussions – discussions which must come to involve very much larger numbers of people if they are to generate effective action.

I have organized this concluding part as five short chapters, although the divisions are inevitably to some extent arbitrary. These deal respectively with so-called social forestry (chapter 26), with some of the promising work being done in agroforestry (chapter 27), with the involvement of ordinary people in forestry and related activities (chapter 28), with forestry aid and development (chapter 29), and with the roles of professional foresters and the importance of a declared forest policy (chapter 30).

One area that gives grounds for hope, but also requires scrutiny, is the enthusiasm in the 1980s for 'social forestry'. A number of university forestry faculties now offer courses in social forestry, and many new projects now feel the need to get a social forestry tag attached to them.

The international fashion for social forestry emerged from changing ideas during the 1970s and 1980s, reflected in the titles of the three World Forestry Congresses held in that period: 'Forests for Socio-Economic Development' (Buenos Aires, 1972); 'Forests for People' (Jakarta, 1978); and 'Forest Resources in the Integral Development of Society' (Mexico City, 1985). Similar concerns are also evident from the increasing attention given to forestry for helping the rural poor, under such various titles as: forestry for community development; agroforestry; village forestry; farm and community forestry; forestry for rural development; and, perhaps most comprehensively, social forestry. The phrases reflect a growth of social consciousness and conscience. But what does 'social forestry' mean? Although (indeed, perhaps because) it lacks any clear and agreed meaning, 'social forestry' has gradually come to cover any kind of forestry activity directed to social needs. What, then, does 'social' connote? Is it a matter of the purpose of planting, whether for local subsistence needs, for the market, or for protection purposes? Is it a question of who owns the planted land or its products? Is it a matter of whether decisions are made by professional foresters or by others? One definition which has won a measure of acceptance runs: 'tree planting and management, at the farm, village or community level, by or for small farmers and the landless'. A positive aspect of this definition is its emphasis on who benefits. But in fact many social forestry projects go awry precisely in the sense that their benefits are derailed and do not go to the intended beneficiaries.

A few examples will serve to illustrate the complexities of defining and targeting such projects. Much of rural India so lacks fuel that it relies on dried cattle dung and agricultural residues. The soil, deprived of the nutrients which should have been restored to it, steadily deteriorates. What could be more sensible than to establish plantations to provide both wood for industry and for domestic fuel? Just such a scheme, however, badly misfired. It was so profitable for the larger farmers to grow and sell wood to industry that they switched from growing food crops to growing wood. Growing wood is much less labour-intensive than farming grain. But over half the rural population was landless, or had too little land to support the family, and thus depended for a living on casual employment on the land of the richer farmers. The switch from grain to wood meant that employment was gone. Thus a well-intentioned project left most of the rural people worse off than before.

Again, 'forestry for community development' projects are often regarded as a category of social forestry. But, like most community development projects, they have often been based on the naive assumption that the village is a community. However, most villages in the Third World (like most villages in Britain) are a tangled web of kinship ties, property and debt links, formal and informal obligations, and power relationships. When help is offered from outside it often polarizes the situation and benefits the more powerful, more literate and more vocal at the expense of the poorer elements within the community. Such asymmetries became clear from one study of energy use in a Bangladesh village. This showed only too vividly why the benefits did not reach the intended recipients: the 'landless' subcommittee of the programme was chaired by a member of the largest landholding family.

Another illustration of how things can go badly wrong has been reported from Pakistan where the fuelwood shortage was so intense that the Forest Department in a particular area had 50 000 forest offences pending in the courts. To meet the shortage, a pilot project of fuelwood planting was launched to test out suitable species and techniques and to work out strategies which would involve the local people. Three categories of land were involved: *khalsa* (state land), *shamlat* (community owned land), and *malkiat* (privately owned land). It was decided to include all three in the pilot project. What the project failed to understand was that, over the preceding decades, the *shamlat* had been partitioned, appropriated and privatized by the richer and more powerful families. These latter had not registered the *de facto* appropriation in order to avoid land tax. The advent of the project sent them racing to register. Thus they not only established title to the land, they got it afforested free. They even demanded protection for the new forests they had acquired free of cost. Meanwhile, the smaller peasants shied away from any form of participation in the pilot scheme: there was no guarantee that they would ever see land, wood or cash from the sale of wood.

The World Bank has supported a number of fuelwood plantation projects. But they are a good example of how the Bank's ideological predispositions present obstacles to social forestry. The Bank understands that as fuelwood becomes scarcer it becomes dearer. It is then the poorest whose food goes uncooked or who go short of food in order to buy fuel. From a social point of view the need is for more and cheaper fuelwood. But the World Bank, on the other hand, sees higher fuelwood prices as the best means of enticing entrepreneurs to enter the business of commercial fuelwood plantations.

In some parts of the world trees enter into very complex property and social relations. Louise Fortmann and John Bruce (1988) have drawn attention to the great variety of relationships between land, trees and people in Africa. Tree tenure and land tenure are by no means the same thing. Four different sets of rights in trees can be distinguished: the right to own or inherit, the right to plant, the right to use and the right of disposal. In some places the situation is so complex that different families within the same village may have customary rights to different parts of the same tree. There are also many areas where the very act of planting and successfully rearing a tree constitutes, by custom, legal title to the land on which it is planted. Small wonder, then, that government planting schemes which ignore this are doomed to failure; the locals root out the government-planted trees at the first opportunity lest they forfeit their land rights.

Experience of 'social forestry' schemes is now beginning to accumulate rapidly. Unfortunately many of them have done little to improve the lot of the rural poor. But there are a number of honourable exceptions and – more importantly – there is a growing disposition to examine critically the likely effects of new schemes. Test and pilot projects often reveal dangers which can be overcome by appropriate safeguards.

27   Agroforestry

Agroforestry, mentioned above as a category of social forestry, is a new name for practices which are very old – the combination, in time or space, of tree growing with growing crops, raising animals, or both. It need not necessarily be small scale: it can be big business. For example, after a certain point, animals can safely be grazed in young tree plantations until the canopy closes and grass is suppressed. The combination of sheep and large plantations of *radiata* pine in Australia and New Zealand has proved highly successful. Another example, intermediate in scale between capitalist and peasant agriculture, is to be found in the rubber plantations of Malaysia, many of which are held in modest holdings of about 40 ha. Here the young plantations are intercropped with bananas and pineapple until the rubber tree canopy closes. It has also been discovered that, beyond that point, the cost of keeping down weeds in the plantations can be reduced by introducing sheep and poultry.

Nevertheless, the real reason for the increasing interest and research in agroforestry is that on many forms of marginal land a sustainable peasant agriculture can only be practised if it is combined with tree culture. At several research centres, and notably at the International Council for Research into Agroforestry (ICRAF) in Kenya, real progress has been made with sustainable agricultural systems, particularly now that emphasis has shifted to the careful study of what peasants themselves have already learned to do.

The *temporal* arrangement of crops is almost as old as agriculture itself. In medieval England the manorial three-field system comprised a food crop, a drink crop, and a year of fallow. Shifting cultivation, the earliest form of agriculture practised in the forest and still widespread in tropical forests today, is essentially temporal agroforestry. So is *taungya*, or 'agri-silviculture', the system devised by colonial foresters to reafforest cleared land. In this system indigenes were accorded temporary lease of land on which to grow their own crops on condition that they planted and tended tree seedlings issued by the Forest Department. When the tree plantation was established the small croppers were obliged to move on. *Taungya* has not disappeared with decolonization. But without some security for those who clear the land it can amount to forced labour.

Spatial agroforestry takes many forms, and includes the planting of trees round borders, alley cropping, shade trees, and the random mix of food, fodder and fuel trees with shrubs and staple crops that is found in home gardening.

ICRAF has stated its central aim precisely: to foster research on the place of woody perennials in combination with crops or animals to solve the problems of small farmers, especially in the tropics. 'Woody perennials' is not simply a synonym for trees; it encompasses palms, shrubs, bamboos, bushes, lianas and the like. Moreover, ICRAF perceives its objective as lying in the agricultural domain, even though agroforestry relies heavily on forest science and has been most vigorously encouraged by professional foresters. It is interesting that this approach was what enabled Chinese foresters to win over Chinese peasants to forestry. They, too, had a catholic interpretation of forestry as including not merely timber trees but trees and woody perennials for all purposes (orchard crops, tea oil, bamboo groves, and so on). Similarly, Chinese foresters encouraged and demonstrated intercropping.

ICRAF has recognized that agroforestry is not simply a matter of solving technical problems. It is also necessary to understand the socio-economic (and hence the political) context within which farming is practised. This has led it to devote special attention to the study of tree and land tenure systems. Under ICRAF's aegis research is being extended to more ecological zones though it is still concentrated in Africa. There is urgent need for similar research centres to investigate all aspects of trees which can improve farming: food and fodder, shade and shelter, soil protection and soil nutrients. Ideally, each centre should draw upon a web of outstations, located among differing ecological situations and social structures. Research of this kind has become all the more important because day by day the area of land in traditional and sustainable agriculture is dwindling. Because suitable use of trees can do so much to improve soil structure and composition, and curb the loss of soil and moisture, agroforestry offers the best hope for helping farmers to find sustainable (and in time more productive) agricultural practices.

These areas of research are only just beginning to receive the attention they warrant. Indeed, since the mid-1980s there has been a tendency for 'social forestry' to concentrate on trees for fuelwood. Agroforestry offers less attraction, since much of the work in this field must necessarily be experimental, tentative, and in the first instance small-scale. And once transferable techniques are devised, there arises the problem of demonstrating and extending them under circumstances where they may cause frictions between different strata of society.

For the most part new agroforestry techniques must be used by those who possess land. Yet a rising proportion of Third World people in the countryside have no land at all. Thus it is vital that wherever it is intended to satisfy their land hunger by using presently forested land, sustainable agroforestry techniques should be developed and thoroughly proved in pilot projects. Yet, regrettably, it is precisely those governments which drive their rural landless into forested land who pay least regard to discovering how such land can be sustainably farmed.

'Agroforestry' is not a new, magic password. Nor is it simply the interface between agriculture and forestry. There is no sense in which 'universal' agroforesters can be trained. However, it is possible to give men and women a trained familiarity with the multitude of ways in which trees and shrubs can support cropping and animal husbandry, under widely differing ecological conditions and no less diverse social structures.

28 Involving people in forestry

Projects to help the rural poor cannot succeed without the involvement of the rural poor themselves. But often they do not participate. Baljit Malik (1980) has explained why:

For most governments to organize peasants means either to control them in settlements, or organize the more economically viable among them in co-operatives or through various community development programmes. Both these types of efforts have usually been imposed from above, with very little peasant participation. Moreover, it is now a well known fact that most co-operatives or representative bodies like 'Panchayats' at the village level in India have been dominated by the rural rich who have stolen the lion's share of the inputs and outputs of most development programmes for their own benefit.

Rural development projects (including those with a forestry or agroforestry component) must have built-in safeguards if the benefits are to reach the right people. The most important factor which inhibits the small farmer from making heavy labour investments in land improvements is insecurity of tenure. If his tenure is uncertain or at the mercy of a large landowner his incentive to improve the land is weak.

However there are many situations where simply persuading individual farmers to adopt new techniques will not stop the decline in productivity. Substantial investments in social capital are needed, the components of which will vary with circumstances (terracing, check dams, watershed afforestation, irrigation canals, dykes, dune fixation, shelter belts, windbreaks, and so on), but the major input of which will generally be human muscle power. Large benefits can flow from this investment, but they usually accrue to different individuals in different degrees. And they are not immediate, but deferred.

Major works of land reclamation, land protection, and land improvement require considerable organizing ability. The massive inputs of labour needed will be forthcoming only if there is a sense of identity between the rural people and those who govern them. This has happened in Third World countries which have carried out a genuine land reform, involving land redistribution. The China model, for example, elicited much admiration. It may have lost some of its early lustre, but the unprecedented labour effort which went into the taming of the rivers and the Great Green Wall stemmed from a sense of identity between leaders and led. In the early days most local activists worked as hard as, and lived a life not very different from, those whom they urged into action. Although, through ignorance and poor organization, some of the effort was wasted, recognizable benefits ensued, and China became able to feed itself.

But in most of the Third World the rural poor who have either no land at all or insufficient land to support them are becoming more numerous every year. They are today the principal instrument of forest destruction. The problem will not go away by encouraging them to cut deeper into the forest, or by ill-conceived transmigration schemes. And famine relief which saves children today only for them to die tomorrow fails to touch the underlying situation. The plight of the rural poor in countries like Ethiopia and Sudan will get worse unless they can be mobilized to bring land back into production and raise productivity on land still farmed.

The sense of identity which spurs rural people into mutual effort must go right down the line. City-trained extension workers purveying orders and advice to farmers often find their advice ignored and their presence resented. It makes more sense to convey new ideas through individuals chosen to represent them by the rural people themselves, whatever their level of literacy.

The role of women

It is difficult today for a man to write about the role of women without being accused either of male chauvinism or of being patronizing. Nevertheless, something has to be said, if only because over much of the drier areas of the Third World women (as wood gatherers) are an important instrument of

Figure 28.1 Men and women from Pipal Koti village in Kumaon at a Chipko meeting. This village has been particularly successful in planting up degraded land and in controlling excessive grass and fodder cutting in the protected areas (photo T. Kowal, Oxford Forestry Institute)

forest destruction, while their labour is everywhere a significant input in the farm economy.

Development assistance first addressed Third World women on the assumption that they were home makers. It stressed better child care, more sensible diets, rudimentary sanitation, and so on. Women's role as providers was overlooked and until recently agricultural extension services directed their efforts solely to men. In fact women's contribution on the farm is much greater than was formerly assumed. However, from the standpoint of bringing about change what matters is not only how much work they do but how big a part they play in decision-making: in determining what crops should be grown and how any cash income should be spent.

This varies greatly, between countries, within countries, from tribe to tribe. In many parts of the world women are still chattels, a source of labour and reproduction, with a negotiable value. Often, even if not mere chattels, they can neither inherit nor own land. Over most of the Third World they still remain subordinate and politically excluded, even where nominally enfranchised. Even in the few Third World countries where the central power is committed to pursuing social justice for women there is still a long hard road to travel before women free themselves from their traditional subjection. Polygamy, bride price, clitoridectomy, child marriage and suttee do not disappear by decree.

But even where women appear to be politically excluded they may not be without influence. By tradition, women in Nepal are not members of the village *panchayats*. However, forestry assistants promoting community forestry schemes discovered that they met with success only when their discussions with the local *panchayat* were complemented by discussions, posters, films and so on addressed to the women of the village.

Where adult males are absent for long periods, women often control agricultural operations. Sometimes they appear to have a better understanding than men of the agriculture-supportive role of trees. For example, in some areas of the foothills of the Himalayas, the Chipko movement (hugging trees to prevent them being felled; see chapter 17 and figure 28.1) depends mainly on women, since most of the men are seasonally absent as migrant labourers. Their action has done much to raise the standing of women in both the family and the community. There is perhaps a parallel here to the recent accession of women into the forestry profession in the rich countries; it is generally accepted that they have shown themselves more sensitive to the non-wood benefits of the forest than many of their male counterparts.

29 Forestry aid

Today nearly all forestry aid has assumed the mantle of social forestry. It is therefore instructive to consider how forestry aid has changed from its early days.

Forestry was an integral part of FAO's concern from its foundation, during World War II. But in the early years after the war forestry aid played only a very small part in development assistance. Funds became available for agriculture but they were largely directed into irrigation projects, dams and tubewells, demonstration farms, livestock institutes and the like. Most of these projects ignored the role of forestry in agriculture, in soil protection, and in land improvement. Forestry itself was reckoned too long-term a business to warrant either requests for aid from Third World countries, or funding from the development agencies.

When forestry aid did start on a significant scale it was largely concerned with identifying and surveying forest resources which could provide log exports or feed new forest industries, thereby saving costly imports or providing export earnings; with educating and training cadres;

or with establishing new man-made forests to provide a basis for future industrial development. These were not, of course, the only kinds of projects to be conceived and proposed. But they were the kinds which Third World governments were interested in accepting or promoting, and which the development establishment (the World Bank, and multilateral and bilateral development assistance programmes) were most interested in financing.

The upsurge in aid for pre-investment surveys and kindred projects in the forestry sector, when it came, was a response to the world-wide expansion in the market for wood products which attended post-war reconstruction and a sustained period of buoyant economic growth in the rich countries. What was happening, in effect, was that the development assistance agencies were helping to identify forest resources which could serve the interests of metropolitan forest industry giants anxious to extend their resource base and product range; at the same time local staff were being trained to facilitate their operations.

A few new forest industries were established in the Third World. Equipment manufacturers in the industrialized countries were able to dispose of machinery and plant, some of which was becoming obsolete in their main markets. The flow of survey information which became available enabled loggers to start operations in many previously unlogged forests. There followed the spectacle of the governments of newly independent countries lucky enough to possess tropical forest vying with each other to attract foreign operators into their forests, while foreign operators used all means, fair or foul, to get their hands on the richer and more accessible resources.

By now the World Bank had become concerned about the small farmer, who had been passed by in the boom of optimism which accompanied the so-called Green Revolution. The Green Revolution – more accurately, the wider adoption of high-yielding crop varieties, varieties needing greater inputs of water, fertilizers and pesticides – had been facilitated by the 'generosity' of the giant fertilizer industries embarrassed by temporary excess production. It spelt increasing prosperity for the better-off farmers, but misery for the small farmers, and growth in the numbers of hungry rural landless.

It was not that the technical staffs of the agencies were blind to the needs of the small farmer and the rural landless. It was that the principal funding sources set their ideological stamp on the kinds of projects considered acceptable. They favoured export-led development (especially in those unprocessed raw materials in demand in the First World), and held to trickle-down notions about development: that is, they presumed that if the better-educated and more efficient farmers prospered, the new cropping patterns and new technologies would rapidly spread, and hence the whole economy would eventually feel the benefits of the new prosperity.

But prosperity did not trickle down. The more powerful, more educated, more accessible farmers prospered – the ones who could obtain credit, could afford fertilizers and pesticides, could carry the risk of new crops and new technologies; the others went to the wall. Often yields went up while more people went hungry. On the one hand, fewer but bigger farms; on the other, marginal cultivators and ever more rural landless, dependent on casual employment on larger farms. And, as we have seen from the examples in previous chapters, this meant accelerating forest destruction.

There were some efforts to persuade Third World governments to adopt projects to ease the lot of the rural poor. In a number of these the significance of trees to their welfare was recognized. But most Third World governments were uninterested in such projects. Their rural poor had neither guns nor lobbies.

Many people still take 'aid' to be a sacred word. But aid is a loose term covering all kinds of grants, loans, and credits, for both goods and services. For many intergovernmental transactions the word 'aid' is a misnomer. In any case official development aid is now in decline, as governments of the rich countries attach more strings to their 'aid' – strings designed to corner markets and exert political influence. The World Bank remains the main source of funding development projects. But the World Bank is a bank like any other. It borrows money on the world market which it must repay with interest. And it makes loans, for purposes which it approves, to Third World (and other) governments, loans which those governments in turn must repay with interest. And although it does offer soft loans (with lower rates of interest and deferred repayments) it finds increasing difficulty in raising funds from the richer countries for this service.

'For purposes which it approves': herein lies the catch. In the World Bank and other development agencies there are many professionals who understand what development ought to mean. They do their best to ensure that the projects which the agencies finance are designed to achieve elementary aims of human welfare. But they come up against a number of obstacles, of which the first lies in the Bank itself: it is the loans officer, not the technical officer, who has the final say. In addition the Bank's general lending policy is heavily influenced by the political sympathies and antipathies of its chief funders, particularly the USA.

Moreover a Third World government borrowing from the World Bank (or elsewhere) may accept stipulations which oblige it to take active steps to improve the condition of the rural poor, but it may well accept them with tongue in cheek, knowing full well that the Bank does not allow its technical officers either the time or the means to effectively monitor what the government actually does with the loan.

Nonetheless, there are Third World governments who have received development aid which they have used knowledgeably, effectively and honestly. And there have been a number of instances of both forestry and rural development programmes which have been well designed and properly utilized. But the stark reality is that the situation has now been reached in many Third World countries (and is fast approaching in others) when nothing short of massive land rehabilitation and land improvement projects will retrieve the situation. These will not yield early or easily measurable returns, and they are not the kind of projects which most aid programmes have supported. Because the principal input is labour, and because returns are bound to be deferred, such projects require deliberate resource transfers for long periods to governments which are capable of organizing and mobilizing popular participation.

There is today a growing awareness in the rich countries that environmental destruction poses a threat no less serious than that of nuclear holocaust, and that those living in the affluent countries are as much under threat as the poor of the Third World. If this awareness grows and governments who are prepared to base their policies on it come to power, there is ample scope for nation-to-nation transfers that can help to halt the destruction of soil and water resources, to restore and raise land productivity, and to support community effort to these ends among the rural poor. Most such land-use and land-rehabilitation programmes will have a forestry component; in many of them the forestry contribution will be decisive.

30 Foresters and forest policies

My arguments so far in this part may sometimes have made it appear that I feel that the best of worlds would be one in which forestry as a specialist area of knowledge, and forest policies, should be dissolved in a general upsurge of popular involvement in planning the use of the natural environment, including trees. In fact, specialist professional knowledge has an indispensable role in forestry and, for reasons that I explain below, formal and explicit national forest policies are a condition of effective popular involvement.

The forestry profession has taken some hard knocks since the 1970s, particularly from environmentalists. Its response has been subdued, partly because so many of its members are state employed. But in countries where the profession is well organized there has been an attempt at serious self-examination.

Like all professions the forestry profession seeks to secure the interests of its members, while ensuring that its members deliver acceptable standards of service. As the sciences on which forestry rests proliferate and advance, it becomes increasingly complex to decide how to reach a defined set of objectives. At one time it was taken for granted that anyone who had reached a satisfactory standard in a prescribed list of disciplines, and had demonstrated his or her ability to combine them in a satisfactory programme (a working plan), could be regarded as a qualified forester. Today, however, additional requirements are set in a number of countries before a forester is licensed to practise. If licensing is by the state, and ensures that foresters working in the private sector take heed of the public interest, this is no bad thing. Licensing by the profession, on the other hand, tends to encourage foresters to believe that they, not society, should prescribe forestry's goals.

Younger foresters have long felt the need to broaden the concept of forestry and address new problems thrown up by a changing society. Student pressure has helped alter forestry curricula, giving enhanced importance to the social sciences and curbing the incessant pressure for more technological detail. The men and women leaving forestry schools today may know a little less about tree physiology and wood anatomy than the generations which preceded them, but they have clearer ideas about what societies want from their forests, and how those wants could be satisfied. Where the forestry curriculum has responded to changing needs, forestry education can be a valuable preparation for living in modern society, embracing as it does interrelations between people, the natural resources on which they depend, and technology.

So far this part has dealt primarily with the Third World. But broader concepts of forestry are needed everywhere. In the affluent industrialized countries, even in those where the forest industries represent a principal pillar of the national economy, the time has come to dispel the notion that forestry is mainly about tending woodyards. Foresters can do more than this. They *do* do more than this. Nevertheless their full contribution has not yet been forthcoming. Why? One reason is that foresters have allowed their employers to set them over-narrow perspectives. Another is that they have not been sufficiently active in helping society to fix its goals. They have a key responsibility in providing society with understanding of the opportunities of and constraints upon natural resource use. It *can* be difficult for lay men and women to grasp the trade-offs involved in resource-use decisions, particularly if these are wrapped up in jargon, but none of the issues is so complex as to be beyond the understanding of the average citizen if professionals take the trouble to express themselves in comprehensible terms. Those who speak in jargon either have something to hide or do not themselves understand.

Those branches of forest science which are concerned with producing suitable wood cheaply for large forest industry complexes are relatively well funded. In many forest-rich industrialized countries the state bears much of this expenditure, even though the principal beneficiary is private industry. Compared with these expenditures, the volume of research funds devoted to non-wood benefits of the forest is scandalously small; it is lamentable that much of the information and research concerning environmental issues is collected and funded by non-governmental 'green' organizations.

Professional forestry in much of the Third World stands in even more radical need of change. Most Third World countries adopted not only the forestry objectives but also forestry institutional models from the First World, either left behind by colonial powers or pressed upon them by past development assistance. And there are still many Third World governments (even among those committed to social justice) which fail to recognize the scale and diversity of the contribution which forestry could make. Not surprisingly they also fail to recognize that the contribution needed cannot come from forest departments organized along traditional lines and staffed by men trained as professional foresters in the narrow sense. Indeed, though this may sound heretical, there are countries where a useful first step would be to abolish the existing forestry department and disperse its staff, after retraining, to the countryside.

As previous chapters have explained, trees have manifold roles to play in helping Third World countries to feed themselves: in halting the downward spiral of land degradation; in reclaiming and rehabilitating land; in protecting land from wind and water erosion and in rebuilding soil fertility; as intrinsic parts of sustainable agricultural systems, especially under marginal conditions; and in providing food, fodder, fuel and building materials. Bjorn Lundgren has rightly observed that there is no 'global' forest problem, save in a purely statistical sense; there is a whole range of local problems that require different solutions based on different strategies.

This is why the key person is often not the forester or other specialist but the one who links the local community to the store of expertise and acts as catalyst in getting things under way. It matters little whether he or she is labelled activist, agitator, village representative or what-have-you. Whoever provides this two-way link must be close to the community in distance, in understanding its problems and in life-style. It is only through such people that foresters or others can gain an understanding of problems and suggest possible solutions.

The training and definition of forestry specialists also needs adapting to concrete needs. Some newly independent countries which found themselves with no professional foresters started to train foresters by giving supplementary training to students who had completed the first two years of an agricultural degree course. This 'bootlace' operation may be quite valid, provided it is underpinned by intermediate technical training in both agriculture and forestry. But there is no general blueprint for training foresters. First World models are almost certainly inappropriate. But so may be the models of other Third World countries. The scope, content and method of forestry training should be arrived at by working backwards. The starting point is to identify the most urgent tasks to be carried out and how the people who are to carry them out can be reached. Then step by step it will be possible to work out the levels of training required and the appropriate content. Those being trained may or may not be labelled 'foresters', but they will have acquired an effective range and depth of knowledge of the ways in which trees and woodlands can serve rural people.

The purpose of forest policies

If the world's governments were circularized concerning the forest policies they are pursuing, the replies would be an incredible hotchpotch of ministerial statements, preambles to statutes relating to forestry, formal objectives of forestry departments, and extracts from annual reports. In fact there is scarcely a country which has a formal, thought-out and declared forest policy, any more than it has a thought-out conservation strategy. Pressure has been mounting for countries to adopt long-term conservation strategies, and the International Union for the Conservation of Nature has offered its services to governments which seek help in drawing one up. A number of countries have accepted this invitation: in most of them work is still in progress; in a few the strategy has been completed and published.

Obviously, a forest policy should be a principal pillar in any conservation strategy, since forests are not only an important renewable resource in themselves, but they decisively influence other resources on which a country depends: air, water, soil. Yet the conservation strategies adopted to date, and the elements of forest policy they include, consist of pious aspirations, rather than being a set of specific targets linked to declared social objectives and accompanied by detailed programmes.

Pious aspirations are better than nothing; they at least provide some evidence that governments take the issues seriously. But what the strategies so far adopted represent is simply the most satisfying consensus which pooled environmentalist knowledge and experience could press upon politicians. In other words, they are the outcome of specialist lobbying at the top rather than the result of mobilized pressure from below – that is, from an informed citizenry. Thus they represent little advance on the forest policies pressed on governments by top public foresters.

A strategy that does not have quantitative targets and time scales for achieving them is certainly better than no strategy at all. But numbers and times are important; they generally mean that someone has examined the implications, in terms of resources needed, of the courses of action proposed. Targets and time scales will in any case need adjusting – in the light of progress made, of resources actually available, and of society's changing needs. The other important reason for putting quantified flesh on to strategic bones is that the figures can then be checked for internal consistency. If, when put together, they make nonsense, then it is clear that the strategy is not to be taken seriously but is simply a propaganda exercise.

The starting point for developing any forest or conservation strategy must be social objectives. It must provide for specified goods and services to go to specified groups by specified dates. That means finding out what people want, and foreseeing what they are likely to want; it does not mean deciding what they ought to want. And 'people' means all people, not just pulp and paper industries, large forest owners, speculative builders and bird-watchers. Of course, many people do not know what they want from the forest or are ignorant of what it does or could provide. That is why a campaign to inform and involve people is necessary, in the period when the policy is being revised and fleshed out and before it becomes fixed. The campaign must also seek to involve those rural people, especially important in Third World countries, who know very well what they need from the forest but have great difficulty in articulating their needs precisely and making their voices heard.

Thus the creation of a forest policy is a process which should involve all groups and institutions with a direct or indirect say in the forest or with responsibility for implementing the policy. It should not be hurried, both because its purpose is to educate and to engage, and because it must lead in due course to legislation and to machinery for enforcing compliance. Justice and democracy both require that the policy should be fully discussed, and this means that it must be set out in language which can be readily understood.

A forest policy will not satisfy everybody, nor should it aim at doing so. Claims on the forest often conflict. What has often happened in the past is that the groups able to exercise most influence have asserted their own claims over others'. The forestry profession, to its credit, *has* had some successes in protecting forests for future generations; today's foresters should also take up the cause of the weaker sections of society dependent on the forest.

It is no longer adequate for forest policy to be a general line of intention, faintly discernible from statutes, ministerial statements, and administrative decisions. Governments, whatever their constitutional form, seek to stay in office. That is why so many of the decisions they take are ones of expediency, unrelated to long-term objectives. The lack of a declared national forest policy has in many countries made forestry the Cinderella of government departments, with no assurance that activities begun today will be funded or continued tomorrow. A forest policy may not prevent government actions which are politically expedient but which run counter to the long-term national interest. But with a thought-out, detailed and formally adopted policy it will be easier to expose and resist such actions.

A clear forest policy is one condition of a truly social forestry. Forestry today must encompass the art and science of harnessing forests, woodlands and trees for human betterment. This is true for all countries, whether rich or poor, temperate or tropical, well forested or tree-barren. In every form of society and in almost every environment trees have services to render. Whoever controls the use of land, the way in which that land is used has an impact on the lives of others. This is particularly true of forested land. Where that impact may be adverse, either immediately or in the long term, it should be subject to social control so that the long-term community interest prevails.

That is why there can be no acceptable delimitation of 'social forestry' as a particular area of forestry science and practice. All forestry should be social.

Bibliography

The bibliography contains both works cited and some others I have drawn on or profited from. Items which are particularly useful as further reading are marked with an asterisk (*).

*Calder, Nigel (1984) *Timescale: An Atlas of the Fourth Dimension*, Chatto and Windus, London.
*Caufield, Catherine (1985) *In the Rainforest*, Heinemann, London.
Cobb, Richard (1975) *Paris and its Provinces, 1792–1802*, Oxford University Press, London.
Davis, David Brion (1984) *Slavery and Human Progress*, Oxford University Press, London.
De Ste Croix, G. E. M. (1981) *The Class Struggle in the Ancient Greek World*, Duckworth, London.
*Eckholm, Erik P. (1976) *Losing Ground: Environmental Stress and World Food Prospects*, W. W. Norton, New York.
Food and Agriculture Organization (1985) *Forest Resources 1980*, Food and Agriculture Organization, Rome.
Fortmann, Louise and John W. Bruce (1988) *Whose Trees? Proprietary Dimensions of Forestry*, Westview Press, Boulder CO.
Galeano, Eduardo (1973) *Open Veins of Latin America: Five Centuries of the Pillage of a Continent*, Monthly Review Press, New York.
*Goudie, Andrew (1986) *The Human Impact on the Natural Environment*, 2nd edn, Basil Blackwell, Oxford.
Ramachandra, R. (1985) 'Forestry and social protest in British Kumaun, *c.* 1893–1921', in R. Guha (ed.) *Subaltern Studies: Writing on South Asian History and Society*, XI, Oxford University Press, Delhi.
*Harrison, Paul (1987) *The Greening of Africa: Breaking Through in the Battle for Land and Food*, Paladin, London.
*International Institute for Environment and Development (1987) *The Brundtland Report: Our Common Future*, Oxford University Press, London.
James, C. L. R. (1980) *The Black Jacobins*, Allison and Busby, London.
Kiernan, Victor Gordon (1974) *Marxism and Imperialism*, Edward Arnold, London.
Kulkarni, Sharad (1983) 'The Forest Policy and the Forest Bill: a critique and suggestions for change', in Walter Fernandes and Sharad Kulkarni (eds) *Towards a New Forest Policy: People's Rights and Social Needs*, Indian Social Institute, New Delhi.
*Lappe, Frances Moore and Joseph Collins (1986) *World Hunger: Twelve Myths*, Grove Press, New York.
McCracken, Eileen (1971) *The Irish Woods since Tudor Times: Their Distribution and Exploitation*, David and Charles, Newton Abbot.

Malik, Baljit (1980) *An Asian Panorama of Peasant Oppression*, IFDA Dossier 19, September/October.

*Meiggs, Russell (1982) *Trees and Timber in the Ancient Mediterranean World*, Oxford University Press, Oxford.

Myers, Norman (1979) *The Sinking Ark*, Pergamon Press, Oxford.

*Myers, Norman (1984) *The Primary Source: Tropical Forests and our Future*, W. W. Norton, New York.

*Myers, Norman (ed.) (1985) *Gaia Atlas of Planet Management*, Pan Books, London. [A vivid and compact summary of the world's resource problems.]

Novak, Alfredo Ernesto (1981) 'Development and justice', paper presented to the International Council of Voluntary Agencies General Conference, Colombo, Sri Lanka, November 1981.

*Quaker Peace Service (1988) *Sharing World Resources – Which Ways Forward?*, Quaker Peace Service, London.

*Rackham, Oliver (1986) *The History of the Countryside*, J. M. Dent, London. [Like Rackham's other writings, this history of the British countryside is a delight to read.]

Richardson, Stanley Dennis (1966) *Forestry in Communist China*, Johns Hopkins University Press, Baltimore MD.

Richardson, Stanley Dennis (1986) *The Cotchell Report: On the World's Largest Timber Industry Frontier. A report covering the production and consumption of forest products in China: future requirements and trade prospects*, Cotchell Pacific Ltd, Hong Kong.

*Timberlake, Lloyd (1985) *Africa in Crisis*, Earthscan, London.

*Tucker, Richard P. and J. F. Richards (eds) (1983) *Global Deforestation and the Nineteenth-Century World Economy*, Duke University Press, Durham NC.

Westoby, Jack C. (1987) *The Purpose of Forests: Follies of Development*, Basil Blackwell, Oxford.

World Bank (1977) *Forest Sector Policy Paper* (Report no. 1778, September 1977), World Bank, Washington DC.

Wyatt-Smith, John (1982) 'The agricultural system in the hills of Nepal: the ratio of agricultural to forest land and the problem of fodder', Occasional Paper no. 1, Agricultural Projects Services Centre, Kathmandu.

Index

Figures in italics refer to illustrations and diagrams.

Index by Meg Davies